The BEANPOT

The BEANPOT

Fifty Years of Thrills, Spills, and Chills

BERNARD M. CORBETT

Northeastern University Press
BOSTON

Northeastern University Press

Library of Congress Cataloging-in-Publication Data

Corbett, Bernard.
    The Beanpot : fifty years of thrills, spills, and chills / Bernard M. Corbett.
        p. cm.
    Includes index.
        ISBN 1-55553-531-3 (alk. paper)
    1. Beanpot (Hockey tournament)—History. 2. Hockey—Massachusetts—
Boston—History. 3. College sports—Massachusetts—Boston—History. I. Title.
        GV848.2.B42 C67 2002
        796.962'09744'61—dc21   2002007680

Designed by Peter M. Blaiwas/Vern Associates, Inc.

Composed in Minion and Franklin Gothic by Vern Associates, Inc., Boston, Massachusetts. Printed and bound by Quebecor/World, Kingsport, Tennessee. The paper is Utopia Matte, an acid-free stock

MANUFACTURED IN THE UNITED STATES OF AMERICA
06 05 04 03 02   5 4 3 2 1

Dedication

To my departed father, Mitchell B. Corbett, starting goalie on the 1950–51 Brown University freshman team and a 1959 graduate of Boston University. I dedicate this book to him for teaching me that—in the same way "all politics is local"—all hockey is Beanpot.

In Memoriam

To John Cunniff (1944–2002), the singular sensation of the tournament's half-century. May the icy road rise to meet you as you dash to the net. The "Madman of the Beanpot," forever rest in peace.

Contents

As boys growing up in the early 1960s in suburban Boston, we fell in love with college hockey. This was just before Bobby Orr and the Big Bad Bruins changed everything. Before all those MDC rinks went up. Before every Bruins game was brought into our living rooms on TV 38.

It was a time when the winters were colder. And it was a time when we skated outdoors—on ponds or uncovered rinks—more than we skated indoors. If we wanted to play the game indoors, we had few choices. The Lynn Arena. The Boston Skating Club. The Boston (now Matthews) Arena. The universities.

In Arlington, a particularly hockey-mad suburb, we also played a lot of street hockey. And since we hadn't yet been won over by the likes of Espo and Cheesie and Hodgie, when we played, we were the Beanpot schools. We were Eagles and Terriers and Huskies and the Crimson.

We sent half-frozen tennis balls covered with a layer of sand and salt flying around the streets and driveways, with someone providing play-by-play.

"Kick save by Ferreira! And what a Beauty!"

Before today's beautiful replica jerseys were even imagined, we took white cotton sweatshirts and, with colored markers, decorated them with a red BOSTON and our favorite number. The last *R* and *N* in NORTHEASTERN always seemed to be a little smaller than the rest of the letters. The Boston College and Harvard shirts looked a little funny because our red markers were the closest thing to maroon (or, excuse me, crimson) we could find.

If we weren't aping our favorite collegians on the ice or in the streets, we could be found in the Arena or at the Garden, sometimes watching our heroes, sometimes on the stairway landings continuing our games between periods. With a crushed soda cup and hockey stick remnants, both extracted from a nearby trash can, we could have a game under way within seconds of any period's buzzer. That is, of course, with the notable exception of the obligatory break for French fries at the Arena.

As special as the Bruins would soon become, college hockey was even more magical. The fact that some of the players came from our hometown and actually wore the Arlington jersey made it all the more fantastic. We never dreamed we could be pros. But if a guy from our town could play college hockey and play in the Beanpot, well, maybe we could too.

Later, when we made the high school team and got to play at the Garden, the dreams of college hockey seemed so real and possible. And then it happened. We got into colleges, made the teams, and some of us, truly blessed, played in the Beanpot.

The celebration of the Beanpot's fiftieth tournament gave many of us a chance to revisit our own Beanpot experiences. Fans, administrators, refs, coaches, and players—we all have memories of great moments and great games. For those of us who had a chance to compete for the 'Pot, the experience made us feel like members of a private club. For those who actually won it, that club was pretty exclusive.

The guardians of the Beanpot Tournament have maintained and nurtured this unique and special event for five decades. We can only hope that, as the world of athletics and our society change, the Beanpot's future will pass along into the hands of others who will appreciate what it means to so many in the local hockey community.

In late February 2002, a few weeks after Beanpot number 50, I attended a regular-season game at Matthews Arena. After doing a between-periods interview on the Huskies' student radio station, I started off in the direction of the rear stairway. There, just in front of the stairs, two kids were rolling around on the floor with broken sticks and a soda cup covered in white tape.

"What a save by Gibson!" said one. As I watched with an amused look on my face, the kids stopped for a second and looked up at me. Briefly, they wondered what I was staring at, then went back to their game.

As I walked onto St. Botolph Street, I remembered being the kid making those saves and doing play-by-play in that same building almost forty years earlier. I remembered how my dreams came true. And I hoped that if those kids dreamed about someday playing in the Beanpot, they, too, would realize those dreams and that the event would still be what we celebrate today.

—Joe Bertagna

I often wonder what the experts say about the power of first impressions. Can something that happened long ago hold a firmly entrenched place in overall memory, especially if you were just a child at the time?

Well, I am here to testify for the benefit of the field of psychotherapy that first impressions are indeed very powerful.

I attended my first college hockey game at age seven. Jack Parker was the BU captain. The Terriers defeated the University of New Brunswick 13–3 at the Boston (now Matthews) Arena.

My parents and grandfather were all BU graduates. My father and mother began attending games on a regular basis and became season ticket holders in the early 1960s.

For my first three years as a youth hockey–playing college hockey fan, I cherished my visits to the Boston Arena and some other venues around the old Eastern College Athletic Conference circuit. I even got to see the legendary Ken Dryden guard the Cornell net in the 1968 ECAC Tournament at Boston Garden; Mom, out with the flu, was unable to take her regular shift. That was on a Friday night.

The Garden. The Beanpot. Monday night. "A school night. Too late," was always the parental response to my plaintive pleas to attend. I even had a friend (a BC fan, no less) who was allowed to go to the Beanpot. Nevertheless, my Beanpot dream remained just that.

As a result, my earliest Beanpot memories are tied to a transistor radio. I listened in plain sight until lights out, then under the pillows in the dark to avoid the attention of any intrusive babysitter.

Then the dream came true. The 1970–71 Boston University team was one of the greatest in the history of college hockey. I had attended several of their games over the course of the season, and the Beanpot final—BU against Harvard—promised to be a memorable one. The BU-Harvard rivalry was at its pinnacle. And I was going to the Garden.

I can still remember the excitement and anticipation surrounding the day. That was one fifth-grade Monday that seemed to last forever. Making the trip to the Boston Garden with my parents and mingling with the other grownups was a heady experience for a ten-year-old.

I remember vividly the long walk up the ramp from the west lobby, the smell of popcorn, and the seats in the BU loge section. For a young Terrier fan, the game was great, and I can clearly recall the 4–1 final score, a second straight Beanpot title for BU.

But what stood out most about the game itself was BU killing off a two-man Harvard advantage for two full minutes, and the Terrier captain, center Steve Stirling, and defensemen Bob Murray and Mike LaGarde being on the ice for what seemed to be the entire two minutes and then receiving a spontaneous, rising standing ovation from the

BU corner of the Garden. That left an indelible impression. The Terrier penalty kill was the pivotal point in the game. Thirty years later, this is how I remember it.

While researching this book I went back to the microfilmed game accounts from the Boston newspapers. As I read the eyewitness description of the 1971 Beanpot final, I was at the same time amazed and vindicated by my recollections.

Apparently it's true. You never have a second chance to make a first impression—and that first impression is indelible.

—Bernard Corbett

THE BIRTH
OF THE BEANPOT
1952–1955

Christmas 1952. America liked Ike so much they had just elected the old soldier president. Frank had yet to surrender the stage to Elvis. The *Boston Globe* headlines were dominated by the war in Korea, the impending Brinks trial, and the prospective meeting between the Soviet Union's Josef Stalin and President-elect Dwight Eisenhower. With the Bruins and Celtics idle over the holiday, the upcoming NFL championship game between the Detroit Lions and the Cleveland Browns dominated the sports pages. Boston Garden was anxiously readying itself for the Ice Capades featuring Olympic champion Dick Button, who had recently signed a contract worth $150,000.

On the local sports scene, the Red Sox were without Ted Williams (on his second tour of military duty during the Korean War) for all but six games. They finished nineteen games behind the world-champion New York Yankees, who defeated the Brooklyn Dodgers in a seven-game World Series. The Celtics were still four years away from the arrival of Bill Russell. Professional football had already come and gone—three times—in the forms of the Bulldogs, the Yanks, and the Redskins. On the ice, the Bruins had placed third among the NHL's original six and lost to the Montreal Canadiens in the Stanley Cup finals the previous spring.

Walter Brown, Boston Garden president

(Courtesy of Boston Celtics)

And so it was that, on the day after Christmas 1952, the Boston Arena (the nation's oldest artificial-ice hockey rink) gave birth to its third child: the local National Hockey League (Bruins, 1924–28) and the National Basketball Association (Celtics, 1946) both had originally called the edifice on St. Botolph Street home.

The Beanpot Hockey Tournament was born.

There was no grand design to the future hockey classic's origin. The driving forces behind the tournament's inception were the same as they always were to the quintessential arena manager–entrepreneur of his day, Walter Brown: fill dates and sell tickets.

In October 1937, at age thirty-two, upon the sudden death of his father, George V. Brown, he had become the youngest manager of a major sports arena in the country. A tremendous innovator, the younger Brown's credits included the founding of the Ice Capades (1940) and the formation of the National Basketball Association (1946). His experience in hockey dated back to his management of the 1936 U.S. Olympics squad that competed in Garmisch-Partenkirchen, Germany.

At the time, the Boston Arena, first opened in 1910, operated virtually around the clock as home to all hockey at the amateur level in Greater Boston. Most of the local high school leagues and all four of the major college hockey teams—Boston College, Boston University, Harvard University, and Northeastern University—called the Arena

**Herb Gallagher, Northeastern
University's head coach**
(Courtesy of Northeastern University)

home ice. As a result, a number of college doubleheaders were scheduled there. It had caught the eye of the Garden/Arena Corporation management that when more than one of the four major colleges were on the bill together, the draw improved. The suggestion that perhaps a round-robin tournament could be played among the four local majors had been proposed several times to Brown, most prominently and persistently by Boston University's head coach, Harry Cleverly. Brown remained skeptical regarding the ability of such a tournament to attract sufficient fan support. When an agreement was reached to sell the Boston Arena building to a clothing manufacturer, Brown decided to meet with representatives of the four schools and formally discuss an experimental tournament at the lame duck venue.

Those present at the tournament's founding conclave included Boston College athletic director, John Curley; Buff Donnelli, athletic director at Boston University; Harvard Athletic Association business manager Carroll Getchell; and Herb Gallagher, head coach at Northeastern University. Walter Brown, the Garden/Arena Corporation's president, and his most-trusted associate, treasurer Eddie Powers, represented the venue. Gallagher had been dispatched to the meeting by Northeastern's athletic director, Edward Parsons, because of Gallagher's extensive and varied hockey background. He had starred for the Huskies' varsity (Class of 1935) and had coached the Austrian team at the same 1936 Olympic Games at which Brown had managed the U.S. team.

"I don't remember who suggested the tournament first," Gallagher recalled years later. "We'd had doubleheaders at the Arena and the Garden and somebody came up with the two-night tournament idea. Right then and there we worked out the rotating schedule that still exists, a schedule that gave each college the chance to play each of the other three in successive years. We sat around the table for . . . I think it took us one-and-a-half to two hours . . . and put a clock rotation (based on the seating at the table that day) on it so that rather than try and seed the teams, we agreed to rotate the clock each successive year and you would play one of the other three."

Prior to the 1965 tournament, when asked about that first meeting, Carroll Getchell seemed to remember Walter Brown suggesting the actual name. "I'm quite certain it was Walter, and do you know we went for a few years without a trophy? Then finally, one day, Walter said, 'Why the devil don't we have a Beanpot Trophy?' So now we have this large silver Beanpot." The trophy problem was solved by legendary Garden troubleshooter Tony Nota, who managed to acquire one.

Once an agreement had been reached regarding the playing of the tournament, the next step was to select the dates. "We wanted something in that Christmas–New Year's holiday vacation time," recalled Gallagher. "All four teams practiced and played at the Arena and it was customary to schedule back-to-back games. In fact, practice time was so limited that our teams generally played better the second night after their tune-up the previous evening."

"It was designed as a filler," observed Northeastern's Jack Grinold, the tournament's de facto historian, on the eve of the fiftieth renewal. "I mean it was originally the first two nights after Christmas. It was to help the Arena on off nights."

How much this new venture would help was a point of conjecture. In his game-day advance story on the tournament, a young *Boston Globe* sportswriter named Ernie Roberts remained skeptical about this Beanpot endeavor.

"Yet if collegiate hockey has any argument at all for its continued existence in the Garden after the Arena folds in the spring," Roberts wrote, "tonight and tomorrow night will give impetus to a drive to save the Arena for sports not suits."

Roberts went on to make a fateful prediction. The New England Invitational Basketball Tourney was also scheduled at the Arena later that week. Boston College, Rhode Island and Georgetown universities, and the University of Seattle (led by Johnny O'Brien and his twin brother, Eddie) constituted the field. Roberts flatly predicted that "the basketball tourney will outdraw the hockey gang." He was proven wrong: the hoop crowd numbered half that of the ice followers.

It is significant to note that the first Beanpot gathering was commonly referred to as the New England Invitational Tournament. The feeling was that Brown was keeping his options open for possible changes in the future field. Dartmouth, an Eastern hockey power at the time, was thought to be a potential Beanpot participant. To the Garden/Arena Corporation the political stakes were high with regard to the future of the local college game. Brown's desire to showcase the Arena as an appealing venue for hockey on a national level was firmly at the root of his motivation. There was no hiding Brown's disdain for the scenario surrounding the NCAA hockey tournament, which had begun four years earlier. The Broadmoor Hotel in Colorado Springs, Colorado, was subsidizing, and thus hosting, the annual tournament (in partnership with Colorado College) to determine a national champion.

At the weekly college hockey luncheon prior to the inaugural tournament, Brown seized the opportunity to state the greater objective of this addition to the Boston winter sports scene: save the Boston Arena. "The Arena would already be saved if the NCAA hockey tournament were in Boston," he bluntly surmised. "I believe for the NCAA event the Garden could be sold out for two nights without trouble. It is not too late for the colleges to think of the future of their sport, rather than selfishly of junkets to Colorado Springs."

The Broadmoor was no roach motel. It happened to be, and still is, one of the premier resort hotels in the United States. It kept its stranglehold on the NCAA championship until 1957, but the Arena served as host in 1960, only the third tournament played outside of the Springs.

1952   And so, on Friday, December 26, 1952, some 5,105 intrepid souls—fewer than one thousand short of the Arena's capacity—braved a bitterly cold night to attend the opening round of the first New England Invitational Tournament, sponsored on radio station WVON (AM 1600) by the Beacon Wax Company ("Biggest Floor Wax Seller in New England").

There was considerable media enthusiasm from scribes other than Mr. Roberts. Paul Hines, Jr., of the *Boston Post*, a noted, longtime hockey observer, referred to the tournament as the "most attractive college hockey presentation in a generation." The venerable Leonard M. Fowle of the *Globe* offered that "college hockey fans will have the newest approach yet to the dream set-up they have hoped to see realized for many years. The New England Invitational Hockey Tournament is neither the Greater Boston nor the super–New England and college league which has been often advocated but it is a big step in the right direction to get BC, BU, Harvard, and NU together for the so-called 'Beanpot' Tournament."

The original home of the Beanpot— Boston Arena. Renamed Matthews Arena, today it is home to the Northeastern Huskies.

(Courtesy of Northeastern University)

All four coaches concurred on praising two things: the tournament concept and their opponents. The belief that the tournament could potentially provide a great boost to the city was shared by the entire hockey community.

"Any of the teams can win and I've maintained a good team can knock off any team if keyed up for a particular game," said Boston College coach Snooks Kelley. "My formula for winning is material, coaching, and that indefinable something which I like to call spirit. . . . Take Harvard. We've all seen it has the material, we know it has the coaching, and I'm sure Cooney Weiland is in a position to supply his squad with the spirit of Christmastime."

Ray Picard, Northeastern University goalie, 1952

(Courtesy of Northeastern University)

Northeastern (5-1), led by its all-American netminder, Ray Picard, and bolstered by the return of Walt Saborski, was a slight underdog to BU (2-1-1), a strong offensive team led by future Gold Medal Olympian Dick Rodenheiser (1960). Harvard (2-0) welcomed back forwards Norman Wood and Dick Clasby (perhaps the Crimson's best all-time, all-around athlete), who had injured his back in that fall's Harvard-Yale game. The Crimson were favored against Boston College (1-1), which was in the unaccustomed role of slim underdog. The Eagles' strength was on defense. The first line of Bobby Babine centering right wing Wimpy Burtnett and left wing Jack Canniff had been reshuffled by Snooks Kelley in the aftermath of a 6–4 loss to Brown.

**Dick Rodenheiser, Boston
University forward, 1952**

(Courtesy of Boston University)

 A blast down the alley—after a corner pass out by Ed Hubbard—off the stick of captain Walter Greeley at 3:51 of overtime sent the undefeated Harvard sextet into the finals of the New England invitation tournament last night at the Boston Arena.

The Crimson's opponent in the Beanpot Tourney final at 9 tonight will be Boston University, which subdued Northeastern 4–1 before 5,105. Last night's losers, BC and Northeastern, will meet in a consolation game at 7.

Greeley's goal broke up a tight contest, with Harvard capitalizing on a BC penalty plus the break of having Jack Canniff tumble into his own nets and partially pull Joe Carroll out of position. The Crimson had an early lead, but the Eagles tied it and went ahead 2–1 in the middle period.

Then Dick Clasby sank his second tally of the night when off-balance to send the game into overtime. All Harvard goals were scored by the first line, which looked very impressive. Clasby was on the right wing for Captain Greeley and Ed Hubbard. Ed Richardson did some fine work in the nets and Jeff Coolidge stood out at defense. Larry Babine was the BC sparkplug as captain Wimpy Burtnett, Frank O'Grady, Billy Maguire and Joe Carroll played fine hockey for an Eagle six which was vastly improved over its earlier games.

Boston University dominated its game from start to finish as the Huskies failed to show their usual spark, probably because several players were suffering from an attack of flu. The score might have been larger but for Ray Picard's great work, especially in the first period when he made 18 saves. Different Terrier lines scored their first three goals, off the sticks of Dick Rodenheiser, Paul Whalen and Johnny Burns. Jerry Denning got the fourth on a Rodenheiser set-up before Dick Smith prevented a shutout on a Jim Campion pass in the final minutes.

The BC-Harvard contest hit a fast pace in the opening period. After each had ridden out a penalty, Harvard scored on a pretty play, started when Ed Hubbard took the rubber over the blueline and passed forward to captain Walt Greeley near the right face-off circle. The Framingham pivot stick-handled away from a defender and then shot a 20-foot pass to Dick Clasby, who drove a slap shot just off the ice by Joe Carroll at 13:06.

The Eagles tied it up in three minutes when Frank O'Grady, after a length-of-the-rink dash down the left boards, caught the near corner with a beauty of a shot when Brad Richardson failed to hug the post.

Early in the second period, Sherm Saltmarsh went down the ice close to the boards and sent a pass across the mouth of the Crimson cage to Billy Maguire. The Eagles' second line center converted from about six feet out and just on the right of the cage to put BC ahead.

Dick Clasby tied the game at 6:51 of the third when he caged his own rebound from a failing position about six feet in front of Joe Carroll. The Crimson was the aggressor, except for a few jumps, through the first 15 minutes of this session, and then BC put on a spirited rally which kept Richardson busy until a penalty against Norbert Timmons relieved pressure. Harvard could not tally and the game went into overtime.

The Huskies and Terriers started by covering closely. This made for a slow opening 12 minutes, even though BU was in Northeastern's zone three-quarters of the time. Picard made many saves, several of them sensational, before a series of penalties speeded up the action.

BU could not score with a two-man advantage, but the Scarlet broke through when each outfit was shy a player. Dick Lee set up Dick Rodenheiser with a rebound a couple of feet outside the crease. Picard stopped the Malden mite's first shot, but a second found home at 16:33. The Terriers left the ice leading 1–0.

Following a scrimmage on an uncalled but obvious offside, the Huskies left Paul Whalen uncovered at 4:25 of the second period. After taking Lee's pass, he beat Picard from the left of the cage. BU's third line got in the scoring act near half-time on a double jump which allowed Paul Cleary to set up Johnny Burns on his left for the third goal at 13:34.

Jerry Denning completed the BU scoring in the final session when he converted a perfect pass-out from Dick Rodenheiser at 13:09. The Huskies avoided a shutout with

less than two minutes remaining when Dick Smith swept in on Paul Kelley for a close-up score after taking a pass from Jim Campion.

—Leonard Fowle, *Boston Globe*, December 27, 1952

Despite Harvard's more grueling overtime test the previous night, most experts picked the Crimson to capture the tournament.

"Don't think Northeastern didn't take something out of BU," said Harvard coach Cooney Weiland. "That NU defense is tough and they were giving Rodenheiser a going over.

"This overtime win will help us on spirit, and winning the Beanpot tourney means an awful lot to us. All but two of our squad are from Greater Boston."

"I'd just as soon stay away from Harvard," said the 145-pound Rodenheiser, fatigued from a combination of school, hockey, and full-time work as a gas station attendant. "They're a big, strong club."

The two finalists had previously battled to a 4–4 draw earlier in the season. Now they would clash for the first Beanpot title.

Sparked by captain Walt Greeley's three goals and backed by Brad Richardson's superb netminding, perhaps the best Harvard sextet since George Ford's 1937 team won the "Beanpot" tournament at the Boston Arena here tonight. The Crimson, never headed, prevailed by 7–4 over Boston University as 3,382 watched.

Captain Wimpy Burtnett, Boston College forward, 1952
(Courtesy of Boston College)

Boston College won the consolation game of this New England Invitation Tournament with a hard earned 2–0 triumph at Northeastern's expense. The goals, by captain Wimpy Burtnett and Frank O'Grady, came hard against another great bit of goaltending by Ray Picard.

Previously unsung Brad Richardson from New York City, via Milton Academy, shared the Harvard honors. A determined Terrier sextet threw everything except a Beanpot at Brad in the first period and he turned aside 16 shots, many of them sensational saves. Thereafter he had more stops than Paul Kelley, but, except in two spurts, the BU attack slowed down after that hectic first period.

The Crimson got the only goal of the first period and went ahead 4–1 in the second session. The teams traded scores—three apiece—in the final 20 minutes, although several of the goals, on both sides, were slightly shabby. The triumph, Harvard's first over the Terriers since December 1949, left the Crimson with the only undefeated record—3 wins and a tie—held by a major team in the east.

Harvard tallied one goal by George Chase in the first period and went two up on captain Walter Greeley's score just after the second period started. Tony Cicoria got the Terriers' first goal at 11:34. Greeley scored his second at 14:02, followed by one by Doug Manchester.

Mario Zanetti tallied for BU at 4:21 of the third but Ed Ellis got it back. Greeley's third goal put the game beyond recall as BU picked up two by Paul Whalen and Dick Rodenheiser. Harvard's Ed Hubbard scored the final goal with six seconds left.

The BC-NU game was only two minutes old when a Northeastern shot caught Boston College's Joe Carroll over the left temple. Carroll required six stitches to close the wound and was bruised under a cheekbone. He retired in favor of Vincent Tarky, who shutout the Huskies for 38 minutes before Carroll returned for the final period.

—Leonard Fowle, *Boston Globe*, December 28, 1952

The original Beanpot coaches.
Standing (left to right): Snooks Kelley (BC), Harry Cleverly (BU), and
Herb Gallagher (Northeastern).
Seated: Cooney Weiland (Harvard)
(Courtesy of Beanpot Hall of Fame)

1954   Favorable reviews for the inaugural event delivered the Beanpot Tournament to a more fashionable (and permanent) Causeway Street address for year two. Boston College, the East's third-ranked team, was the pre-tourney favorite as the quartet of schools gathered on consecutive nights early in January 1954.

That close to 8,500 fans attended the tourney's post-Christmas debut in December 1952 augured well for an even bigger gate at the Boston Garden. Instead, a severe Nor'easter reduced the opening-night crowd to a minuscule 711 at the new, more cavernous host venue.

Snooks Kelley's Eagles (8-1) had suffered their only loss to St. Lawrence two weeks earlier at the fledgling Boston Arena Tournament. The concept of the Arena hosting an annual holiday hockey tournament in effect allowed the Beanpot, as it had become known, to find another place on the calendar for its unique, strictly parochial brand of ice warfare. The Arena Tournament invited two teams from outside Greater Boston to compete with two teams calling the St. Botolph icehouse home. Also on the bill for this first tournament were BU, Middlebury, and St. Lawrence.

Early in the season, BC had handled their first-round Beanpot opponents, Northeastern (3-6), easily with a score of 6–0. Skating three lines on a regular basis, the Eagles' overall depth was undeniable. Two-goal efforts by Bobby Babine, Jim Duffy, and John Canniff paced the Eagles offense in an 8–5 victory. After squandering a 4–1 second-period lead, the Eagles rallied back to decide the game early in its final stanza. "That ten-day [actually twelve-day] layoff hurt us and we took Northeastern too lightly," confessed BC mentor Kelley. Nevertheless, the 1953–54 Boston College squad was the first Eagle team to play in the Beanpot finals.

The defending tournament champions from Harvard had garnered a great measure of renewed respect from a dominating 4–0 win over Dartmouth the previous weekend. Skating three lines regularly presented the Crimson with a huge advantage over struggling Boston University (1-6-1) in a rematch of the previous season's title game. Although BU was severely undermanned, aggressive forechecking, solid goaltending by Dick Bradley (thirty-four saves), and two goals from sophomore sensation Jack Murphy of Cambridge kept the game stalemated at 2–2. A goal by Scott Cooledge, with under two minutes remaining in the third period, swung the game to the Crimson skaters, who held on for a 3–2 victory. The first Harvard versus Boston College Beanpot championship clash was established.

A crowd of 2,399 turned out the next evening, one day removed from the tenacious blizzard conditions. Following a scoreless first period, Harvard jumped out to a 1–0 lead on a goal by captain Norm Wood. BC's prolific Jim Duffy notched his first of two goals and set up teammate Bob Gallagher for another goal, securing the Eagles a lead they would not relinquish. "I thought our club looked real good out there tonight," observed BC's Kelley, "especially our defense and of course our goalie, Chick D'Entremont." The sophomore netminder from Stoneham had been criticized by the wily Eagle mentor for his inconsistent play and had responded with an impressive overall performance.

Most formidable of all the Eagle skaters, though, was their five-foot-four-inch, 124-pound center, Bob Babine. The diminutive BC captain inspired his teammates with his relentless on-ice demeanor. His spectacular, streaking breakaway goal, with 3:45 left in regulation play, had given the Eagles a critical two-goal advantage at 3–1. A second marker by Duffy, with one second remaining, set the final count at Boston College: 4–Harvard: 1. The Eagles had captured their first Beanpot and won the first of many memorable battles with the Crimson for all the beans.

"They capitalized on their scoring chances and we didn't. That was it," offered Harvard coach Cooney Weiland. "We had our scoring opportunities, but when you can't put the puck in the net you can't expect to win. One of our boys was in all alone just before the second period ended but couldn't do anything." The Eagles' Beanpot victory would commence an undefeated stretch run that would take BC to the NCAA tournament in Colorado Springs for the third time in six years.

1955   The third meeting of the Beanpot schools would complete the "once around the table," first-round rotation established at the tournament's initial organizing session. The defending champions from Boston College (7-6) were without the services of several injured players, including leading scorer Bill Leary of Arlington. But Boston University (3-14) had endured a thirteen-game losing streak that ended with a 6–3 win over Army immediately before the tournament. As a result, the Eagles remained a decided favorite in the first ever all–Commonwealth Avenue Beanpot clash.

A gathering of 2,560, a slight increase over the previous year's final-round crowd, witnessed a torrid Eagle offensive onslaught. After squandering a 4–1 lead, BC posted the first of five unanswered third-period goals on a tally by sophomore Joe Moylon. Forward Ed Coakley deposited his second goal of the night just short of the five-minute mark of the third period. The Eagles never looked back in their 9–5 demolition of their oldest rival.

The opening semifinal game of the first Beanpot Tournament to be held during what has come to be the time-honored, traditional month of February was a showcase for the first true icon of Beanpot history. Compiling a record of 7-2-1 prior to their mid-January exam break, Harvard's number three–rated team in the East was primed for a return to action versus a 3-10 Northeastern team they had already defeated twice. It was less the Harvard team and, to a far greater extent, one Harvard player, who had captured the imagination of the local hockey community.

William J. Cleary, Jr., a bona fide hometown Harvard hero from Cambridge, had begun his association with Crimson athletics selling programs in front of venerable Harvard Stadium. After graduating from Belmont Hill in 1952, Cleary embarked on a half-century career with Harvard University as a two-sport athlete (hockey and baseball). He followed this with a stint as assistant coach to his mentor, Cooney Weiland, and a nineteen-year tenure as head coach highlighted by delivering the

Billy Cleary, 1955 tournament MVP

(Courtesy of Harvard University)

The Birth of the Beanpot 1952–1955

nation's oldest university its first-ever NCAA team title (1989) in school history. He would culminate his career in the Square as the school's athletic director for eleven years of unprecedented growth. While Cleary would also officiate at several Beanpots, his on-ice exploits during his only appearance as a Beanpot player remain unsurpassed, towering over the accomplishments of many who have participated in the annual mid-winter celebration during the intervening half-century.

Cleary's initial appearance on the hallowed Garden ice established marks that still stand as tournament records today, in all probability never to be broken. His five-goal and two-assist opening game performance set the Beanpot records for goals and points in a single game. As a result, Harvard overwhelmed Northeastern 12–3 and earned the opportunity to dethrone the reigning champions from Boston College the next night. The two teams had split a pair of matches earlier in the season but it remained to be seen if anybody—even Snooks Kelley—had an answer for the incomparable Billy Cleary.

 Billy Cleary, Harvard's greatest player of the decade—perhaps the best since George Owen—won the annual Beanpot tournament for the Crimson at the Garden last night with a goal at 1:24 of overtime after Boston College almost stole the game with a torrid two-goal rally in the last minute and nine seconds. The score was 5–4.

Chick D'Entremont, Boston College goalie, 1955

(Courtesy of Boston College)

Cleary, who was voted the tournament's most valuable player and the only unanimous choice on the All-Beanpot six, contributed two goals and two assists despite as close coverage as any college player has been subjected to this season.

Boston College, beaten a month ago by an 8–2 tally and playing without its star, Billy Leary, turned in one of those inspirational performances for which coach John Kelley's teams are famous.

More than once the Eagles had the Crimson hanging on the ropes in a contest in which they jumped Harvard to score first and twice rallied to tie the count—the last time with two goals by Dick Dempsey when the game was seemingly lost.

The windup came with Harvard's Tom Worthen in the penalty box and the Eagles storming the Crimson end of the rink. Cleary picked up the rubber along the right boards, 10 feet inside the Harvard blueline, and raced down the boards with a lone Eagle in hopeless pursuit.

Billy came in on Chick D'Entremont, and took his time to fake the BC goalie to the left, before firing the rubber home.

—Leonard Fowle, *Boston Globe*, February 9, 1955

The Pioneers

It started as an excuse to get out of the house and tell a few lies among friends. A group of men, all approaching or just charging into their seventies, who shared a common bond. Much like the tournament itself, the idea of a fiftieth-anniversary reunion for the participants from the first Beanpot tournament took shape with no grand plan in mind. The town of Framingham, the current or former residence for many of these pioneers, became a monthly meeting place for the six committee members, who included at least one representative of each of the four Beanpot schools. They began to formulate a plan. Would this be a formal reunion event or something as informal as the organizational meetings? Once the current Beanpot committee found out about the efforts of these pioneers, a formal event it became.

Bud Purcell, 1952–53 Huskies captain, organized the fiftieth Beanpot reunion.

(Courtesy of Northeastern University)

They gathered on a blustery late-January afternoon, at the appropriately named Legends Club at Boston's FleetCenter, current home to the Beanpot. The group, comprising thirty-nine original Beanpot skaters and thirty-six assorted wives and family members, included Northeastern's 1952–53 captain, defenseman Bud Purcell, who was the first to speak on behalf of his assembled teammates. "Northeastern standing first can't help but remind me of a biblical reference—'The Last Shall Be First,'" said Purcell, acknowledging Northeastern's fourth-place finish in December 1952. "It's wonderful to see all you fellas together again. I can't wait for the seventy-fifth."

Next up was Boston College, represented by Joe Carroll, a former goalie. "I can't help but remember today how excited Snooks would get about the Beanpot," said Carroll. "It's a great tournament and I know it will go on forever." Carroll also singled out his gentlemanly teammate, Billy Maguire, who "never got penalties" but was whistled off in the third period of the Eagles' opening round game with BU. The resulting power play goal by Harvard's Walt Greeley proved to be the game winner. Fifty years later, the fact that the official was Billy Cleary, Sr., remained a hot topic for discussion.

Dick Rodenheiser of Boston University, a Terrier all-American and member of the first "miracle on ice"—the 1960 U.S. Olympic hockey team that won the gold medal in Squaw Valley—talked of the camaraderie shared among "kids who played the game," with a half-century of reverence. "I'm glad I'm up here speaking now," Rodenheiser observed. "Then the Harvard team will come here and talk for about an hour. They all have speeches in Greek!"

Among his teammates in attendance was Paul Whalen, a career coach at Berwick Academy in Maine, who had a forward named Mike Eruzione on his 1972–73 team.

Last to approach the podium was Brad Richardson, chairman from the Harvard contingent, who, in a politically correct tone, thanked all the wives in attendance who had "heard about the Beanpot for fifty years." He then pointed out the Harvard captain, Walt Greeley. If the distinguished MVP of the first Beanpot tournament looked as if he could still lace 'em up and play, it was probably due to the fact that he is still playing. Two months short of his seventieth birthday, Greeley plays competitively, with over fifty skaters, at his hometown rink, Loring Arena in Framingham. Walt's tournament days are also far from over. He recently competed in the Senior Olympics at Lake Placid, New York, as well as in tournaments in Minnesota and Canada. The Beanpot as fountain of youth is personified by Greeley, its original outstanding performer.

SNOOKS AND COONEY
THE BOSTON COLLEGE–HARVARD RIVALRY 1956–1963

**C H A P T E R
T W O**

The Boston College–Harvard rivalry defined the first decade of Beanpot hockey, as two legendary coaches made the title game their personal birthright.

John "Snooks" Kelley and Ralph "Cooney" Weiland were already established hockey icons decades prior to the Beanpot's arrival. The route they traveled to their respective positions behind the Eagle and Crimson benches couldn't have been more different, but their relative successes bore a strong resemblance and fostered a tremendous on-ice rivalry between the two schools.

Kelley, an Irish Catholic from Cambridge and a standout athlete at BC High, was the varsity hockey manager at Boston College for three years before becoming a "playing manager" during the 1927–28 season, his senior year. The 1928 Boston College year-book described Snooks as "a peach of a center iceman. Not the fastest man in the world on skates, our fair-haired Cantab more than excelled by his proficiency in carrying the puck and his earnestness."

In 1933 Snooks stopped playing for the Boston Hockey Club and returned to his alma mater as a volunteer coach. For the next four decades (interrupted only by a World War II stint in the Navy), until his retirement in 1972, Snooks Kelley guided his beloved Eagles into battle, changing the face of college hockey by becoming the first coach to win five hundred games. Kelley's 1949 BC squad became the first Eastern school to win a National Championship. His record—eight Beanpot titles—remained the tourney standard until 1992.

A member of the Boston College and United States Hockey halls of fame, Kelley was noted for a fire-and-brimstone oratorical style directed both at his own team and at the audience at the Beanpot luncheon, where he originated the "Beanpot Charge," an annual rallying call.

Cooney Weiland arrived on the Harvard campus in 1950. The Seaforth, Ontario, native, a former Stanley Cup–winning player (1929 and 1939) and coach (1941) with the National Hockey League's Boston Bruins, could not have been more of an out-sider to the college game or to the world of academia. The first half-century of Har-vard coaches prior to Weiland had all been former Harvard centermen. The hiring of a non-Harvard man and a former professional player and coach was quite a radical change of policy (although athletic director Bill Bingham had chosen John P. "Stuffy" McInnis, first baseman in Connie Mack's famed 1911 Philadelphia Athletics "Million Dollar Infield," as head baseball coach in 1949).

After going through a brief adjustment period during his first two seasons, which ironically preceded the first Beanpot, the former center of the Bruins' fabled "Dynamite Line" put together an impressive résumé that included 315 wins in 21 seasons. Among the victories were five Beanpot titles, beginning with the inau-gural competition in 1952. Weiland, a member of the National Hockey League Hall of Fame, will forever hold a unique place in Boston sports lore for his accom-plishments at both the professional and collegiate level on the hallowed Garden ice.

As different as two coaches could be in their backgrounds, Snooks and Cooney shared a fierce loyalty to their respective schools and an endless list of humorous anecdotes.

Always looking to give his team an edge, for example, Snooks was extolling the virtues of an opponent in his passionate style before a game at McHugh Forum one evening. Finally, one of his players stood up and asked the coach how he knew so much about the other team, which was from upstate New York and hadn't played in Boston previously.

"I know," the coach said matter-of-factly. "I scouted them on the radio."

On the other bench, Cooney was ever an equal as a character. Before a trip to the NCAA tournament one year, a local television sportscaster asked Weiland what he thought about the University of Minnesota, the Crimson's next opponent.

"Well, they got a lot of lakes there," the Harvard mentor replied in a deadpan manner. "And it's pretty cold, so I would think they have some pretty good hockey players." The days before videotape and endless breakdown of game films was truly a more innocent time.

Boston College forward Jim Tiernan, 1956 MVP

(Courtesy of Boston College)

1956   Weiland's Harvard squad entered the 1956 tournament as defending champions. Despite a 7-7 overall record, the Crimson had the advantage of a four-game winning streak. By comparison, their first-round opponents from Boston University arrived on a three-game losing streak and minus three players, who had been lost to scholastic ineligibility.

In the other first-round matchup, Boston College, with an 11-2 season mark, arrived intent on recapturing the title. An inconsistent Northeastern team (8-8) that had played BC evenly into the final minutes of a 3–2 loss earlier in the season would attempt to engineer a Garden upset.

The two first-round matches were played before a crowd of only 2,500—a dramatic decline from the 5,654 witnesses to Cleary's exploits the previous year.

Boston College skated to a 7–1 win over Northeastern in the opening game. Scoreless for almost two periods, the Eagles took the lead on the first of two goals each by Jim Tiernan and Frank Quinn. A patented BC offensive explosion (five goals) followed in the third period. The Eagles extended their all-time series dominance of Northeastern to a gaudy 40-2-3.

Harvard dominated the late game. A depleted BU team, playing without captain Jack Murphy, who was sidelined with a broken jaw, proved to be no match for the Crimson. A balanced scoring attack featuring six goals from six different players catapulted Harvard back to the title game by a 6–1 final count over the Terriers.

Forty-eight hours later the two teams were ready to meet for the third straight year to decide Boston collegiate hockey supremacy.

While the players on both teams voiced pregame confidence, Kelley and Weiland took a more cautious approach. The prospects for an overtime period to decide the winner seemed to be a legitimate concern for both men.

In a spirited battle before a crowd of four thousand, the Eagles gained a measure of revenge and regained the Beanpot crown with a 4–2 victory over Harvard. Led by captain Ed Carroll's two goals and one assist, BC recovered from an early Harvard scoring strike by Mario Celi to take the lead for good early in the second period on a goal by Frank Quinn. First-round offensive standout Jim Tiernan of Boston College, a Providence, Rhode Island, native, netted a third-period goal and was selected as the tournament's MVP.

Snooks Kelley's strategic use of a "floater" at forward paid major dividends in the BC attack. The technique of playing a forward behind the opposition's defense at the offensive blue line was a favorite play of the wily Kelley, who often advocated a quick-striking offensive approach to the game. But the Eagles' overall depth proved to be the deciding factor, as Harvard's Weiland was forced to use just two lines as the game continued. The Beanpot was back on Chestnut Hill. In March, the Eagles would return to the Broadmoor in Colorado Springs, Colorado, to make their fifth NCAA tournament appearance.

1957 Boston College entered the 1957 tournament with an injury-plagued squad. A Northeastern squad that the Eagles had routed 12–3 a month earlier provided the opening-round competition for the second consecutive year. Paced by the offensive exploits of Roslindale's Joe Celeta (four goals), the Eagles cruised to a 6–0 win over the Huskies that could have been more lopsided if not for the stellar goaltending of NU's Ed Kerr.

The nightcap of the opening round promised a much closer matchup, with both Harvard (9-2) and BU (10-4) enjoying successful seasons. In a stunning turnabout, the Terriers rallied from a 3–0 deficit halfway through the game to score five unanswered goals and advance to the finals by a 5–3 count. It was the Terriers' seventh straight win after a 4-4 start to their season. The stage was set for the first all-Commonwealth Avenue championship game in Beanpot history. The sixty-first meeting between the two ancient Green Line rivals, who began competing in ice hockey during World War I, would be played for all the beans in Boston.

A more stable BU team looked to unseat the defending champions from the Heights on the following Tuesday. The Eagles' woes had mounted due to illness, eligibility trouble, and previous injuries.

The Terriers burst from the gate quickly, taking a 2–0 lead on a pair of goals by Sarge Kinlin. A miscue by BU goalie Hank Levin (thirty-two saves) in the second period proved costly, as he inadvertently swept a shot by BC's Ned Bunyan into the net on an ill-fated clearing attempt. The Terriers later regained their two-goal advantage (3–1) after two periods but were unable to stem the Eagles' torrid third-period onslaught. BC drew even, at 3–3, on markers by Dick Kane and Don Fox, only to witness Kinlin's completion of his hat trick with just 1:40 remaining in regulation. It was simply not the Terriers' night, however, as the irrepressible Bunyan combined with Kane and Fox to tally his second goal with just 53 seconds remaining in regulation time. The tenacious Eagles would strike for the deciding goal at 2:24 of overtime on a Joe Eclat shot from the right boards that trickled through the legs of BU's beleaguered netminder Levin.

The frustrated Terriers had been denied the title for the second time in as many final appearances. BC's Eclat followed Tiernan as tournament MVP. The Snooker's high-flying Eagles had become the Beanpot's first back-to-back champions.

1958   The 1958 tournament became the first to be played on what has become the familiar "first-two-Mondays-in-February" format.

Coach Harry Cleverly's Terriers (11-2) came into the tournament's opening round replay of the 1957 overtime final versus Boston College as one of the nation's most prolific offensive teams. At the other end of Commonwealth Avenue, the Eagles were an uncharacteristic 5-5-1.

The other first-round game projected Harvard as a huge favorite over Northeastern, a squad they had humbled 11–0 a scant four nights earlier.

In a game that the *Boston Globe*'s Leonard Fowle described as "one of the sport's most startling reversals of fortune," the Huskies advanced to the Beanpot final for the first

1958 NU players (left to right) Arthur Paresky (one goal), Ed Kerr (forty-three saves), Donald Cronin (three goals and one assist), and George Lambert (one goal and four assists) keyed the upset of Harvard.
(Courtesy of *Boston Globe*)

time in tournament history with a stunning 5–4 victory. The sensational forty-three-save netminding effort of Ed Kerr and the offensive combination of George Lambert (one goal, four assists) and Don Cronin (three goals, one assist) propelled the denizens of Huntington Avenue to the marquee game the following Monday.

"Northeastern was up and Kerr sure had a great night," offered Harvard coach Cooney Weiland in the aftermath of the Crimson defeat. Weiland had been openly second-guessed for his decision to start his number-two goalie, Dick Cleary.

Could lightning strike again in the guise of a second upset? Boston College coach Snooks Kelley, considered the master strategist of the college game at the time, certainly thought it could. The Eagle mentor had always brought out the best in his teams when they played against BU. Two weeks prior to the Beanpot, the Terriers had needed a six-goal, third-period offensive explosion to turn back the Eagles 7–4.

The best college hockey crowd (6,117) of the season witnessed a BU-BC classic that wasn't decided until Terrier all-American center Bob Marquis broke a 4–4 deadlock with the game-winning goal halfway through the third period. With a pair, BU forward Bill Sullivan was the Terriers' only multiple-goal scorer. Coach Kelley had no excuses in defeat. "Al Pitts was great," Snooks said, referring to his goalie. "Everyone carried out his assignment."

Above: Bob Marquis, Boston University forward, scored the game-winning goal that put BU in the 1958 title game.
(Courtesy of Boston University)

Below: 1958 Boston University line (left to right) Dave MacLeod, Bill Sweeney, and Bill Sullivan (MVP)
(Courtesy of *Boston Globe*)

The Terriers had slain their personal dragon. Although "amazed at the first game," BU's Cleverly insisted his team would not be taking Northeastern lightly.

The underdog Huskies would enjoy unprecedented adulation during the week between games. Coach Jim Bell, a former NU player himself, and the youngest of the Beanpot coaching fraternity in Boston, was elated over his squad's come-from-behind win.

"There's only one win that could be greater than that over Harvard," explained Bell. "And that would be over Boston University next Monday in the Beanpot final."

Jim Bell, Northeastern University head coach, pictured as NU player.
(Courtesy of Northeastern University)

Praise for the Huskies' accomplishment came from all corners. "Northeastern should be an example to all underdog college teams in the future," observed Cooney Weiland. "I don't think the Huskies will ever play a finer game."

On the ice, the heavily favored Terriers tuned up for their Causeway Street recital with a 9–3 romp over Army. Meanwhile, Coach Bell juggled the Northeastern lineup. Two defensemen by trade, Connie Harrington and Walt Harney, were moved to the Huskies' first line in order to neutralize the dangerous Marquis.

The Terriers had handled NU in the teams' two previous meetings but had been upset by the Huskies late in the 1956–57 season. The only thing the Beanpot fans could be sure of was that a new champion would be crowned on the Garden ice. The exclusive Harvard-Boston College hold on the 'Pot would end.

A disappointing crowd of only 4,784 turned out for the "dog fight" between the Terriers and the Huskies. Local sportswriters speculated that a BU–Harvard final would have doubled the gate. In the consolation game, Harvardian Bob Cleary's dominant offensive efforts (three goals, three assists) sent the Eagles to an unfathomable double Beanpot loss, 7–3.

 Boston University is the new Beanpot champion. The Scarlet won the trophy for the first time by thumping a game but outclassed Northeastern by six in the Garden last night by a 9–3 score.

Bill Sullivan led the Terrier attack with a hat trick, matching one by Bobby Cleary in the preliminary game. Two other Terriers hung up double tallies, Don MacLeod collecting one each in the first and second periods and brother Dave sinking two in the final session.

Bill Sweeney and Bob Marquis got single goals for the Terriers as Jack Carruthers, Larry Creighton, and Bob Dupuis each had three assists.

For part of the opening period, the fighting and close-covering Huskies made trouble for the victors. Even after Sullivan's pair of tallies, NU threatened when Jim Walsh scored at the 15-minute mark, but Don MacLeod's first goal allowed the Terriers to leave the ice leading 3 to 1.

Then three goals in a minute and 25 seconds early in the second period wrapped it up. . . . Art Paresky made the contest respectable again with a pair for Northeastern only 20 seconds apart in the final period when BU was leading 8 to 1.

—Leonard M. Fowle, *Boston Globe*, February 11, 1958

1959 Normalcy would return the next year for one-half of the Beanpot's dominant early rivals, as Boston College arrived at the first Monday in February with an 11-3 record ready to take on a sub-.500 (5-6-2) Harvard team.

The Eagles recovered from a slow start to defeat the Crimson, 6–4, with an impressive stretch run. A similar Terrier rally from an early 2–1 deficit offset the heroics of Northeastern's Art Chisholm (two goals and two assists) in a 7–4 BU victory, as all-American center Bob Marquis (two goals and two assists) matched the Husky's offensive numbers.

Although Northeastern University's Art Chisholm was arguably the best all-around performer in tournament history never to play in a championship game, the chunky Arlington native was the last cut of the 1956 U.S. Olympic hockey team and a charter selection for the Beanpot Hall of Fame (1995).

(Courtesy of Northestern University)

The tournament title showdown between BU and BC brought a crowd of 8,180 to the Garden. The Terriers, seeking a repeat of their 1958 success, were, instead, buried early in the proceedings. Boston College jumped to a 4–0 advantage after one period and never lost command of the game. The old Snooks Kelley "floater play" sprung Billy Daley for a breakaway goal on a pass from sophomore defenseman Tom "Red" Martin only forty-eight seconds after the opening face-off. A wild brawl late in the game, which began with BC captain Joe Jangro and BU's Forbes Keith squaring off, led to six player ejections—three on each side.

The Eagles had gained revenge for a 5–1 loss to the Terriers earlier in the season. In addition to grabbing the local college hockey bragging rights represented by the Beanpot, BC took a major step toward Eastern supremacy with the 7–4 victory. It was the Eagles' fourth title in seven years. His thirty-two-save performance in the title game distinguished Boston College netminder Jim Logue as first nonforward to be named tournament MVP.

After a two-year absence, BC would return to the NCAA tournament in March 1959.

Jim Logue, Boston College goalie and 1959 MVP

(Courtesy of Boston College)

1960   The dawning of a new decade produced the tournament's largest crowd to date (10,909) on opening night, 1960. The Terriers (11-3) and Eagles (10-4-1) renewed their rivalry in the first round.

Two-time all-American center Bob Marquis (two goals, two assists) and goalie Barry Urbanski of Danvers (forty-two saves) turned in stellar performances for the Terriers in leading BU to a 5–2 win. But, for the second consecutive year, a BU-BC brawl marred the proceedings. A high-sticking duel between BC's Billy Daley and BU's Paul Hughes triggered a melee that resulted in nine ejections. The eighteen minor penalties whistled by referees Frank Bell and Eddie Barry established a Beanpot record.

In the other semifinal, a surging Harvard team won its seventh straight over Northeastern by a score of 5–3, as Dave Morse, a Hingham native, notched two goals and one assist. The championship game would feature BU and Harvard for the first time since the tournament's inaugural year.

A disappointing crowd of 5,713, barely better than half the turnout for the opening round the week before, turned out for the championship-night doubleheader. The consolation game between Boston College and Northeastern grabbed the headlines. The forever-underdog Huskies, in the words of the *Boston Globe*'s Ernie Roberts, "stole the show and the hearts" of the Garden hockey throng with a 6–5 victory over Boston College. It was Northeastern's first win over the Eagles in nine years.

Unfortunately, the game was spoiled by an ugly postgame altercation regarding a buzzer-beating attempt by the Eagles to tie the game and involving two Boston College players, the referee, and the goal judge.

Northeastern's first line of ironman Art Chisholm (the tournament's leading scorer with two goals, five assists, and seven points), diminutive Gerry Cronin, and Larry Weisbach delivered a victory that the team's coach Jim Bell referred to as "the biggest of my career, either as a player or coach." Chisholm absolutely dominated the proceedings, playing more than half the game, assisting on four goals, and scoring the game-winning goal with less than two minutes to play.

The evening's title match was highlighted by a stirring third-period Harvard rally. Trailing 2–1, the Crimson got goals from Dave Grannis and Stu Forbes, who banked a shot off a BU defender past Terrier netminder Barry Urbanski. Final score: Harvard 3, BU 2.

The biggest hero of the Harvard championship, the Crimson's third in the tournament's eight-year history, was nineteen-year-old sophomore goalie Bob Bland. The

Noble and Greenough School product, from Chestnut Hill—the heart of Eagle territory—stopped twenty-six Terrier shots while stonewalling Boston University's prolific all-American center Bob Marquis.

Named the tournament MVP and following his ninth win in ten previous starts, Bland remained humble amidst the postgame celebration, deflecting credit to his teammates. The Crimson goalie surprised the assembled media by proclaiming that Coach Cooney Weiland, who some thirty years earlier had established the National Hockey League record of forty-three goals in forty-four games for the Boston Bruins, was the toughest goal-scorer he had faced. Bland confessed that Weiland "scores on almost every shot in practice" and thus got him properly prepared to face a player of Marquis' considerable ability.

Whatever it took from the irascible coach, the Crimson began the decade in triumph.

1961   Harvard (11-3-1) was placed in the always-precarious role of Beanpot favorite in 1961. Cooney Weiland's skaters shook off the rust of their exam break with a 2–1 victory over Cornell, unloading fifty-seven shots on Big Red goalie Laing Kennedy. The veteran coach cautioned that his charges would have to "play much better" to beat BU in the tournament's opening game.

The Crimson were just barely able to survive as tourney favorites by forging a miraculous rally as the Terriers became too conservative with their 2–0 lead. Third-line senior winger "Cowboy" Ted Ingalls, the pride of Sheridan, Wyoming, became the unlikely hero. After scoring just two goals in the previous fifteen games, Ingalls deposited goals twice in less than a minute; first on a slap shot off a face-off, then on a rebound flip shot over BU goalie Barry Urbanski from an original point shot by defenseman Bob Anderson.

The Terriers were firmly in command of the overtime period until Harvard's Jim Dwinnell decided the game with a shorthanded overtime game-winner. The 3–2 win allowed the Crimson to advance to the title game for the third straight year. The first participant of the Boston hockey crowd's prospective dream final was in place.

Ingalls was undeniably the story of opening night. The Crimson senior center had spent his previous summer as a ranch worker in his native Wyoming and entertained his teammates with stories of his rodeo experiences, which even included bronco riding. A two-year member of the "Hatchet Line," with Dean Alpine and Tom Heintzman, Ingalls did not allow a bruised hip sustained in a goalpost collision deter him from his first two-goal game at any level of hockey.

Boston College had tuned up for its Garden visit with an 8–2 victory over Colby College and its head coach, Jack Kelley, who would later become a prominent figure in Beanpot history upon his return to Boston University the next season.

The Boston College–Northeastern main event was the most one-sided contest in Beanpot annals. Only 5,800 saw the Eagles dismantle the Huskies 15–1, as forwards Ed Sullivan (five goals) and Billy Hogan (four goals) combined for an incredible nine goals to help the Eagles exact their Beanpot revenge for the 1960 consolation game defeat. The

Barry Wood, Harvard hockey star, 1931

(Courtesy of Harvard University)

low attendance figure was a direct result of a severe weekend storm that dumped fourteen inches of snow on the region. Boston was enduring its worst winter in ninety years, but the Beanpot would live to see a bigger blizzard.

The Garden was prepared for the possibility of a college hockey sellout for the first time since 1931, when Harvard fans had filled the building to see Crimson star Barry Wood, a football all-American, ten-letter winner, and perhaps Harvard's greatest athlete, take on Yale.

Boston College's pre-Beanpot-championship week began with a 10–2 win over Dartmouth's Big Green, the three-hundredth career win during the twenty-five-year tenure of head coach Snooks Kelley, the winningest college coach in America. And Harvard extended its overall winning streak to eleven in a row, with a 9–2 win on the Hanover, New Hampshire, home rink of the Big Green.

"When the Garden runs out of two-dollar seats for a college hockey game, man, that's news," commented the *Globe*'s Jerry Nason, designating the Beanpot final the most intriguing of any winter sporting event on the local scene.

By the morning of the game, all the two-dollar seats were gone, as were the tickets in every other price range. Harold Kaese wrote, for the *Globe*, of "the gathering interest in college hockey," as the Beanpot reached the Garden's magic sellout figure of 13,909 for the first time in tournament history.

The two previous meetings between the two teams had resulted in a pair of Harvard wins (2–1 and 4–1). The Crimson's tight, close-checking style managed to contain the explosive BC offense, and the stellar play of netminder Bobby Bland allowed Harvard to succeed with the conservative strategy.

The formidable Eagle offense, led by Billy Daley, Billy Hogan, and Jack Leetch, would test goalie Bland and the Harvard defense, led by stalwart Bob Anderson.

 Boston College wrested the Beanpot crown from Harvard with a tense 4–2 victory in a championship final that boiled with action from the opening face-off last night before the Garden's first 13,909 crowd for college hockey in 30 years.

Sophomore Billy Hogan was BC's man of the hour as the Eagles offered new proof that the old adage about "the third time never fails" is still true. The former Belmont Hill star scored the first goal of the night on a magnificent individual effort, then assisted on the next two before center Billy Daley sealed the verdict with 2 1/2 minutes to play.

Sharing in the heroics was goalie Jim Logue, a seasoned senior who continually drew the noisy crowd's applause with one sensational stop after another. In all, the ex–Malden Catholic

Billy Hogan, Boston College forward and 1963 MVP

(Courtesy of Boston College)

ace kicked out 30 shots. His Maroon mates, really making the most of their opportunities, forced the Crimson's Bob Bland, also brilliant, to make but 17 saves.

Harvard's defenders, playing without three regulars, just couldn't cope with BC's speed, hustle, and determination. Coach Cooney Weiland's crew, possessors of 2–1 and 4–1 wins in the first two meetings with BC, were without the services of defenseman Harry Howell and forwards Bill Beckett and Dave Crosby. Howell was stricken with appendicitis yesterday morning while Crosby was out with an ankle injury and Beckett was sidelined with a cut thigh. BC played without Paul Aiken, shelved with a bruised shoulder.

There was nothing cautious about the style of play by either side in the hard checking title tussle. It was wide open, held-for-leather hockey with the crowd constantly roaring its approval.

Hogan sent the Eagles soaring on the road to their seventh straight the hard way. He blocked a clearing pass just inside Harvard's blue line, shoved the disc past one defender and stick-handled through two more to sweep in alone and trigger a sizzling backhander from 12 feet out at 17:30.

The Johns equalized early in the middle frame after an apparent score by Dave Morse was disallowed near the four-minutes mark. Referee Bill Stewart ruled the rubber was kicked in; but Teddy Ingalls, hero of the first-round triumph over BU, made Crimson faithful forget this disappointment with a bona-fide 15-footer from the right, after Dean Alpine won a fight for possession along the boards and fed his linemate perfectly.

BC went back in front at 12:19 on a screaming 35-footer from the left boards by Jack Leetch that hit the strings before Bland could make a move. Hogan also figured in this tally, making the pass out that set up Leetch's shot.

There was no slow down in the third period, also played at a furious pace. BC's lead went to 3–1 when Hogan won a face-off draw, and fed Capt. Tom Martin for a 45-foot bomb at 10:58. Harvard matched this one when Dean Alpine poked one in with a diving shot at 11:49, but Daley streaked the length of the ice at 17:31 to circle behind the net and tuck one past the surprised Bland at the left post. Streams of paper and debris sailed onto the ice as the final buzzer sounded and the happy BC skaters mobbed Logue. . . . The victory lifted BC's record to 14-3-1 and left Harvard with a 14-4-1 slate.

Billy Daley, ranked eighth in tournament career scoring, Boston College

(Courtesy of Boston College)

The din was deafening and both the BC and Harvard bands were blaring away when the presentation of the tournament trophy to Martin and Coach Snooks Kelley by Walter Brown set off another wild demonstration as a finishing touch to the 9th annual event.

—Jim Carfield, *Boston Herald*, February 14, 1961

1962 The Garden's magic number of 13,909 was reached again for the opening night in 1962, the tournament's tenth anniversary. In a rematch of the previous year's final, Harvard's potent first-line duo of Gene "The Edmonton Flyer" Kinasewich (one goal and three assists) and Tim Taylor (two goals and two assists) led the way to the finals with a 6–1 victory over Boston College.

The early match between Boston University and Northeastern featured a three-goal third-period rally by BU. Right winger Ken Ross's second goal of the game, with 39 seconds remaining, delivered the Terriers to a championship-game date with Harvard.

BU coach Harry Cleverly had the unenviable task of preparing his team to face a heavily favored Harvard team. "We have been having a tough year but we can salvage it all by knocking off Harvard," offered the BU mentor.

Red Martin: The 58-Minute Man

There are iron men—tireless individuals who put forth an effort in sports that some-how reaches above and beyond conventional endurance—and then there is Boston College defenseman Tom "Red" Martin.

A two-time all-American (1960 and 1961), an All-East and All-New England selection in each of his three varsity seasons (1959–61), a member of the 1964 U.S. Olympic team, and twice a Beanpot champion, Red is best remembered for his extraordinary feat of endurance in the 1961 championship game versus Harvard. During an epic battle between the two power brokers of the tournament's formative years, Martin played fifty-eight of the sixty minutes of the title match.

"I was always in good condition," Martin recalls. "I had the ability to make a quick recovery when there was a lull in play. I had played sixty minutes at Clarkson and St.

Tom "Red" Martin, Boston College

Iron Man

(Courtesy of Boston College)

Lawrence the year before. I had confidence in my ability. It was easier in the Garden that night because of how warm the building was. The other rinks [Clarkson's Walker Arena and St. Lawrence's Appleton Arena] were much older."

A native of Cambridge, Martin was clearly the "one that got away" from Harvard and coach Cooney Weiland. The Crimson thought they had the inside track on recruiting the All-Scholastic skater and excellent student from Cambridge Latin. "I was able to skate at Watson Rink [Harvard's home ice] quite often," said Martin. "I got to know Cooney and the Clearys very well." The informal practice time with the Harvard skaters further honed Red's estimable skills.

When the time came for college selection, Harvard seemed to be a perfectly familiar fit for the hometown hero. Until the oratorical power of Boston College's Snooks Kelley wielded its influence, that is. The ever-impassioned plea of the Eagles' head coach regarding the importance of a good Catholic boy's receiving a good Catholic education at the school on the Heights won over Martin's good Catholic parents and thus swung the Beanpot balance of power.

On the afternoon of the 1961 Beanpot championship game, Martin drove to Milton to pick up his girlfriend, June, who later became Mrs. Martin. Although this was long before the Big Dig, traffic was still a constant Greater Boston nuisance. Already behind schedule, Martin capped his game-day excursion with a flat tire en route to the Garden.

Upon his eleventh-hour arrival, Red was greeted by a head coach who resembled a pacing expectant father. The game began and Martin left the ice only once, for a two-minute hooking penalty in the second period. "With the speed of today's game there's no way you could do what I did," observed Martin, looking back over four decades.

Despite the lack of any real rest, Red had enough in the tank to score the game-winning goal. "I remember the goal so clearly because I didn't score many," added Martin (23-111-134 career scoring totals). "Billy Hogan [1963 Beanpot MVP] won the face-off and was able to get the puck back to me. I was a right shot at the left point and I was able to deke the first defender and slip the shot inside the left post." Red became the first defenseman to be named the Beanpot MVP.

BC versus Harvard "was a great rivalry back then," said Martin. "It was the first Garden Beanpot sellout, 13,909, and they were hanging from the rafters. I'm proud of the fact that we played at a time that the tournament curve was just beginning to peak. Today the [media] coverage is tremendous. It's also become such an important alumni social event. For many people they're the only games they see all year."

As president for the past twenty-two years of Cramer Productions, a marketing and communications company, Martin follows his beloved Eagles closely, now that he has time to sit and watch.

In front of only 4,500, Harvard dominated BU, winning by a decisive 5–0 margin for its fourth Beanpot title. Kinasewich (one goal and one assist) and Taylor (two goals) would again be key contributors, but Romuald "Ike" Ikauniks (two goals) entered the ranks of what would become a long line of unlikely Beanpot heroes—and postgame stories of interest.

Ikauniks had begun the season on the junior varsity team for not exhibiting enough confidence, according to Coach Weiland. But a plea by captain Dave Grannis was later acknowledged by Weiland, and the bruising sophomore was moved to the varsity.

Ikauniks, a bulldozing 200-pound left wing out of Crookston, Minnesota, shocked the Terriers with his first goal just 13 seconds after the opening face-off. Ike's second goal came with 3 seconds remaining in the second period and staked Harvard to an insurmountable 3–0 lead. The Crimson outshot the Terriers 48–11, forcing BU goalie Glen Eberly to make forty-four saves.

The considerable efforts of Gene Kinasewich (two goals and four assists in both games), who finished tied for the tourney's scoring lead with linemate Tim Taylor (four goals and two assists), earned Kinasewich tournament-MVP honors. The Alberta native became the first Canadian-born player so honored.

1963 The most closely contested first-round matches in tournament history highlighted the 1963 Beanpot. A gathering of just 6,961 attended the opening night of the eleventh annual tournament. Once again, without the lure of a BC-Harvard showdown, ticket sales suffered.

The first opening-round game, featuring a soaring Boston College team (13-3) and a sputtering Boston University squad (5-9), held little capacity for surprise. The diligent Terriers had other ideas. The Eagles slipped by BU at 3:17 on an overtime goal by Billy Hogan, with a nifty set-up by linemates Paul Aiken and Jack Leetch. Hogan appeared to be too deep for a clear shot, but was able to squeeze his shot just inside the goalpost off BU goalie Glen Eberly's ankle. Boston College would make its eighth trip to the marquee game.

In the second first-round game, Harvard (9-2-2) needed come-from-behind dramatics of its own to thwart 6-11 Northeastern's upset hopes by a 4–3 count. Crimson forward Bruce Thomas supplied the decisive goal in overtime, with help from linemates Barry Treadwell and Baldwin Smith. The estimable thirty-eight-save effort of NU goalie Gus Capizzo was for naught.

For the sixth time in eleven years it would be a people's choice clash between Boston College and Harvard to determine Boston bragging rights for another winter. And the fans responded, as the BC-Harvard match delivered a sellout for the third straight year.

 A determined Boston College hockey team proved beyond any doubt that it's the top hockey team in the East when it came from behind to nip Harvard 3–1 and win the Beanpot championship before 13,909 Garden fans, including Gov. Endicott Peabody.

Harvard, defending Beanpot champ, couldn't cope with BC drive and power, especially its first line of Billy Hogan, Paul Aiken, and Jack Leetch. Hogan, for his outstanding part in the victory, was chosen Most Valuable Player.

This was the "Game of the Year" for both teams. Boston fans have been looking forward to this one since the season got under way. They were justly rewarded with a bruising, hotly-contested game between a pair of outstanding sextets. . . .

The victory boosted BC's record to a very impressive 16-3. Harvard's loss was its third of the year.

Midway through the first period the Eagles suffered a near disaster when Hogan slammed into the boards in front of the BC bench. His right knee buckled under him.

Harvard took advantage of the situation and punched in the first tally at 10:58. Gene Kinasewich, brilliant Canadian forward, kicked in Ron Thomson's lengthy shot, and BC goalie Tom Apprille couldn't come close to the disc.

Hogan responded to treatment on the bench, then came back to spark the club to an outstanding uprising.

Harvard was hit hard when Bill Lamarche, its leading scorer, was sidelined at 2:16 of the second period. Lamarche was dumped hard at mid-ice and re-injured his knee. He was forced to sit out the remainder of the game.

At 14:33 of the middle stanza, Pete Flaherty put the Eagles on equal footing. He picked up a pass from John Marsh and bombed it into the strings, off Godfrey Wood's elbow.

Just before the frame ended, Apprille made a brilliant save on Ike Ikauniks, who was stationed just outside the crease. This seemed to take some of the zip out of the Crimson.

Hogan was all over the ice in the torrid third chapter. At 5:56, he put his club out front to stay when he passed off to Paul Aiken, who was in close. Aiken hit the target with his short punch shot. At 15:32 it was Hogan once again who led the charge. He swept past the Crimson defense, down the left lane. While still 35 feet out he fed a strike to Leetch who went roaring in. Leetch slashed the disc home from 10 feet out.

The game nearly ended in an uproar when Hogan was dumped hard. He bounced up after treatment on the ice, then with only 12 seconds remaining, staved off Harvard's belated thrust.

He was well enough to sport an ear-to-ear grin when presented with the MVP trophy.

—Milt Greenglass, *Record American*, February 12, 1963

Harvard took a measure of revenge with a victory over the Eagles in the ECAC championship game a month later, but the era of the Boston College–Harvard rivalry as the marquee attraction had come to an end. Eighteen years would pass before the two would meet again in the tournament's title game.

O Canada!

Gene Kinasewich burst onto the Boston hockey scene from Edmonton, Alberta, at a time when controversy often clouded the participation of Canadian hockey players at Eastern colleges.

Kinasewich was the second youngest of thirteen children. Gene's parents died when he was ten, leaving him to be raised by his older siblings. Through his older brother Orie, who played hockey at Colorado College, Gene had an opportunity to leave his Edmonton Oil Kings junior team and attend Deerfield Academy, in Massachusetts.

From there, Kinasewich was accepted at Harvard. After a lengthy eligibility battle that sacrificed a season, Gene was declared eligible in time for his sophomore year. That season, the smooth-skating Harvard left wing shone as the 1962 Beanpot Tournament's brightest star.

Playing on the same line with standouts Tim Taylor (now head coach at Yale) and right wing Ike Ikauniks, Kinasewich helped Harvard rout archrival Boston College by a score of 6–1, then shutout Boston University 5–0. Kinasewich and Taylor shared tournament scoring honors, with the Edmonton native garnering MVP recognition.

Gene Kinasewich, Harvard University forward and 1962 MVP
(Courtesy of Harvard University)

Kinasewich's most vivid memory of the Beanpot involves Boston College star Jack Leetch. "He was so tough to move, almost impossible to get around," Kinasewich remembers. "As a sophomore, I swore at him out of frustration. He knocked me down as if to say 'That'll teach you, kid.' I was flat on my back staring up at the banners in the rafters." He picked himself up off the ice, though, to lead the Crimson to their fourth Beanpot title.

Kinasewich has yet to hang up the blades. He remained an active member of the Gloucester Bombers hockey team, which included a number of former Beanpot skaters such as Harvard's 1989 MVP, Lane MacDonald, and former Northeastern coach and Harvard player (class of 1969), Ben Smith.

"The spirit that surrounds the event is unparalleled in college sports," says Kinasewich of the Beanpot.

Billy Hogan, Center of Attention

Billy Hogan remains one of the most honored players in Boston College history.

Growing up in Cambridge and playing his prep hockey at Belmont Hill, Hogan was a highly proficient offensive player throughout his three-year career, scoring 130 points (58 goals, 72 assists).

In leading the Eagles to the NCAA tournament in 1963, the prolific forward garnered All-New England, All-East, and All-America recognition and received the prestigious Walter Brown Award as the best American-born college hockey player in New England.

From his first Beanpot appearance in 1961 through his MVP performance in 1963, Hogan was right at home in front of February's Causeway Street crowds. Billy finished among the top Beanpot scorers of all time, with nine goals and four assists for thirteen points, including a 5-2-7 line, in 1961, to lead the tourney in scoring as a sophomore.

Hogan played on two Beanpot championship teams (1961 and 1963) and fondly remembers the rivalry between Boston College and Harvard.

"We all knew each other very well," Hogan recalls today. "It was such a close rivalry [with Harvard and Gene Kinasewich], always good, solid hockey. It seems like we'd meet four times every year: twice in the regular season and once each in the ECACs and the Beanpot. The big crowd, the Garden atmosphere really made it special."

After graduation Billy served as a Naval officer and was decorated for heroism in Vietnam. For the past twenty-six years, Hogan has been employed by Clestra, Hauserman, a manufacturing company based in Cleveland, Ohio. He and his wife, Jane, live in the Cleveland suburbs.

"I feel particularly honored to be inducted [into the Beanpot Hall of Fame] the same year as Cooney Weiland," Hogan commented with pride.

FROM "THE MADMAN" TO "THE MENTOR"
1964–1972

There seemed to be no end to the Eagles' supremacy as Snooks Kelley smoothly navigated his way through his third decade as Boston College's head coach.

The Eagle-Crimson rivalry had reached its pinnacle in 1963. For the first time ever in the same season, the same two teams played to decide both the Beanpot and the newly established ECAC championships. Despite losing the ECAC title contest by a 4–3 score to Harvard, Boston College made a sixth appearance in the NCAA tournament within the friendly confines of home ice, their own McHugh Forum.

One of only two Eastern teams (along with Renssalaer Polytechnic Institute, in 1954) to win an NCAA title (1949), Boston College had established itself as the marquee program in Eastern college hockey.

While the Eagles prided themselves on their exclusive all-American roster, Kelley's formula for success was a simple one, his recruiting strategy less than elaborate. He concentrated on mining the rich, fertile terrain of Greater Boston hockey. Snooks often had the run of the premier local talent and didn't need to look much beyond a twenty-five-mile radius of the school's Chestnut Hill campus. If a blue-chip recruit could connect to the Green Line trolleys from his own front door, there was a distinct possibility that he would land at Coach Kelley's front door.

The caliber of play on the local high school hockey scene was consistently at the highest level, with origins tracing back to the nation's first organized league, the Greater Boston Interscholastic.

Across the river at Harvard, the Crimson's success was also closely tied to tradition. Hockey had been part of the fabric of winter life at New England's elite preparatory schools since the origins of the game itself in North America. Since they began play in 1897, the Crimson had focused on this deep pool of talent. It was no coincidence that the hero of Erich Segal's best-seller *Love Story* was Oliver Barrett IV, Deerfield Academy graduate and Harvard hockey player. Oliver was merely following a well-trodden path. But Harvard also took pride in the diversity of its recruits throughout the United States and Canada.

1964   As the 1964 tournament approached, the Eagles and the Crimson appeared to be on a familiar Beanpot collision course, with both schools as slight first-round favorites over Northeastern and Boston University, respectively. "Wide open," offered BU coach Jack Kelley on the tournament field, "but Harvard and Boston College are still the teams to beat."

"The Beanpot is the greatest intracity rivalry in college hockey anywhere in the country. . . . Records, personnel don't mean a hoot. Anyone can win," reminded Snooks Kelley.

In fact, the field would feature four of the top six–ranked teams in the East, with Harvard ranked second, Boston College third, Northeastern fifth, and Boston University sixth.

In the opening game of the first round, a feisty Northeastern squad was even with Boston College, at 4–4, early in the third period, but a goal by BC's E. J. Breen and a pair by Eddie Downes propelled the Eagles to a 7–4 victory.

The nightcap of the doubleheader turned out to be a long journey into night for the 8,396 fans in attendance. The Boston University–Harvard match ended at 4:34 of the second overtime period and 12:29 A.M. on a goal by Lyman Carter, a Terrier forward from Winnipeg, Manitoba, via Stockton (California) Junior College. Carter's dramatic tally from a goal-mouth scramble sent the Terriers to the finals, for the first time under second-year head coach Jack Kelley, by a score of 3–2.

The Terriers had witnessed the disappearance of their 2–0 first-period lead when Harvard's Billy LaMarche registered the tying goal in the third period. The BU victory ended a nine-game Crimson winning streak in the series that dated back almost five years to March 2, 1959.

This was not the first brush with sudden death heroics for the Terrier junior forward, son of a retired Baptist minister. Carter had set up a game-winning overtime goal earlier in the season in a game versus Boston College.

Richie Green, defenseman for Boston University

(Courtesy of Boston University)

"There was a rebound and I just swept the puck to the right corner. I backhanded it," said a grinning Carter surrounded by weary Terriers in the locker room. There was all-American defenseman Richie Green, who had logged a Red-Martinesque seventy minutes of ice time; and there was sophomore goalie Jack Ferreira (thirty-four saves), who had performed brilliantly in his first Garden appearance. For the third time in the tournament's twelve-year history, the Terriers and Eagles would match up to decide the championship.

Another sophomore had made his first Beanpot appearance in the opening game. Boston College forward John Cunniff's Beanpot career started quietly, with no goals and one assist. Wearing number two, he was one of three sons of a South Boston longshoreman from East Second Street. Cunniff would personify the Eagle prototype of "local-skater-becomes-Beanpot-legend."

The Commonwealth Avenue title bout between BU and BC matched the Garden sellout mark of 13,909, reached for the first time in the 1961 championship game. The BU and BC football programs had drifted in opposite directions and suspended their series in 1962, a development that placed ever-greater attention on the hockey rivalry between the two neighboring schools.

Beanpot pregame speculation rated the game razor close. The Terriers broke from the gate fast, leading 2–1 after the first period and 4–2 going into the third stanza. But the penalty-killing combination of Cunniff and Phil Dyer of Melrose proved to be potent offensively.

A power play early in the third period afforded the Terriers an opportunity to put the game away. Instead, the

Eagles narrowed the advantage to one on a shorthanded goal by John Cunniff, who burst out of the defensive zone with the Terriers pressing to accept a Ralph Toran pass and deposit a shot from twelve feet out.

Cunniff's tally ignited an Eagle rally as Pete Flaherty tied the game 2:03 later. A power-play goal by Paul Lufkin on a redirect of a Toran shot gave the Eagles their first lead of the evening with less than four-and-a-half minutes remaining in the third period. BC then converted shorthanded for the eventual game-winner at 17:25, as the ever-dangerous Cunniff beat a BU defender to a loose puck and scored. The final Cunniff goal proved to be the game-winner, as BU's Bob Martell got one back for the Terriers at 18:37. Martell's break-away bid for the tie one second before the buzzer peeled inches wide of the BC net. The Eagles had prevailed once again, with a 6–5 score.

"Of course we know that our first job is to stop the other team from scoring or getting good chances. But we're not out there just to play defense. We're ready to move on the attack whenever we get the opportunity," Cunniff pointed out. Named the Beanpot MVP for his efforts, the man with the hardest shot in the East had established himself as the fastest gun in Beantown.

1965   The balance of power would continue its shift in the direction of Commonwealth Avenue the following year. A prospective rematch in the final between the Terriers (16-4) and the Eagles (16-3) was clearly the first choice of the Boston hockey crowd. In the opening round, BU would face a Northeastern team (12-7) that had played the Terriers very toughly during Jack Kelley's brief tenure as head coach.

A first-night crowd just short of capacity was treated to a marathon duel of epic proportions. The game stretched to a third overtime before BU's Fred Bassi, a seldom-used sophomore winger from Niagara Falls, Ontario, corralled a lead pass from defenseman Tom Ross, split the Husky defense, and skated in to beat NU goalie Gary Thornton (forty-seven saves) on a low shot, with 52 seconds remaining, for a 5–4 victory. The plucky Huskies overcame two-goal deficits twice to draw even with the Terriers in the final minute of the second period on defenseman Dan Turcotte's second tally of the game.

The Eagles and Crimson (5-10), forced to sit anxiously through the lengthy first game, were also destined for an extra session. The Eagles' hero, sophomore forward Jerry York, notched the game winner at 2:51 of the first overtime, converting a pass from linemate Fred Kinsman. The favorites had survived—barely.

For their efforts, Snooks Kelley rewarded the Eagle skaters with the first day off issued in twenty-nine years. His Terrier counterpart and namesake, Jack Kelley, also granted his beleaguered team a day of rest.

The following Monday, the third consecutive Beanpot sell-out throng of 13,909 jammed the Garden for the much-anticipated matchup of the East's top-two college hockey teams. The Eagles and the Terriers treated the fans to a display of the college game at the highest level.

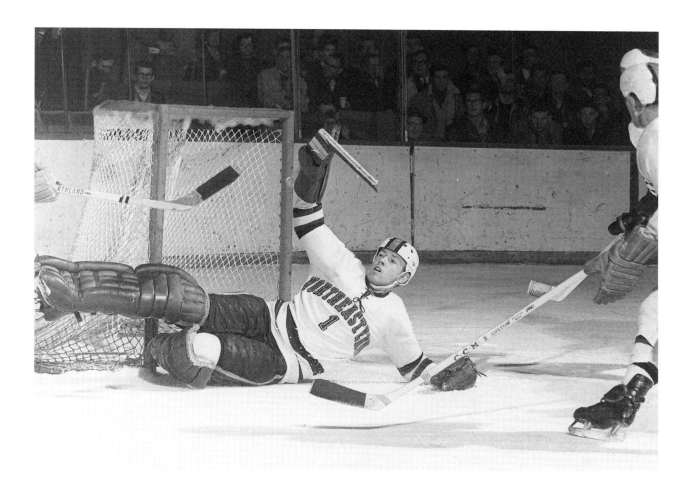

Gary Thornton, Northeastern Huskies goalie

(Courtesy of Northeastern University)

BU jumped to a 2–0 lead only to allow BC to rally, evening the proceeding at 3–3 as they entered the third period. John Cunniff solidified his selection as the only back-to-back tournament MVP in the tournament's fifty-year history by placing the Eagles in front to stay with his second goal of the evening. The second goal of the game for another South Boston native, BU's Dennis O'Connell, at 12:10 of the third period, got the Terriers back within one.

A frenetic third period was defined by the efforts of Boston College goalie Pat Murphy, who made seventeen of his forty saves in the final twenty minutes. The Eagles had prevailed once again, capturing their unprecedented third straight Beanpot crown and their eighth in the tournament's thirteen-year history.

 ### The Madman of the Beanpot

The worst thing that happened to John Cunniff Monday night was winning the silver platter that is engraved to the most valuable inmate of a mental ward called the Beanpot Hockey Tournament.

Until he got the prize, Cunniff had steered through the night of shrieking hysteria untouched. He is a rough and ready kid out of Southie who wears No. 2 because he's from 2d St. He does some boxing, and he can take a punch. But when the announcement came that he was lifting another platter out of the Garden—to go with the one

Boston College forward and two-time MVP John Cunniff

(Courtesy of Boston College)

from the previous year—his Boston College comrades swarmed him.

Snooks Kelley, his coach, belted him and the rest of the Eagles started whacking him and everybody from BC in the frothing-at-the-mouth mob of at least 15,000—no matter what the fire laws say—wanted a piece of him. That is the kind of brotherly love you get in a nuthouse when you've scored two goals in the biggest game of your life. Cunniff loved it. He stood there getting belted and smiled, enjoying it the way Hurricane Jackson used to eat up being punched.

The worst thing that happened to Boston University was Cunniff. None of the Terriers got close enough to push him around the way his buddies did after the game. The Eagles knew they were going to win when he scored his first to shove them ahead 3 to 2. They had been behind 2 to 0. This goal was a masterpiece that shook the Terriers seconds after they had benefited from a penalty.

Cunniff seized the moment when the BU's were formulating plans to assault to sneak away from the group casually. In an instant the BU's knew they'd been had as Fran Kearns pushed him a pass at the blue line. Cunniff was gone and it was just he and John Ferreira, the BU doorman, playing the game as nine others watched.

With a magnificent fake he pulled Ferreira from the net—as though he had a vacuum cleaner instead of a stick—and inserted the puck into the right corner.

Cunniff was born with a silver spoon in his hand that turned out to be a hockey stick. He was also born, apparently, to preside over the Beanpot madness during his term at BC. They may as well have the platter engraved for him next year and make it about the size of the Garden clock.

The Beanpot syndrome affects increasing numbers in our town every year. You can't get a ticket unless you can scream like an elephant who has forgotten his mate's birthday. And if you don't scream every second, an usher comes along to throw you out—or pronounce you dead.

A trumpeter in the BU band stood up and blew his brains out on "Blues in the Night" between the first and second periods, and that's what the BC's had until Cunniff decided it was platter time. After he got going the BU crowd all wanted to blow their brains out, but not with a trumpet.

Our enemies think Americans are soft, but if we could send the appreciators of BC hockey to Viet Nam, they'd chase Ho Chi Minh back up his trail. The hypertensive roar when Bob Kupka started the Eagles' scoring in the third period would have shattered windows in the Soviet embassy in Washington if the wind had been right.

It is lovely to go mad every once in a while, though—perhaps there is therapy in madness. For the next Beanpot tournament I've ordered a hound's-tooth check straight-jacket for me and a silver platter for John Cunniff. He says that instead of planning an acceptance speech, he'll try to keep his left hand high. It is ever dangerous for Cunniff to make his people so insanely happy.

—Bud Collins, _Boston Globe_, February 16, 1965

1966   The Terriers skated into the 1966 tournament with an impressive 17-4 record that included a 9–2 shelling of Boston College in the only pre-Beanpot meeting of the two ancient rivals.

Boston College had struggled through the early season. They had survived injuries to several key players, including the incomparable Cunniff, and had recently rebounded to win three straight. "It will take a tremendous effort to knock off a team like BU," Snooks Kelley commented prior to the Beanpot's opening round. His counterpart at BU, Jack Kelley, emotionally stated his own Beanpot aspirations. "It's greater than the Eastern [ECAC] championships. I'd rather win this tournament than any other."

The opening game of the first round featured a stellar goaltending performance by Harvard's Bill Fitzsimmons (thirty saves) in a 5–1 victory over Northeastern, with the Crimson scoring twice on the power play and twice while shorthanded.

The Garden sell-out standard number of 13,909 was reached again for the marquee first-round matchup, in which the Terriers and the Eagles dueled once again. This

The Coaches Kelley—Snooks (BC) and Jack (BU)—whose rivalry took center stage in the mid-1960s

(Courtesy of Sports Museum of New England)

time, a trip to the finals, and not the title, was on the line. The Garden faithful were treated to perhaps the wildest momentum swings in tournament history.

 Boston University, sparked by Fred Bassi, Mike Sobeski, and Bruce Fennie—who scored two goals each—and the outstanding goaltending of Jack Ferreira, overcame a 3–0 deficit to defeat Boston College, 6 to 4, in the semifinal round of the Beanpot Hockey Tournament at Boston Garden before 13,909 Monday night.

BC jumped off to a 2–0 first period lead on goals by John Cunniff and Dick Fuller.

South Boston friends and neighbors John Cunniff (BC) and Dennis O'Connell (BU) greet each other after the 1966 semifinal game; BU defenseman Tom Ross, 1966 tournament MVP, is at far left.
(Courtesy of Boston University)

Cunniff, who was voted the Beanpot MVP award the last two years, scored at 3:24 while the Eagles were shorthanded. Cunniff scored from the right lane from 30 feet out. Phil Dyer and Paul Hurley assisted.

Fuller scored at 12:30 when he nudged one in from the crease after Jack Moylan dug the puck out of the right corner and centered it.

Fuller let go a torrid shot minutes later which goalie Jack Ferreira stopped with his head. Ferreira was protected by his mask, but he was a TKO victim for a few minutes. He returned to the nets, though.

BC upped its lead to 3–0 at 6:53 of the second period when Jerry York rapped in a rebound from the crease. Allan Keirstead and Gordie Clarke assisted.

The Terriers kept digging, their forechecking improved and they managed to score three times before the middle period ended.

Fred Bassi scored his 24th goal on a power play at 9:35. Pete McLachlan fired in from the right point to Bruce Fennie. Fennie's shot was stopped by BC's Pat Murphy, but Bassi knocked in the rebound.

Fennie put BU back in the game at 14:14 when he scored unassisted. Fennie caught the far side with a 45-footer from the left lane.

Mike Sobeski made it 3-all at 19:14 when he whipped in a screened backhander from eight feet out. Jim Wood and Jim Quinn assisted.

The Terriers pulled ahead 4–3 at 3:26 of the third period on a power-play goal by Sobeski. BC had two men in the penalty box and BU put on plenty of pressure. Sobeski scored when he picked up a Brian Gilmour rebound and put it in the BC cage with a high shot from in close. Pete McLachlan also assisted.

Bassi increased the BU edge to 5–3 at 10:28 when he took a neat pass out from Fennie and scored from in close.

BC stormed Ferreira, but the All-American stood his ground.

The Eagles stayed alive when Moylan scored from the right face-off circle at 12:55 with a low drive. Hurley and Fuller assisted. BU's Fennie put the game out of the Eagles' claws at 18:10 when he took a nifty pass out from Bassi and scored easily. BU had All-American defenseman Tom Ross going for it, too. Ross had been out of action with a broken jaw since before Christmas. . . .

—Bob Monahan, *Boston Globe*, February 8, 1966

At 11:19 P.M., the "We're number one!" chant began to drift down from the east-end balcony as the Terriers claimed their first lead of the night. Three minutes later, with the BU lead now 5–3, the BU faithful changed the chant to "The Eagle is dead." The Beanpot would never be the same.

Tom Ross, Boston University defenseman, receives 1966 MVP Award from Boston Garden President Eddie Powers.

(Courtesy of Boston University)

Kelley's Terriers (19-4) were now in the unfamiliar role of Beanpot favorites for their title match with Harvard (8-8-1). After two years of disappointment, the Terriers vowed that the third time would be the charm. "We seniors have been in the final twice and lost," observed BU's Ferreira. "This is our last chance. We don't intend to waste it." The seniors and the rest of the BU hockey team didn't squander their opportunity.

"We're No. 1," chanted jubilant Boston University rooters after the Terriers had scrambled Harvard, 9–2, in a riotous, fight-filled final of the 14th Beanpot Hockey Tournament before 12,904 at the Garden last night. Six players were ejected for fighting and at times it appeared open warfare would ensue as BU won the cherished Beanpot for a second time. . . .

Terriers head coach Jack Kelley

strikes a triumphant pose.

(Courtesy of Boston University)

Sophomore John Cooke of Regina, Sask[atchewan], and defenseman Pete McLachlan of Newmarket, Ont[ario], each scored two goals for BU, now 20-4 this season and anxious to face Clarkson and St. Lawrence, the upstate-New York teams menacing it for top spot in the ECAC rankings.

Single BU goals were scored by Mike Sobeski, Jim Wood, Captain Dennis O'Connell, Bruce Fennie, and defenseman Don Lumley.

Terrier defenseman Tom Ross of West Roxbury, an All-American last season and playing with a protector on a broken jaw, was voted the tournament's MVP.

Sobeski and two other Terriers, Fred Bassi and Somerville's Jim Quinn, were thrown out of the game for fighting. Three Harvardians also were given the heave-ho— Tag Demment, Bob Carr, and Ben Smith, all sophomores.

Goalie Bill Fitzsimmons kept Harvard in contention during the first period allowing just Sobeski's 14th goal of the season. The floodgates, however, opened in the second period as BU scored five times. Cooke and Lumley added third period tallies. . . .

Officials Ed Barry and Giles Threadgold tooted 24 penalties in the hard-played game. Bassi and Demment were ejected for a second-period fight. Later, Smith and Sobeski tangled several times, finally going after each other at the penalty box. Carr, in an earlier jam with BU's O'Connell, was ejected for grappling with Quinn. These brawls came at 12:44 of the third period.

—D. Leo Monahan, *Record American*, February 15, 1966

The Terriers rode the momentum of their Beanpot triumph to a school record twenty-seven wins and appearances in both the ECAC and NCAA tournaments in March.

1967   Out of the gate fast again the following year, BU, 14-3-1 and undefeated versus Eastern competition, was designated the tournament favorite to repeat in 1967.

Because of a major snowstorm, the Terriers would have to wait a couple of extra days to renew acquaintances with Harvard. The results would be remarkably similar to the

Boston University's "Pinball Line" (left to right): Serge Boily, Herb Wakabayashi, and Mickey Gray
(Courtesy of Boston University)

previous year's final, as the Terriers overwhelmed the Crimson 8–3. BU center Herb Wakabayashi's record-setting five assists paved the way for a BU return to the finals.

The other semifinal provided all of the evening's dramatics. The ever-underdog Northeastern Huskies overcame a 2–0 BC lead and a two-minute, two-man disadvantage to rally past the Eagles 6–5 on Ric Porter's goal at 9:26 of overtime.

A second Husky trip to the championship game, however, would again end in disappointment as BU captured its second straight title 4–0. Rookie netminder Jim McCann, a sophomore from Dedham, was the unlikely Terrier starter due to an injury to starter Wayne Ryan. McCann's unblemished thirty-save performance was the first shutout ever by a BU goalie in Beanpot play. Sophomore Herb Wakabayashi, the diminutive, crafty Japanese-Canadian centerman from Chatham, Ontario, garnered MVP recognition.

The Beanpot was the third title for the 1967 Terriers, following victories in the Boston Arena and Madison Square Garden tournaments earlier that season. The Terriers would advance all the way to the NCAA championship game in Syracuse, New York, before losing to Cornell.

1968   Favored to win a record-tying, third straight Beanpot in 1968, Boston University had to rally from a 3–1 deficit for a 7–4 victory over Northeastern in opening-round action. The Terriers' "Pinball Line"—Herb Wakabayashi centering Serge Boily and Mickey Gray—combined for four goals and seven assists to lead the way to a fifth straight championship-game appearance.

In the other semifinal, Harvard, twice beaten earlier in the season by Boston College (19-4-1), surprised the Eagles with a 6–4 upset victory. The surging Crimson stood between BU and a third straight Beanpot.

The Terriers, equaling the Beanpot accomplishment of Boston College (1963–65), prevailed 4–1 as junior goalie Jim McCann turned aside twenty-five Crimson shots and earned MVP accolades. The Beanpot was presented to Coach Kelley and his senior captain, Jack Parker, a twenty-two-year-old forward from Somerville, who had scored the Terriers' third goal on this night.

1969   The 1968–69 edition of the Boston University hockey team was the second in tournament history to have an opportunity to capture an unprecedented fourth straight Beanpot title. But, as always, the tournament held no promises.

The Terriers had defeated their first-round opponents from Boston College an incredible nine straight times. Indeed, an amazing role reversal between the ancient rivals had occurred during the Terriers' three-year Beanpot reign.

**Jim McCann, Boston University
goalie and 1968 MVP**

(Courtesy of *Boston Globe*)

The offensive heroics of junior Mike Hyndman (three goals), a Quebec native, and the stellar goaltending of the 1968 MVP Jim McCann (thirty-four saves) were the difference in a close-checking 4–2 BU victory over BC before a Beanpot-record crowd of 14,659. The trend continued.

Meanwhile, youth was handsomely served for Harvard. The Beanpot debut of the Crimson's sophomore line—center Joe Cavanagh, left wing Dan DeMichele, and right wing Steve Owen—was most auspicious. The smooth playmaking Cavanagh, with one goal and four assists, simply dominated the Northeastern Huskies in an 8–4 win. Overall, the sophomore trio combined for four goals, with Owen (two goals) and DeMichele (one goal) both key contributors. It was not an unusual night for the precocious line; the three had combined for 46 of Harvard's 101 total goals for the season.

The young Crimson (12-4-1) squad was thus presented the considerable challenge of unseating the three-time defending-champion Terriers. A severe winter storm reduced the crowd to 9,236—the smallest for a Beanpot final since 1962. The fans who braved the elements were treated to a memorable championship game.

 Harvard's hockey team, shocked by a Boston University one-two punch in the third period, came off the ropes with a clutch combination of its own to defeat the Terriers, 5–3, in the finale of the 17th-annual Beanpot Hockey Tournament before 9,236 last night at the Garden.

A goal by junior George McManama, set up by a beautiful feed by Harvard captain Bobby Bauer at 9:19 of the third period, was the winner. The final goal came with 55 seconds left into an empty net by sophomore Joe Cavanagh.

The Beanpot's all-time leading scorer, Joe Cavanagh, was 1969 MVP as well.

(Courtesy of Harvard University)

Cavanagh was voted the tournament's most valuable player by a vote of writers, radio and TV men. . . .

BU had been favored to win this one, but Harvard, winner of five straight games going in and eight of its last nine, was not to be denied.

The pace was hectic throughout as befits a Beanpot final, but it reached its crescendo in the third period.

Harvard went in leading, 2–1, getting goals from Dan DeMichele and Cavanagh to offset a blast by BU captain Billy Hinch.

The Terriers came roaring out for the third period, and began pressing Harvard hard. Bruce Hatton finally got the puck in front and flipped it over Bruce Durno, who played a great game for Harvard, to make it 2–2 at 7:17.

Now little Herb Wakabayashi, in an absolutely sensational effort, went in from center ice alone, split the Harvard defense, and on one skate beat Bruce Durno to give the Terriers the lead. The time was 8:03.

Harvard's situation did not look good. But in a little over a minute the Crimson had come back to end the game. Ron Mark, fed by McManama from behind the net, got a little flip up over McCann and it was tied once more, 3–3.

The Crimson poured back into the Terriers' zone and Bauer, controlling the puck, gave it to McManama dead in front, and cashed it in at 8:33.

BU pressed and harried the Harvards, but Cooney Weiland's men kept coming up with the puck and clearing the zone as time ticked by.

With 55 seconds left, Terrier coach Jack Kelley yanked McCann with a face-off at Durno's right. In all, there were four face-offs in the Harvard end but none was productive until the last one backfired. Cavanagh, who was doing the facing for Harvard, was moving forward when the puck hit a BU player and bounced to center ice. Joe pounced on it and rammed it in from the right side near the face-off circle to clinch the Pot.

—Jack McCarthy, *Herald Traveler*, February 11, 1969

1970   The Beanpot entered its third decade with another record-setting crowd on hand for opening night 1970. A throng of 14,835 packed the Garden for the Boston College–Northeastern/Boston University–Harvard doubleheader.

In the early match, the Huskies had no answers for Boston College's classy senior centerman Tim Sheehy. The native of International Falls, Minnesota, a tiny hamlet on the Canadian border, paced the Eagles' offense with three goals and one assist. BC netminder Jim Barton handled all twenty-one Northeastern shots in a 5–0 shutout win. A spectacular forty-save effort by Northeastern goalie Dan Eberly, the second member

Dan Eberly, Northeastern goalie, 1970

(Courtesy of Northeastern University)

of the family that would donate the Beanpot tournament's goaltender's award, would be for naught.

The late game, a rematch of the 1969 final, was a contest of dramatic momentum swings. Boston University watched a 3–0 first-period lead disappear by virtue of a Crimson comeback. With overtime a distinct possibility, Terrier co-captain Dick Toomey redirected a Steve Stirling shot into the Crimson net with 2:25 left in the third period. The Terriers added an empty-net goal for a 5–3 final count. BU would play in their seventh straight final under Jack Kelley.

Local hockey faithful were at a fever pitch for the first all–Commonwealth Avenue final since 1965. This time, an unlikely offensive hero would emerge for BU. A third-period hat trick by Terrier junior Wayne Gowing rallied the Terriers to a gritty 5–4 victory over the Eagles. After a one-year hiatus, the Beanpot returned to BU.

1971   Jack Kelley's Scarlet-and-White Terriers skated into the 1971 tournament with perhaps their best-ever squad. One of the only teams close to BU in the East was Harvard. Fittingly, the two would be separated in the first round of the annual midwinter rite of passage.

Boston University and Harvard confirmed their respective status as prohibitive favorites by completing the most one-sided first round in tournament history.

In the early game, Steve Doloff, a sophomore center from Melrose, notched a hat trick to lead the Terriers' offensive onslaught to a 12–2 drubbing of Northeastern. The Terriers peppered beleaguered Husky netminder Dan Eberly with fifty-six shots.

The nightcap of the opening-round doubleheader featured a six-goal third-period explosion by Harvard en route to a 10–4 victory over Boston College. Harvard's 1969 sophomore line heroes—Joe Cavanagh, Steve Owen, and Dan DeMichele—now seniors, scored two goals apiece. Cavanagh, the Crimson captain, added four assists, establishing a Beanpot record of nineteen career points.

The Crimson (12-4-1) professed to be unimpressed with BU's gaudy 21-1-1 record entering the tournament final. In fact, Harvard had battled the Terriers to a 4–4 draw in their only previous meeting back in December. Another record-setting college hockey crowd (14,994) crammed the Garden to the rafters to witness the championship summit.

 Boston University's high-geared hockey team outskated and outdefensed a battling Harvard sextet to win the 19th annual Beanpot championship before a wildly cheering record crowd of 14,994 at the Garden last night. . . .

BU forward Wayne Gowing, 1970

(Courtesy of Boston University)

It was the third straight BU Beanpot championship and sixth in the last seven years for the Terriers, who added to their prestige as the East's No. 1 team with a record of 22-1-1.

It was far from an easy game for the fast-skating, hard-hitting Terriers, however, although they never trailed in the contest.

Paul Giandomenico put BU ahead with an eight-footer from in front of Harvard goalie Bruce Durno at 6:31 of the first period. But Harvard came back to tie the score with Dave Hynes hitting an open net at 4:15 of the second period.

A power-play goal at 19:45 by Capt. Steve Stirling, who also had two assists and was voted game MVP, proved the eventual winner with third-period goals by Steve Doloff at 6:42 and Toot Cahoon at 12:46, putting it out of reach of the frustrated Crimson, whose record now is 12-5-1.

There were a total of 22 penalties in the game, 12 against Harvard and 10 against the Terriers. Ten of the infractions were levied in a wild second period that saw BU stand off the potentially potent Harvard attack with just three skaters for a span of 2:25.

"It's been about four or five years since we've had to play so many minutes of shorthanded hockey," said BU

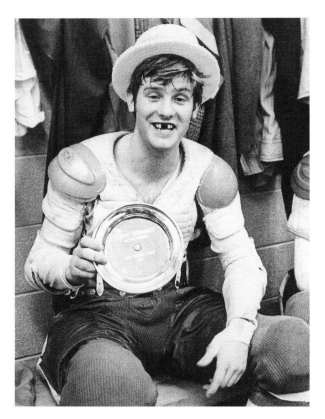

Boston University center and 1971 MVP, Steve Stirling

(Courtesy of Boston University)

coach Jack Kelley. "We proved that we work on another phase of the game that many people don't see.

"I was pleased to see us keep our cool with all those penalties. It will be hard to move us out of the No. 1 spot now."

This defensive excellence, plus the fact that the Terriers completely throttled the Crimson's high-scoring line of Joe Cavanagh, Dan DeMichele and Steve Owen, was the difference.

Some fine goaltending by Dan Brady, who turned aside 27 Harvard shots, also was a factor. The Terriers fired a total of 31 shots at Durno, who couldn't be faulted on any of the four BU goals. Both teams had been waiting for this game since they played to a 4–4 tie at Harvard's Watson Rink on Dec. 9. They came out breathing fire and kept the capacity crowd on the edge of its seats for 60 minutes.

The walls were shaking when Giandomenico slid the first score past Durno and continued to rattle in the second period when a total of seven penalties—three on Harvard and four on BU in less than five minutes—failed to slow the tempo of the game.

Hynes scored Harvard's only goal with both teams at full strength after Bill Corkery steamed down the left side and accidentally felled Brady outside the net, leaving an open shot for his sophomore linemate.

Successive penalties to Bob Havern and Jay Riley proved the Crimson's undoing, however. The Crimson was shorthanded for almost three minutes and Stirling finally stuffed a rebound from Bob Murray behind the sprawling Durno.

Terriers goalie Dan Brady makes a save against Harvard in the 1971 final.

(Courtesy of Boston University)

Doloff's goal that provided the cushion for the Terriers was the prettiest of the night.

The Melrose sophomore was fed near his own face-off circle on a pass from Mike LaGarde to Murray and carried it the rest of the way himself down the left side, cruising to the middle to slip behind four Harvard defenders. He beat Durno cleanly from 15 feet out.

"That goal really took off the pressure," said Kelley.

And Cahoon's goal on a fine pass from Stirling was just the frosting on the trophy.

—Tom Monahan, _Herald Traveler_, February 23, 1971

1972   There was a remarkable similarity between the seasons preceding the 1971 and 1972 tournaments. In 1972, BU and Harvard were once again the class of Boston and the entire Eastern region.

Harvard's 9-1-1 record placed them slightly ahead of the Terriers (10-2-1). For the second consecutive year, the two squads had battled to a 4–4 tie in their only pre-Beanpot encounter, at BU's brand-new Walter Brown Arena. Harvard and BU were the big favorites over Northeastern and BC, respectively, in the opening round.

The smallest first-night crowd in eight years (8,159) witnessed an auspicious night for the prospective finalists. Harvard, the defending ECAC champions, handled Northeastern with relative ease, 8–3, as sophomore Dave Hynes tallied a pair of goals and his classmate, netminder Joe Bertagna, turned aside twenty-seven Husky shots.

Meanwhile, an inspired Boston College squad battled the reigning Beanpot and national champions from Boston University only to fall 4–2. BU's senior captain, John Danby, scored twice and fellow senior Dan Brady posted twenty-five saves.

The Beanpot hype reached an unprecedented level during the prechampionship-game week. Harvard and BU would be meeting for the championship for the fifth time in seven years and BU would be making a record ninth consecutive title-game appearance. Ticket demand was at an all-time high. The Boston press noted a story about one Harvard graduate traveling back from Stockholm, Sweden, just to see the Beanpot.

 Ever-hustling Boston University won the Beanpot hockey championship for the third straight year at steaming Boston Garden last night as it defeated Harvard, 4 to 1, before a capacity crowd who took part in a massive yell-in, swing-in and thrill-in.

The championship game, well played by both clubs, was marred by the calling of 19 penalties by officials Bobby Barry and Joe Albert.

The Terriers, now the top team in the East with an ECAC record of 13-2-1, were sparked by Capt. Jake Danby (two goals and an assist) and goaltender Dan Brady, who made 31 saves. They shared the tournament's Most Valuable Player award.

Other BU scorers were Ric Jordan and Thunder Thornton. Harvard's goal was scored by Andy Burns in the closing minutes.

This 20th edition was spectacular despite the penalties. BU scored three times on power plays and, despite the fact it had 11 penalties, it proved it can stop the power play, too.

BU's success while shorthanded was due to the work of Brady and the penalty killing of Danby, Guy Burrowes, Ron Anderson, Dave Wisener and the entire defensive corps. It was a thing of beauty.

Danby initiated the scoring at 12:18 of the first. BU had the man advantage, Harvard's only penalty of the period, and clicked when Danby rammed home a 12-footer from the slot after taking a neat pass from Anderson.

BU's second goal came at 3:02 of the second while the Terriers had a 4–3 manpower edge. It started with Danby winning a draw to the left of Harvard goaltender Joe Bertagna and passing to Bobby Brown on the right point. Brown slid the puck over to Ric Jordan who smashed home a 55-footer.

At 7:28 of the third, Albert called a holding penalty on BU's Bobby Murray. The house nearly came down with a roar of disbelief.

The Terriers scored their only regulation goal at 11:10. That's when Thornton picked up an Anderson rebound and hit from right out in front.

The fourth goal was Danby's at 13:03 while the Terriers had another 4–3 manpower edge. He skated in alone on Bertagna, made several nifty moves and scored from three feet out. The entire BU section started to yell "We're Number One," the band went wild, and it was a little like New Year's Eve.

—Bob Monahan, *Boston Globe*, February 15, 1972

The Beanpot was the first of three Terrier championships won on the Garden ice in 1972. The following month, BU captured both the ECAC and NCAA titles. They remain the last team to win the NCAA tournament in consecutive years.

In the Beanpot consolation game, the last coached by Eagle mentor Snooks Kelley, who had announced his retirement effective at the end of the season, Boston College defeated Northeastern 5–4.

It would also be the final Beanpot game for BU's Jack Kelley, who had agreed to become coach and general manager of the New England Whalers of the fledgling World Hockey Association. Fittingly, both Kelleys would exit the Beanpot stage as winners: Snooks with his 497th career win and Jack with his sixth Beanpot title.

One Beanpot era was ending—and another was almost ready to commence.

The Boy from New York City

Dennis O'Connell spent the first twelve years of his life in the environs of 95th Street and Second Avenue in New York City. "Now they call it the Upper East Side. We used to call it one block from Harlem," said O'Connell. Before moving to South Boston in 1957, the sum total of his experience on ice had been a brief twirl in figure skates on Wollman Rink in Central Park. All of his hockey had been of the roller version, sewer cover to sewer cover, on the streets of Manhattan. Between the ages of ten and twelve, Dennis spent most of his time in a full-leg brace as a result of a left knee problem. "It was difficult to walk the five blocks to school," O'Connell remembered. "The sisters allowed me to eat my lunch at school."

Assimilation into the close-knit enclave of South Boston wasn't easy. His braces discarded, O'Connell began to spend all his time at a local park that was flooded all winter for endless games of shiny hockey. His roller-hockey experience had developed his stick skills, but the aspiring young hockey player needed to catch up on his skating ability. "There was a group of Boston firemen that rented the ice at the Boston Arena between 2 and 3 A.M. on Saturday night," said O'Connell. "A group of us would go over and play them every week." One of the group was a player of considerable talents from M Street. His name was John Cunniff, one of O'Connell's best friends from the Southie neighborhood.

As a freshman at Christopher Columbus High School, O'Connell tried out for the varsity hockey team. Then-retiring coach John Gallagher, a former Boston College star, was still in charge of selecting the team for incoming coach Warren Lewis, another Eagle all-time great and a fellow member of BC's 1949 National Championship team. "The day after the tryout I checked the list," said O'Connell. "My name wasn't on it. I knew Gallagher was leaving, so I showed up at the next practice anyway. Lewis liked me and kept me on the team."

As an Irish-Catholic kid from South Boston, Dennis dreamed of attending only one school after his outstanding career at Christopher Columbus—Boston College. But Snooks Kelley suggested he attend prep school. Meanwhile, Jack Kelley's top assistant, Bob Crocker, offered O'Connell a full scholarship to Boston University. Dennis accepted and became a member of Jack Kelley's first recruiting class at BU. Cunniff, after a year at New Prep, went to Boston College—on a football scholarship.

In 1963, as a BU freshman, O'Connell witnessed his first Beanpot and was in awe of the Billy Hogan–led Eagle championship team. The next year the upstart Terriers faced the Eagles in the finals and Cunniff, the crafty lad from M Street, broke the Terriers' hearts. The same script played out the next year. "He always seemed to save his best games for us," O'Connell said of his close friend Cunniff, the two-time MVP.

Despite the two February disappointments, there was no denying that Jack Kelley was building the Terrier program into something very special. A 25-6 record and ECAC semifinal appearance in 1965 led to a confident start to the 1965–66 campaign, with now senior O'Connell assuming the captaincy.

The 1966 Beanpot would match the Terriers and the Eagles in the first round. "We had beat BC 9–2 early in the season after having the whole team over for some of my mother's macaroni the night before," the captain said. "Cunniff was playing with a bad shoulder. Snooks Kelley described the loss of John Cunniff as 'beyond the scope of human comprehension.' I remember Jack Parker [a sophomore center on the 1966 BU team] saying to him later on that he knew he was good—but a seven-goal difference!"

The Terriers would finally slay the Eagle dragon and dominate Harvard in the tournament final. "After losing twice we were on a mission. Coach Kelley was very intense. We were heavily favored and we didn't let up," O'Connell recalled.

At the end of the game the seniors—goalie Jack Ferreira, defensemen Tom Ross (the 1966 MVP) and Vic Conte, and forwards Bruce Fennie, Jim Todaro, and Captain O'Connell were on the ice as the final seconds ticked down on Terrier Beanpot frustration. "When they presented me the trophy with Coach Kelley I skated it over to the corner of the building where our fans were celebrating and held it up. We then did a victory lap with the Beanpot. Every year during the victory lap my wife reminds me that 'you and your guys started this.' "

THAT SEVENTIES SHOW
1973–1977

A Kelley-less Beanpot was a peculiar sight in 1973.

Boston College looked to a past all-time great to lead their program. Len Ceglarski had been a sophomore member of the Eagles' 1949 National Championship team. An all-American forward, the Walpole native also captained the 1950–51 Eagles his senior year, and was an outstanding second baseman for BC baseball, teaming with shortstop (and future Red Sox manager) Joe Morgan to form a stellar double-play combination. As the head hockey coach at Clarkson from 1958 to 1972, Ceglarski compiled a record of 254-97-11. The Eagles' "coach in waiting" at Potsdam, New York, was primed for a return to Chestnut Hill.

Down the street, Boston University looked outside their immediate hockey family and hired RPI head coach Leon Abbott as their new leader for the 1972–73 season.

In 1972, Len Ceglarski replaced Snooks Kelley as Boston College's head coach.
(Courtesy of Boston College)

Both Ceglarski and Abbott were placed in the unenviable position of replacing coaching icons. One year earlier, Harvard had looked to Cooney Weiland's assistant, former Crimson, and 1960 Olympic gold-medal legend Bill Cleary to succeed the former Boston Bruins all-time-great player and coach. Suddenly, the veteran Beanpot mentor was another former Bruins player—Northeastern head coach Fern Flaman, who had followed Jim Bell to begin the 1970–71 season.

The atmosphere surrounding the tournament was dramatically altered by the departure of a circle of the most affable, engaging, and successful Beanpot coaches. "Ring out the old, ring in the new" was the tournament theme for 1973.

1973   Boston College approached Coach Ceglarski's first Beanpot—he had never even seen a Beanpot game—having just snapped a ten-game winning streak with an overtime loss at New Hampshire. Yet the Eagles were still rated the favorite versus Northeastern's Huskies, who were playing their best hockey in several seasons.

At the other end of Commonwealth Avenue, Boston University was on a streak of its own—on the ice. The Terriers' six-game pre-Beanpot winning streak had been achieved despite an off-ice eligibility controversy. BU forward Dick DeCloe had been ruled ineligible by an ECAC committee for having accepted an "educational expense" of $189.33 two years earlier, while playing junior hockey in London, Ontario. As a result, BU was forced to forfeit the eleven victories in which DeCloe had participated earlier in the season. The winning streak had begun at the time that DeCloe was sidelined pending a final ruling. With their playoff future subject to the ECAC committee's evaluation of the forfeitures, BU had plenty of additional motivation to topple Harvard, the nation's top-ranked team, in the first round.

The Terriers clearly demonstrated why they were the two-time defending national champions, crushing the Crimson by an 8–3 margin. BU captain Dave Wisener led the Terriers' offense with a hat trick, while sophomore goalie Ed Walsh made his first Garden appearance since his peewee-hockey days a memorable one with a solid performance in net.

In the early opening-night matchup, Boston College freshman forward Mike Powers, a native of Malden, tied a Beanpot mark first reached by Harvard's Bill Cleary, with a five-goal eruption that included the overtime game-winner in a volatile 9–8 win over Northeastern. The game Huskies, playing without their captain, Les Chaisson, miraculously rallied from an 8–3 deficit to force the overtime session. On this particular Garden night, a beleaguered Coach Ceglarski called his players "the worst disciplined team I've ever had."

A record crowd of 15,003 turned out to see if the Terriers, winners of seven Beanpots, could match the Eagles' total of eight, the all-time best.

In a ragged game overall, Boston University center Steve Doloff, a senior, scored twice, for an efficient 4–1 BU victory. Afterward, Captain Wisener openly talked of the turmoil surrounding the DeCloe situation, characterizing the Terriers as being "on a mission." Boston University became the first team to capture four consecutive Beanpot crowns. Mission accomplished.

When Boston Garden President Eddie Powers—who loved the Beanpot beyond all of the annual events that visited his "House of Magic"—passed away that summer, another familiar face left the Beanpot scene. In his honor, the Beanpot was renamed the Eddie Powers Memorial Trophy, the first of which was awarded the following year.

1974   The Athens and Sparta roles that Harvard and Boston University had played were reprised the next two seasons. The schools that had dueled in five of the seven finals between 1966 and 1972 were back at the zenith of their collective prowess.

Jack Parker (at right), three-time Beanpot champion as a player, became head coach for Boston University in 1973.

(Courtesy of Boston University Photo Services)

In December 1973, Boston University followed Boston College's and Harvard's leads, making a coaching change to a former player. Assistant head coach Jack Parker, a native of Somerville and captain of the 1968 Terriers, was named head coach, replacing Leon Abbott. The twenty-eight-year-old Parker was a direct descendant of coach Jack Kelley, having played on three consecutive Beanpot championship teams, from 1966 to 1968, and in two NCAA tournaments (1966 and 1967) under the esteemed former Terrier mentor. Parker had skated the center position for teams that compiled a record of 72-22-4 overall and an imposing 22-1 versus the other three Beanpot schools.

Following a period of considerable upheaval, the coaching fraternity established for the 1974 tournament—Ceglarski (BC), Cleary (Harvard), Flaman (Northeastern), and Parker (BU)—remained intact through 1989, becoming the four recognizable faces on the Beanpot's Mount Rushmore.

Parker's first Beanpot game as a head coach would be a harbinger of many to come. The Terriers surged to a 3–0 first-period lead as all-American goalie Ed Walsh came up with all the big saves in the 6–1 victory over Northeastern.

The other first-round game featured a six-goal third-period explosion by Harvard. The Crimson's 11–6 win turned on a hockey rarity. A call by referees Bobby Barry and Dana Hennigar on Boston College goalie Ned Yetten (forty-three saves) for throwing his stick at a loose puck set up one of the most compelling showdowns in all of sports—the penalty shot. Harvard forward Bob Goodenow proceeded to skate in and calmly beat Yetten to his stick side.

The Eagles stayed close for a while but Harvard's third-period dominance resulted in the most goals ever by a Harvard team in a match against Boston College. Amazingly, sixteen different players scored points in the game. Harvard's Ted Thorndike, with two goals, finished as the game's only multiple-goal scorer.

As usual, the Crimson had skated directly out of exams and into the Beanpot. Because the energy crisis extended the schedule, some players actually were completing their blue books less than four hours before taking to the Garden ice.

An up-tempo final was expected between Boston University and Harvard, two excellent skating teams. The Terriers, riding an eight-game winning streak, were deemed a slight favorite. "We're ready physically and mentally," declared BU's Parker. "We remember how Harvard gave us a hard time in our sixth game of the season." (BU had won 6–5 in Abbott's last game as head coach.)

On the other side of the Charles River, Harvard coach Billy Cleary could draw on his considerable personal experience to comment. "Our guys are anxious and pretty healthy," he said. "I know how they feel because I've played in this tournament, too, and it's one of the biggest thrills in a player's life." The thrills would be plentiful in that pulsating Beanpot final.

 It was a fantastic game, this Beanpot final.

It was played to the accompaniment of constant screaming (from the stands) and at breakneck speed on the ice (from the first second to the last).

It was won by Harvard 5–4, with just 2:37 to play. The real winner was college hockey—for if this Harvard-BU was a typical college game, good heavens, what all you pro fans have been missing. . . .

Harvard won the Beanpot (to end BU's four-year reign), and Northeastern won the consolation game 4–3. It was the Huskies' first victory in a Beanpot game since February 9, 1967. They won it with a spurt of three goals in just 2:26 of the first period and then hung on as BU twice came within one goal of tying the score.

It was a game to make you forget the great college games of the past. It was a game to make you remember almost every minute, to remember a Jimmy Thomas of Harvard (who must have logged as much ice time as Bobby Orr), to remember that Ed Walsh of BU is some kind of goalie. And let us not forget Harvard goalie Jim Murphy and Harvard's defense (they told me it was suspect, but I didn't notice that).

On with the game. There were 12,202 fans there and they barely had time to renew old friendships (Beanpots are reunion games, you know) when BU had a 1–0 lead. It went 2–0, then 2–1, and 3–1 early in the second period.

Suddenly it changed. "The second period," said coach Bill Cleary of Harvard (he won the 1955 Beanpot for Harvard with an overtime goal), "we started beating them to the puck. We play our best when we're behind." Harvard scored three goals to take a 4–3 lead and it scored virtually in every possible way, even-sides, a man advantage, and a man short.

"We could have lost our poise in the third period when they tied it with five minutes to go," said Cleary, "but the kids were great."

"We were down for maybe a second or two," said Randy Roth, the man who scored the winning goal, "but Carr's line went on the ice right after that goal and they attacked and there was no letdown."

Let's get to the third period. Harvard has a 4–3 lead. It's standing around a little, not attacking. With 4:44 to play BU defenseman Vic Stanfield tied the game. He rushed to the net, went right and had the puck against the curve of the side of the goal. He seemed to lose the puck there, came back to it and jammed it between Murray's left leg and the post. It was 4–4 and Stanfield was a hero. His role changed within two minutes. He went for the puck at the BU blue line. Roth beat him to it, rapped it around him off the boards, and broke down the left side.

"Bobby Goodenow was with me and I just wanted to put the shot on the net," said Roth, "and hope he'd be in the right spot for the rebound." There was no rebound, for Roth's 25-footer ticked off Walsh's left leg and soared up high into the net. Harvard led 5–4 with 2:37 to play. The game, you see, wasn't over. Murray had to come out to stop Rickie Meagher at the top of the crease with 1:30 to play. Then BU pulled its goalie and with four seconds to go had a point shot deflected wide.

Harvard forward and captain, Bob Goodenow

(Courtesy of Harvard University)

"Maybe the key goal," said Cleary, "was the short-handed one." Harvard had battled up to a 3–3 tie on goals by Leigh Hogan (with Peter Brown riding his back and taking him to the boards) and Jim McMahon's power-play goal (a 10-footer from the slot).

Goodenow and Roth were killing a penalty and they forced a face-off in the BU end. Goodenow spun around off the face-off and hit a backhander at Walsh and he lifted it

into the net. "Our sticks got jammed on the face-off and I just whacked a backhander at the goal," said Goodenow.

Terry Meagher had the first BU goal from up close and the third, a nice backhander from the inside edge of the left face-off circle. Bill Bishop's six-footer came between them.

It was a hockey game never to be forgotten. . . .

—Fran Rosa, *Boston Globe*, February 12, 1974

1975   The rivalry between the Terriers and Crimson would gain momentum in 1975. After vying head-to-head on Garden ice for both the Beanpot and ECAC titles the previous year (the latter won by BU, 4–2), BU and Harvard raced to the top of the ECAC standings again. Harvard entered the Beanpot a perfect 11-0 in ECAC games. Boston University was 11-1, the only loss being a 7–2 shellacking by Harvard in early December.

The Crimson dominated Northeastern in the first opening-round game, with a resounding 9–0 victory. Harvard forward Jim McMahon was the offensive pacesetter, tallying a third-period hat trick amidst a five-goal deluge.

The other opening-round match—Boston University versus Boston College—was a classic blood-rivalry game. The Eagles (7-11-2) appeared to be a huge underdog to the Terriers (13-3-1) but played BU even for 56 minutes. A goal by Vic Stanfield, on a goal-mouth pass from Bill Burlington with 4 minutes left, proved to be the game winner. The Terriers survived the Eagle challenge with a 5–3 win. An opportunity for both a Beanpot and redemption loomed.

The game preceding the Beanpot final can often be a trap for a talented team caught looking ahead to a Monday night of Garden glory. BU proved that rule when they ventured to distant Hamilton, New York, where they unloaded fifty-five shots on Red Raider goalie Kevin Barry only to get back on the bus a 5–3 loser. Meanwhile, Harvard was a most ungracious host to Vermont. The Crimson came out flying and demolished the Catamounts 10–1.

Nevertheless, it was the callow coach of the Terriers who, years later, professed his unflappable pregame confidence: "In all my years of coaching I've never been more confident of a victory than prior to that game," Parker recalled.

The coach's feeling would prove prophetic.

 For 57 agonizing days and nights, the players on the Boston University hockey team had lived with a nightmare. Every time they would seem to wipe it out with a win, it would automatically reappear. No matter how good they would play, everything they did was weighed against a single night.

It was the night of December 10 in Watson Rink at Harvard. Here was the matchup of the two top teams in Eastern college hockey. It was a no-contest game. It wound up Harvard 7, BU 2, and, as BU captain Vic Stanfield would say last night, "that game was always there."

Boston University defenseman and two-time MVP Vic Stanfield

(Courtesy of Boston University)

"Had it been somebody else," he went on, "maybe it wouldn't have been the same. The Harvard game was so bad. No matter where you went, people always brought the Harvard game up. We'd win. They'd say, 'Nice game.' Then they'd say, 'What happened at Harvard?' Maybe that'll change."

Yes, maybe it will, because last evening before 15,000 steamed-up fans in the Garden, this same BU team, in a performance set off by the outstanding goaltending of freshman Brian Durocher, had its night of atonement in the Beanpot championship. And, guess what? This time it was BU 7, Harvard 2.

"We were mentally ready," said coach Jack Parker. "That beating at Harvard had set badly. We'd keep winning, winning, winning. But all people would talk about was what happened at Harvard. Harvard was the big team. We were winning. But the loss was to Harvard." . . .

The game turned around in an incredible 38-second span early in the second period. After BU had taken a 1–0 lead on a goal at 16:05 of the opening period, Harvard had tied it on a power-play rush 42 seconds into the second period. It was the calm before the earthquake.

Bill Buckton, a sometime-unsung player, started it when he took a feed from Rick Meagher and eased it past Petrovek at 2:53. "He scooped it to me," said Buckton. "He was out of position. I just shot it at the net and it slid past him."

That made it BU 2, Harvard 1. For 21 seconds. Buckton, who scored a pair of goals on his birthday in the Beanpot a year ago, celebrated six days late this year with his second on a pass out from Rick Meagher at 3:14. "He fed it out to me," said Buckton, "and it went under his right arm."

Before the announcement was made on these two goals, freshman Bob Dudley took a cross-ice pass from Buddy Powers and backhanded it into the near side past a stunned Petrovek. "We wound up with a two-on-one," said Powers. "I just threw it over. It was right there. I couldn't believe it."

That was the blitz that was and Harvard missed enough opportunities for a game in on a near breakaway.

BU proceeded to put the champagne on ice with a second three-goal outburst in the third period. Mike Fidler started it at 8:58. Billy Burlington was set up for a goal by Fidler at 12:27 and Rick Meagher, frustrated twice before by Petrovek, finally scored at 14:43 for a 7–1 lead.

—Joe Concannon, *Boston Globe*, February 11, 1975

1976   There would be no BU-Harvard final in 1976. In a tournament wrought with uncertainty, that was a fact. The Terriers and Crimson would play the feature first-round match on opening night.

Harvard had fashioned a seven-game unbeaten streak (5-0-2) prior to the annual pre-Beanpot exam break. The Terriers were holding a familiar position: number one in the ECAC with a 14-2 overall record.

The clash between the champions from the two previous seasons was hardly a master-piece. BU utilized a fast start, with a pair of early goals from co-captains Terry Meagher and Bill Buckton, to hold on for an eventual 6–5 victory. The Crimson out-shot the Terriers 29-22 but were unable to tie the game.

The early semifinal was more of the same for the hard-luck skaters from Huntington Avenue. A struggling Boston College team (9-9-1) appeared to be a potential upset victim for the Huskies (5-11-1), who had been all but mathematically eliminated from postseason consideration. Among Northeastern's eleven defeats were five by a single goal, including one each to their three Beanpot rivals.

The Huskies rallied twice from two-goal deficits, extending the Eagles to the limit in the final minutes. Forcing three face-offs in the Boston College zone during the last 63 seconds, Northeastern fired a barrage of shots at the Eagle net, only to be repelled each time by goalie Paul Skidmore (twenty-seven saves) and the BC defense. An empty-net goal by BC defenseman Joe Augustine, with four seconds remaining, officially sent the Huskies back to their "wait 'til next year" lament for the twenty-fourth consecutive year.

"We had a good attitude coming into this game," said Northeastern captain Duncan Finch. "We went into it even. We'd played BC and knew they weren't better than us."

For three Husky seniors the results on this Monday night were particularly painful. Center Charlie Huck had been flanked by Jim Martel at left wing and Dave Sherlock on the right wing forming the "Huck Line." The trio would finish as the highest-scoring line in Northeastern history but would end their careers without so much as an appearance in the Beanpot final.

The Huskies' "Huck Line" (left to right): Dave Sherlock, Charlie Huck, and Jim Martel
(Courtesy of Northeastern University)

Martel, who finished his career as Northeastern's all-time leading scorer, would have gladly traded the record for a chance to play for the coveted Beanpot. "It's hard to say,

what it's been," Martel said in the dead silence of the Northeastern locker room. "I don't know what it is. Something seems to be missing. I thought we had just as many scoring chances as they did. It's hard. It really is."

Equally frustrated, the Huskies' coach, Fern Flaman, lamented the results: "That's the story of this year. We've been that close to winning games—but the puck turned this way instead of that way. We had our chances."

The interminable wait for Northeastern's Beanpot fortunes to turn around would be extended still further. A BU-BC match would decide the bicentennial year's Beanpot.

The Eagles, once the tournament's dominant team, had endured eleven long years without a Beanpot title. The ghost of John Cunniff was still haunting them.

In January 1976, the first meeting between the two teams had been an example of college hockey at its best. The Terriers managed to hold on for a 4–2 win, with two late goals, one into an empty net. "We played a good game the last time against them," said BC coach Len Ceglarski, "because we did a good job of forechecking. I think we can skate with them."

"I think BC is one of the best offensive teams around," offered BU coach Jack Parker. "They move the puck very well. They've played well in the tight games. Last year, they didn't believe. Now they do. And they're winning."

But could they win on the Garden ice against Parker's team as it made its thirteenth straight appearance in the final, looking for its ninth crown in eleven years?

 He had never seen a Beanpot game until last week, never sampled the Boston collegiate clan war that sets brothers against each other for two weeks every February.

He is only a freshman, a lanky, quiet goaltender with long sideburns, but at midnight yesterday, everyone who filed out into Causeway Street was hoarsely whispering his name.

It had taken 10 years, five straight tournament losses to Boston University, and too many 6:15 consolation games. But last night, Boston College's hockey team had its ninth Beanpot, a 6–3 stinger over BU before 12,250 at the Garden—and another February savior.

His name is Paul Skidmore, and all he did was keep the Terriers at bay until teammates Bob Ferriter (two goals), Joe Mullen (two), Richie Smith and Kevin Bartholomew rallied to win it for him.

He made 43 saves in all, 18 of them in a crazy first period, when a Bartholomew slap shot gave BC the lead with two seconds to play.

Nobody thought it would hold up, even after Smith and Ferriter scored shorthanded goals 34 seconds apart to put BC ahead, 3–0, barely five minutes into the second period.

Paul Skidmore, Boston College goalie and 1976 MVP

(Courtesy of Boston College)

Not against this team. Not in this building. Not in this tournament. BU had owned them in the Beanpot—last winter, six years out of seven, nine of the last eleven. BU would find a way to win. Wouldn't they?

Not last night, even after the power play goals by Terry Meagher and Gary Fay had cut the deficit to 3–2 with 18 minutes to play. Skidmore, who had carried the Eagles into the final two minutes of their 4–2 loss at Brown Rink last month, simply negated everything.

With 14:12 to play, Ferriter knocked in another goal on his own rebound. The Eagles, behind Skidmore, killed off a two-man BU advantage for 44 seconds with seven minutes to play. And after Terry Meagher chopped BC's margin to 4–3 at 15:20, here came freshman Joe Mullen, who had missed a pair of first-period breakaways, with the clincher 73 seconds later. Nothing else mattered—although Mullen would add a sixth goal (18:56) into the empty cage 14 seconds after goalie Brian Durocher (24 saves) was pulled.

"The fifth goal was the turning point," BU coach Jack Parker said. "Up until that point, I thought we were going to come back. We had a number of golden opportunities. And I didn't think Skidmore could keep it up much longer."

It came down to Skidmore, persistence, forechecking—and luck. BC coach Len Ceglarski's car had been stolen earlier in the day, and with it, the Eagle game plan. "Briefcase, papers, everything," Ceglarski said.

Yet did it really matter? After a few dozen years, the Eagles knew what they had to do to stop a BU varsity. You forechecked them. Knocked them off stride. Pinned your offensive hopes on the initial rush, hoping your shooters could find daylight.

And you hoped your freshman goalie didn't glance up and notice the people, and the lights, and the bedlam.

"I'd heard of the Beanpot," Skidmore would say. "People talked a lot about Harvard and BU—what super teams they were, how they always won it. How BC had their time, back when it started. And I thought, maybe it's our time again. . . ."

For once, BU was playing catch-up, glancing nervously at the Garden clock, hurrying its passes, hitting the post. For once, BC people were going home champions.

"This," grinned Richie Smith, "makes up for everything."

—John Powers, *Boston Globe*, February 10, 1976

Above: In the 1976 tournament, Boston College forward Richie Smith led the Eagles in scoring.
(Courtesy of Boston College)

Right: BU defenseman Peter Brown battles BC forward Paul Barrett in the 1976 final.
(Courtesy of Boston University)

1977   As the Beanpot geared up to celebrate its silver anniversary in 1977, the field was perhaps the most wide-open in the tournament's history.

In the Monday-night opener, a BU team (10-8-1) that had shaken off the effects of a five-game season-opening losing streak matched up with the ever-hopeful Huskies. Northeastern (8-10) kept it close with a goal by Dale Ferdinandi late in the second period, making it a one-goal game at 4–3. From that point, BU's only three-time all-American center, Rick Meagher (three goals and two assists), initiated a six-goal final stanza with a score off a dash from his own zone. The BU blitz resulted in a 10–5 victory, a fourteenth straight trip to the feature game for the Terriers, and another fruitless first Monday in February for the Huskies.

The other semifinal, between Harvard (9-8) and the defending champions from Boston College (14-6-1), remained deadlocked into the final minute, when a most unlikely Beanpot hero emerged. Crimson soccer captain Lyman Bullard, a recent call-up from the junior varsity, made a centering pass from behind the BC net that found its way to Harvard center George Hughes. The former Malden Catholic standout put the puck behind Boston College goalie Paul Skidmore with twenty-nine seconds remaining. The Crimson added an empty-net goal with one second on the clock for a 4–2 final score. Harvard was back in the final, seeking their first title in three years.

As the BU-Harvard rivalry grew, so did the friendship between the teams' two head coaches, Harvard's Bill Cleary and Boston University's Jack Parker. But even friendship had its limits when the Beanpot was at stake. Cleary recalled a tennis match between the two on the morning of a December 1974 game won by the Crimson, 7–2:

An unlikely Beanpot hero—Lyman Bullard, Harvard soccer captain

(Courtesy of Harvard University)

"So I called him the morning we were going to play that year [February 1975] in the Beanpot," recalled Cleary years later, "and I said, 'I've got some tennis time, do you want to play?' He said, 'Hell no. After what happened the last time, I'll never play you again on the day of our game.' "

Parker's new tennis policy worked well. In the seven games since the court confrontation, BU had reeled off seven straight wins by an aggregate score of 49–24.

Harvard senior goaltender Brian Petrovek had played in six of the seven losses since the last Harvard victory, during his sophomore all-American season. The team's early-season encounter—a 3–2 overtime victory at Harvard's Watson Rink—was the Terriers' first win after five defeats.

The Garden had unquestionably become home away from home for BU. The Terriers arrived on Causeway Street having won eighteen of their last twenty-four overall matches (twelve of fourteen versus Harvard) on the home ice of the National Hockey League's Boston Bruins. An up-tempo, fast-paced game was expected, with the Terriers a slight favorite to reclaim the title wrested from them the year before. Would Cleary or Parker celebrate a happy Valentine's Day?

 To call it a spectacular Beanpot final would be redundant. All Beanpot finals are spectacular.

And it was more than a hockey game. Harvard won from Boston University, 4–3, in the sold-out (14,597) Garden last night. For the Beanpot is a symbol beyond a hockey game. It is the whole college scene packed into the Garden. Bands blaring, people cheering, people drinking and a steady noise.

This was a college hockey classic. A game played with the exuberance and resiliency that belongs to youth, and with the aggressiveness that belongs to the sport.

It was a game of changing tempos. The first period was cautious—and inevitably scoreless. The second period was reckless—and inevitably produced five goals. The chippiness that developed in the second period carried into the third and came to an end as the pressure of a tie mounted.

Harvard won this game, the record will say on a goal by freshman Jon Garrity from Milton Academy at 12:12 of the third period. Bill Hozack and Garrity had created a two-on-one situation. "The defenseman went to Hozack," said Garrity, "and he laid a perfect pass on my stick. In that situation you don't have time to think of anything except shooting the puck. I shot as soon as I got it and hit the top corner."

Then it was the tournament's most valuable player, goalie Brian Petrovek of Harvard, who took turn after turn at saving the championship of the Charles River.

"I'm too tired to talk about the game," said Petrovek. "It was a great game and I'll tell you I didn't know we had scored two shorthanded goals until somebody told me in the dressing room after the game."

Harvard scored two shorthanded goals in the second period to go from a 2–1 deficit to a 3–2 lead. "The second one," said coach Bill Cleary of Harvard, "was the key one." And it was a goal that never should have been scored.

Bill Horton had taken a pass and broken in on BU goalie Jim Craig from the left. He whistled a shot at him. Craig, at the top of the crease cutting the angle, caught the puck.

"He made a really great save on it," said Horton. But there was no whistle. "I kept waiting for the whistle," said Craig, "and people kept bumping into me." Finally, the puck was knocked out of his glove and it dribbled into the goal.

Harvard University goalie Brian Petrovek won the MVP and Eberly awards in 1977.

(Courtesy of Harvard University)

"After he made the glove save," said Horton, "I kept going to the net. He was juggling the puck, so I knocked at it with my stick. The puck fell out and was just barely moving. I was urging it on and it dribbled into the goal."

That put Harvard ahead going into the last 20 minutes and BU had to come out attacking. The Terriers did and, at 5:34, tied the score on John Bethel's goal. Bob Dudley was trying to pass the puck out of the right corner, and it struck a Harvard player's skate and went directly to Bethel 12 feet out in the slot to the left. He didn't waste any time. He pulled the trigger and the game was tied.

Harvard's other shorthanded goal had come off the stick of freshman Jack Hughes from a step inside the blue line. It was a seeing-eye shot that found its way by many legs and to the goalie's left.

Dave Silk, with a 40-foot slap shot from the right boards to the wide side of the goal, had started the scoring in the second period. Harvard tied it on Gene Purdy's finish of a goal-mouth pass from Bryan Cook on a power play. And BU went back into the lead on Mike Eruzione's power-play goal at 11:08, also on a good pass to the right top of the crease.

It was an extraordinary hockey game—and perhaps such games are not commonplace at any level. It was right and just that the silver anniversary of the Beanpot should have produced such a game. When better college hockey games are played, they'll be played in the Beanpot. . . .

—Francis Rosa, *Boston Globe*, February 15, 1977

In consecutive years, Boston College and Harvard had ridden the performances of two outstanding goaltenders to Beanpot glory. Boston University had become the Beanpot's schoolyard bully. Anytime the bully gets his nose bloodied people cheer. The parochial Beanpot battles were no exception. How would the bully (BU), or any of the other kids on the playground, fare in the face of Mother Nature's overwhelming fury?

The next year held the answer.

Jack and the Beanpot

A self-described gym rat, he came from nearby Somerville—by his own admission
"Basketball City USA," not the original "Hockeytown USA" (Melrose), where he
would later reside. As a kid, his favorite team on the local winter sports scene was the
Celtics, not the Bruins. His hockey number at Boston University was 6, in honor of
Celtics center Bill Russell, his all-time sports idol. He didn't see his first Beanpot until
his freshman year at Boston University, 1965—the second act of the John Cunniff
MVP Show.

Such is the pre-Beanpot history of coach Jack Parker, the tournament's all-time winningest coach and the fourth-winningest coach in the history of college hockey, with 655 victories.

Coming to the game relatively late, especially by today's standards of skate fittings in the maternity ward, Jack Parker became one of the top high school hockey players in Greater Boston upon graduating from Catholic Memorial in 1964. At Boston University he broke into the lineup as a sophomore (freshmen were not eligible) and never left. A competitive, defensive-minded, dogged, forechecking center, Parker was the prototypical BU hockey player for coach Jack Kelley. He played on teams that compiled an overall record of 72-22-4, went to the NCAA Final Four twice, and won three Beanpots, as captain accepting the trophy in 1968. Before his arrival, BU had won the 'Pot once (1958) in the tournament's first thirteen years.

After coaching at the high school level for one year, Parker came back to campus to be an assistant coach to Jack Kelley. In the 1970 Beanpot final, BU was trailing their bitter rivals from Boston College 4–2 entering the third period. "I can remember coming in and ranting and raving about how we cannot lose this game," Parker recalled. "Wayne Gowing [a junior winger from Kitchener, Ontario] went out and scored a hat trick in the third period." The Terriers prevailed 5–4.

An assistant coach to Kelley for Beanpot and NCAA championship teams in 1971, and for a "Triple Crown" (the Beanpot, the NCAA, and the ECAC titles) in 1972, Parker remained on the staff with new head coach Leon Abbott for his Beanpot victory in 1973. Then, the sudden removal of Abbott in December of the same year thrust Jack Parker into the head coach's role at age twenty-eight.

Harvard was an ECAC power at the time. The young coach's best friend among the fraternity of head coaches was Harvard mentor Bill Cleary. "I knew him from the time he was an official," said Parker. "He helped me out with scouting reports on opponents . . . everything." Only in hockey. Two coaches at two of the top programs in the nation sharing information. This would probably not occur in ACC basketball or SEC football.

In Parker's first Beanpot title game, there was Cleary on the other bench, coaching Harvard to a 5–4 victory. "Vic Stanfield [tournament MVP in 1973 and 1975] missed an unbelievable chance at one end and they came down and scored," recalled the BU head coach.

The following year Harvard was the number-one team in the nation, with BU slotted at number two. Harvard had defeated BU 7–2 early in December. "I was never so confident of winning—and winning big—as I was that night," Parker recalled wistfully. "There was an electricity in the dressing room. I was talking to a friend of mine who was a gambler about twenty minutes before the game and told him how confident I was. After the game he congratulated me and said, 'If you ever get that feeling again, please get to a phone.' "

And so the incredible success has continued through the first two February Mondays of Jack Parker's life. Blizzards, hot goalies, "retirements," and returns. "I remember how difficult it was to tell the team," said Parker of his "last" Beanpot, in 1989.

Since his brief stint as BU athletic director, Jack and his Terriers have simply owned the tournament, with ten victories since 1990. "I think back to 1991 and what a great year [it was] for college hockey. Sixteen players [eleven from BU, five from BC] that played in the final played in the NHL," said Parker. "And Travis Roy being on the ice and having Chris Drury and Billy Pierce present him [with] the Beanpot [in 1997]. That was a very emotional moment."

It never gets old but does, sometimes, get a little strange. "After we won in 1999 I was walking to the postgame press conference with Steve Nazro [Beanpot tournament director]. I turned to him and said, 'this is getting eerie.'

"I think it was important to the tournament that someone else won last year [2001]. BC was the best team. They proved it by winning Hockey East and the NCAAs. That [the best team's winning] doesn't always happen."

To what does the coach attribute the Terriers' success in this tournament?

"We always seem to be playing better in the second half of the season," said Parker. "I think that's part of the tradition of our program. If this tournament was played in December, I don't know if our record would be anywhere near the same."

Could there be something else, an intangible perhaps, for the coach from the home ice named after Beanpot- and Boston Celtics–founder Walter Brown, a man who grew up in a basketball hotbed, a rabid Celtics fan who idolized Bill Russell? Basketball experts have theorized about the Celtics mystique and the ghosts that aided them in times of greatest need. Well, maybe that leprechaun has a dog. A Terrier, of course. And Jack Parker is the only one allowed to feed him.

THE BLIZZARD
AND THE BEANPOT
1978

CHAPTER FIVE

Boston University exhibited season-long perfection in anticipation of the 1978 Beanpot gathering: nineteen games and nineteen wins for Jack Parker's squad as January skated into February. Although thirteen of the Terrier wins were by one- or two-goal margins, a 19-0-0 record was still difficult to argue with.

If the Terriers' upperclassmen needed any extra motivation, they looked no further than their two consecutive 'Potless Februarys. Upset victories by Boston College and Harvard (neither of which qualified for the 1976 and 1977 postseasons) were difficult to grasp for the team that had won the ECAC tournament and advanced to the NCAA championships both years. In fact, during Parker's first four seasons behind the Terrier bench, BU had engineered a string of four consecutive ECAC titles and NCAA tournament appearances—but only one Beanpot. A Boston College team (16–5), on a recent roller-coaster ride despite its impressive overall record, blocked the Terriers' road back to the finals.

In the early opening-night match, an uncharacteristically optimistic Northeastern squad (9-9-1) was a popular choice to upend 10-7 Harvard. The Crimson had been routed by Northeastern to the tune of a 14–5 score in the game prior to their traditional January exam break. Coaching the only completely healthy team entering the tournament couldn't help making Northeastern's Fernie Flaman feel upbeat. "I think we stand a shot of making it into the finals," Flaman observed. "I know Harvard was hurting a lot when we beat them. But we played so well in that game that I think we still would have won if Harvard was at full strength.

"This NU team is much different from others I have had," he added. "We have a lot of scorers for a change. We have seven players with ten goals or more and most years we have two, three, or four. We've cut down on our penalties too—at least fifty percent from last year. That's a very big factor."

Something else loomed as the biggest factor of all, however. The *Boston Globe*'s front-page weather pun for February 6, 1978, spoke volumes: "You Sled It!—snow, wind, snow ending." The "snow, wind" part proved to be 100 percent accurate; the "snow ending" prediction was more like wishful thinking—at least for a few days. The Boston winter of 1977–78 was already one of the harshest in memory. On Friday, January 20, the weekend that BU and BC had last renewed their on-ice acquaintance, a record twenty-four-hour, twenty-one-inch snowfall descended on the city. The citizens of Boston had already absorbed some body blows, but were in no way prepared for the knockout combination Mother Nature was about to land.

There was no effort to conceal from Beanpot ticket holders the weather prospects on this February day: snow, with temperatures in the twenties, under a heavy-storm watch beginning in the afternoon; gale-force coastal winds gusting higher by the afternoon into the night; a wind chill of 10° below zero during the day, plummeting to 25° below at night. Frostbite was a very real danger. The most revealing piece of information was the speed and direction of the wind: 15 to 25 miles per hour from the east backed by winds out of the west at 25 to 35 miles per hour. Every New Englander, from grade-schoolers on, and almost every Beanpot fan knew what that meant: Nor'easter.

Even though the Blizzard of 1978 wreaked havoc across New England, it didn't stop the Beanpot.

(Courtesy of *Boston Globe*)

By the time the evening edition of the *Globe* for February 6 hit the streets, the weather note warned simply, "Brace Yourself!" The forecast for southern New England was for eight to sixteen inches of snow. "A rapidly developing storm off the Mid-Atlantic coast will likely become a vicious Nor'easter this afternoon." At 1:15 P.M., the athletic directors of the four schools met at the Sonesta Hotel in Cambridge. All 14,000 seats were sold. Harvard was in an impossible situation because its game versus Cornell, in Ithaca, New York, the following Wednesday couldn't be rescheduled, lending no flexibility to the tournament committee's decision. On top of that, Boston Garden management had no available alternate dates, so, all warnings considered, the Beanpot would be played as scheduled. Any rational observer might have assumed that the Beanpot would be played to a near-empty house, but anyone who shared these sentiments didn't know the Beanpot or its indomitable disciples. A crowd of 11,666 showed up on Causeway Street determined to observe their sacred midwinter hockey ritual.

Against the backdrop of the worst storm of the century, Harvard rallied from a 2–1 deficit against the Huskies to seize the lead for the first time, with 6:26 remaining in the second period, on captain Bryan Cook's second goal of the game, this one on the power play. The precarious 3–2 advantage would hold up until Northeastern sophomore center Wayne Turner rerouted a shot by defenseman Mike Holmes with under six minutes to play in regulation time. In the first minute of overtime, on the extra session's first shot, Harvard forward Gene Purdy carried the puck into the Husky zone, faked inside, swung around the net, and got behind NU goalie Ed Arrington to stuff the puck home. Despite outshooting Harvard 29–19 and having the better of the play late in the game, Northeastern remained the snakebitten dog. For the eleventh straight year, the Huskies had failed to make the finals.

"What do you have to do to win? We had two disallowed goals. If we play badly it's one thing. But we didn't. This is my toughest Beanpot loss," said a dejected Fernie

Flaman. "This is the best NU team I've ever had and I really thought we had a good chance." At least the Huskies and their beleaguered coach had a "good chance" of getting home safely after completing the early game.

By the time the Terriers and Eagles took the Garden ice, the rumors inside the building regarding the storm's intensity were matching the swirling winds outside. Undaunted by the weather—or any other fact—the methodical Terriers burst from the gate quickly, to take a 4–1 lead, with all-American, 1976 Olympic team defenseman Dick Lamby assisting on three of the four goals. But Boston College responded to trim the Terrier lead to 4–3 after one period. Until 13:52 of the second period it was Beanpot business as usual. Then, for the second time, the lights dimmed ominously. A momentary fading had occurred during the first game's overtime, but this was much more serious. The game was halted as repairs were made. After a twelve-minute delay, play resumed with the overall quality of lighting less than desirable. A third flickering several minutes later led to full power finally being restored. Some 3,500 hardy hockey fanatics remained in the building. The prospects of being snowbound at the Garden didn't seem to faze them.

There were no lapses of power on the ice for the Terrier skaters, however. The torrid offensive onslaught continued as BU extended their lead to 8–4 after two periods. The loss of all-American goalie Paul Skidmore to a groin injury midway through the second period added to the Eagles' misfortunes. The Terriers added four more in the third period against Boston College's backup netminder Mike Cronin. BU also took advantage of a depleted Eagle defense that was minus two regulars. The injuries forced Boston College coach Len Ceglarski to move all-American forward Joe Mullen back to the blue line. In all, ten Terriers scored goals and fifteen recorded points to complete a 12–5 dismantling of the Eagles. Boston University forwards Tony Meagher and Bob Boileau were the only Terriers to score twice.

Art Moher, then the "voice of Boston University Hockey," would later say that, "in a dominant season, [BU's] relentless performance versus BC was a signature moment of the season along with the NCAA semifinal victory over Wisconsin." The Wisconsin game would be followed by the Terriers' National Championship showdown with the Eagles in Providence, Rhode Island.

The Terriers were in the Beanpot finale for the fifteenth straight year. In the postgame locker room, BU junior defenseman Jack O'Callahan spoke for all of the still-unblemished 20-0-0 Terriers: "We had them at the end of the second period," said O'Callahan, "and we killed them in the third. Did we kick them in the tails or what? It's the Beanpot. We've been stung in it the last two years. We look at it as three seasons. The Beanpot is one."

For the next several days, the real world, let alone the sports world, was placed in a state of great uncertainty. As Greater Boston slowly navigated its way back to normalcy the following Monday, an official announcement regarding the fate of the 1978 final was made. "We all agree that it is the best for the fans [to postpone the finals]," said tournament director Steve Nazro of the Boston Garden. "We've sold 14,500 tickets, and with the driving ban on in Boston, poor road conditions in some areas, and . . . public transportation not back at full strength yet it just seemed the right thing to do for the safety and comfort for all concerned." After consideration by the various parties, the Beanpot was moved to the uncharted waters of March.

In the interim, Yale ended BU's (23-1) dream of a perfect season. Harvard (12-12) dropped five straight decisions before salvaging a win at Dartmouth the night before the Beanpot showdown. "We played two games in five weeks," commented Crimson coach Billy Cleary. "Then eight in fifteen days. The frustrating part of all this is we've played well. We just haven't been scoring."

Although assured of the number-one position for the upcoming ECAC playoffs, BU had been far from impressive in recent outings. "Mentally we aren't sharp at all," said Coach Parker. "I think the Beanpot final will tell us a lot about how we'll play in the playoffs. We haven't played well since the first Beanpot game."

Often-quotable Terrier right wing Dave Silk offered his thoughts on the delayed annual battle for bragging rights: "Everyone's ready to play this one. The Beanpot's

Harvard's George Hughes battles Boston University's Dick Lamby in the 1978 Beanpot brawl.

(Courtesy of *Boston Globe*)

the Beanpot. It's Boston Garden with fifteen thousand people. We could play it the Fourth of July and it'd still be the Beanpot."

The future Olympic gold-medalist's words proved prophetic. The calendar may have read March 1, but there was no shortage of fireworks in the longest-delayed—and the only March—Beanpot game ever played.

 The 1978 Beanpot began in The Blizzard and ended 23 days later in a brawl. But what took nearly a month and the Boston Garden cops to finish was one of the most one-sided tournaments in its history.

Boston University last night finished Harvard's season, 7–1, the same way it had humiliated Boston College a month before in the first round. And while Harvard could take solace by settling some old and personal scores in the brawl that erupted with 3:36 left, it meant very little to BU.

What did mean something was a hat trick from Mickey Mullen, a pair of goals by defenseman Dick Lamby and an exhibition that looked like a coach's dream.

BU came out storming. In fact, were it not for Harvard goalie Jack Hynes, it might have been 6–0 by the time the game was 10 minutes old. Instead, BU ended the first period with but a 2–0 lead on goals by Jack O'Callahan and Mickey Mullen.

After pouring six shots on Hynes in the first 2:20, BU got a power-play opportunity at 3:55 when Harvard's Bob McDonald was called for hooking Dave Silk. Then Silk got the puck back to Dick Lamby at the left point, who in turn slipped it to O'Callahan just inside the line and in the middle, and the BU captain fired it in at 4:17.

At 7:12, Mullen punched in his own rebound and finished a dazzling 3-on-2. Paul Miller made a reverse, behind-the-back pass to Mullen as he broke in from the right. Hynes made the initial save, but Mullen banged in the rebound for his fifth goal in seven games. That may not seem particularly significant. However, the junior from Courtright, Ont., now has a grand total of six goals for the season.

The saga of Mickey Mullen continued in the second period when he got two more goals for a hat trick and increased BU's lead to 4–1. After doing all the blue-collar work in the corner getting the puck back to Bill LeBlond at the point, Mullen broke to the net and had the shot deflect off him past Hynes. The score was 3–0, 3:18 into the period.

Harvard then woke a few of the 14,335 up. Rick Benson won a face-off and flicked a shot past Jim Craig. Some 15 seconds later Benson almost scored again on a deflection. Less than two minutes later, however, Mullen finished the hat trick (giving him seven goals in seven games) tapping in a rebound in a pile-up after another LeBlond shot.

What Mullen did was an example of what makes BU so good—its depth. After all, the 3-M line of Mullen, Miller, and Daryl MacLeod came into the game as the so-called third line, with 17 goals all season. Poor Harvard, it shutout the two name lines for two periods and was down, 4–1.

Jim Craig and Jack O'Callahan celebrate the Terriers' 1978 Beanpot championship.

(Courtesy of Boston University)

With that frustration firmly implanted and the realization that this loss eliminated Harvard from the ECAC tourney, Harvard coach Billy Cleary tried one interesting move at the end of the second period. With a man advantage and 4 seconds remaining, Cleary pulled Hynes for an extra skater. Yup. BU won the face-off and yawned out the clock.

And by then, Harvard had had it. Fortunately for the concessionaires, most of the crowd waited around for the third period, thus giving them another between-periods killing in the popcorn department. By the time the third period was 142 seconds old, Causeway Street was crowded.

What put the game to rest was Lamby coming out of the penalty box and scoring two goals in 31 seconds. Killing off a 4-on-3 Harvard power play, Mark Hetnik broke out of his own end, went around Harvard defenseman Kevin O'Donoghue, held off George Hughes with one arm as he crossed the blue line and fed a one-handed pass across to Lamby breaking out of the penalty box. Lamby finished the play off, then 31 seconds later scored again from the point. Harvard had one consolation. Hey, if it had won and eventually gotten eighth place in the ECAC, it just would have to play BU again.

—Peter Gammons, *Boston Globe*, March 2, 1978

Tales from a Beanpot Blizzard

One of the events that helped shape the Beanpot into the Boston institution it is today took place in 1978. This time, the fans were participants as much as the players, and events took place outside the Garden as well as inside. It was the Great Blizzard—which demonstrated either how loyal Boston's college hockey fans could be or how foolish, depending on the point of view. Starting with my own recollections, the following anecdotes give some idea of how the weather, of all things, contributed to Beanpot lore.

By 1978, I was a Beanpot veteran. I began regularly attending BU games with my family (Mom, Dad, Grandpa—all BU grads) in 1968, when a skinny kid from Somerville named Parker was the Terrier captain. My first Beanpot, in 1971, was truly an event. Although I was still only a peewee in Stoneham's youth hockey program, I had arrived. I was now old enough for a late school night out.

Boston University forward Mickey Mullen was the 1978 tournament's unlikely hero.

(Courtesy of Boston University)

That morning in 1978 was typical of all the Beanpots before I got to BU myself. The anticipation, the excitement—the day could not go by quickly enough, because tonight we were going to the "Gah-den."

My father had been trying to get more tickets for a couple of my friends from Stoneham High. He made a few phone calls from his office that morning. No luck. By the time he got home though, the messages were stacking up. Our friends were following the weather reports and suddenly getting extra tickets was no longer a problem. We had enough for the whole senior class at Stoneham High, if necessary.

By the time we left for Boston, my mother and younger brother had been scratched from the lineup. My father, one of his friends, myself, and two of my friends headed out despite the ever more ominous weather advisories.

Through flickering lights, a rampant rumor mill, and multiple MBTA announcements, we stayed. Heck, BU was really burying BC; there was no way we wanted to leave. Against all common sense, we stayed to the end, worrying about the implications later.

We headed outside into a scene from *Dr. Zhivago*. We made it to what we hoped was our car, buried in a snowdrift in a small parking lot behind the Garden. (It was my mother's car. When we finally got home, all she wanted to know was, is my car all right?)

With the help of some other inhabitants of the same lot, who had similar hopes of not having to call their cars home for the evening, we dug out and got on 93 North, tucking behind a snowplow all the way to our exit.

Needless to say, my friends spent the week at my house. Two February vacations is every high school senior's dream. The best part was, with all the world at a standstill, the sports segments on the local news featured BU's dozen Beanpot goals all week long—a Terrier's midwinter dream come true!

Jack Grinold, associate athletic director for sports information at Northeastern University, then and now, comes clean:

"I have to confess I've lived a lie for a long time. I've always said I've never missed a Beanpot game. You'll see there is an exception.

"Two weeks before the Beanpot, our team routed a pretty good Harvard club at the old, freezing Watson Rink, 11–5. I can remember thinking, don't make them mad. . . . Save a few goals for the Beanpot first round.

"That morning of February 6, I heard about the storm. I was more concerned with the game. I've often talked about my Beanpot experience as me being Charlie Brown trying to placekick with Lucy pulling the football away at the last second. Well, we lost in overtime (3–2), and I can only describe my reaction as a temper tantrum.

"I was muttering many curses as I walked downstairs and jumped into the first cab I saw, showing total disregard for the second game. It wasn't until we weaved our way along for about a half-mile, jerking left and right, that it dawned on me that we were in the middle of a blizzard.

"The cab driver told me just how rough things had been. He also told me that I was his last fare of the night. I was home in Brighton by the time they dropped the puck for the second game. For once, I was lucky to have been so luckless in the Beanpot."

Tom Peters, current associate athletic director at Boston College, was the Boston Garden's marketing director in 1978. As he tells it:

"We heard the weather reports. We knew it was going to be a severe storm, but nothing like what happened.

"From my window on Causeway Street, I could see things were getting worse and worse. I was watching people try to navigate. It was an eerie sight. Despite it all, we had over 11,000 turn out for the game.

"What we didn't need was overtime in the first game [Northeastern and Harvard], then, after the second game started late, seventeen goals. By the time that game ended, I knew there was going to be no way home for me to my wife and young daughter out in Waltham.

"We had over two hundred people stranded in the building. We fed them with the leftover hot dogs and popcorn. All we had to drink was beer. I can remember sleeping on my desk after a beer-and-hotdog bedtime snack. In its own way, there was a party atmosphere in the Garden.

"The next afternoon, I went over to the North Station concourse. Luckily, I found a conductor I knew from my regular commuter train. He said they were going to send a train out to clear the tracks and I could get a ride. I ran back into the Garden and grabbed Steve Nazro and Gary Castletine and told them we had a ride. We ran down, jumped on the train, and off we went. I can still see Steve jumping off at his stop into a snowbank and disappearing!

"I know some people who came for the Beanpot stayed until the end of the week. I was just happy to get home to my family. It was unbelievable."

"It was my final assignment after thirty-seven years in the newspaper business," recalls Cliff Sundberg, who was a sportswriter at the *Boston Post, Boston Daily Record,* and *Boston Globe,* before his fourteen-year stint as sports editor at the *Boston Herald.* "The night before the Beanpot, I was down at the Foxboro Raceway with Dave O'Hara of the AP. He asked me if I could cover the Beanpot. It would pay $25. I said okay.

"By the time the second game ended that night, I knew once I got outside that there was no way out. I went back to the Iron Horse [the popular street-level bar at North Station] and closed the place, then went over to the old Hayes-Bickford and did the same. We had the last eggs in the place. I went back and slept at the Iron Horse.

"The next morning, I ran into Harry Sinden and Nate Greenberg in North Station. They invited me into the Bruins' dressing room and I ended up spending the rest of the week there, with John Carleton [the late Bruins scout] as my roommate. Fortunately for us, the players had left shaving gear and combs, so we were able to stay well-groomed. The Bruins people kept the food coming for us and everyone that was stranded there.

"When I finally got out at the end of the week, I took the train to Kenmore Square—not knowing that I couldn't get to my house at Cleveland Circle. I walked to the Brookline Police Station and got a ride with a nice young couple who helped me shovel out in order to get into my house. I offered them the $20 I still had in my pocket. (I don't think they accepted it.)

"By the time I picked up my car at the Government Center garage, a week had passed. I think they offered reduced rates. Dave got me $40 instead of $25. Not bad, considering the whole thing cost me a couple of lunches."

Now a sports-radio talk-show host on WEEI, Ted Sarandis was an employee of the Boston Garden when the Blizzard hit Boston in 1978. "The Blizzard occurred in an eventful year in Boston sports," he recalls. "The Bruins went to the finals, where they lost in six to Montreal. The Celtics were in their final year before getting Larry Bird.

"As I remember, everyone in Boston anticipated this storm, but guesses of its size varied. I remember [sports photographer] Dick Raphael saying it was just another storm. During the intermissions, people were jammed in the east and west lobbies to see the weather reports.

"The speed of the storm was what caught the fans. Many had thought they could beat the storm home after the Beanpot. Some left early. Some didn't try. I recall that since Nate Greenberg had a room at the Sonesta, he stayed and caught the whole game.

"All things considered, it was the best place to get stranded. You could eat, sleep, shower. As I remember, the ushers were getting paid, too, because the fans were still there.

"Partly because it was the usual people, who knew the building, it was comfortable. We slept in the skyboxes. Concession-vendor uniforms were available for a change of clothes. We were fed with leftover concessions food, then in the 150 Causeway lobby coffee shop. We showered in the locker rooms.

"I remember listening to Mo Harrington, telling stories about the Thirties. TVs were available in the Blades & Boards Club—*color* TVs. I can remember this particularly from the colors of the sweaters [governor] Mike Dukakis wore. A lot of people played cards the whole time—I was down a little. The Fours ran out of food.

"It was quite an experience. I remain good friends still with half a dozen or so of that Blizzard group. We just never knew the storm would last so long."

"I was at the Garden, assigned to cover the early game," says Bob Monahan, who was a *Boston Globe* sportswriter from 1952 to 2001. "Will McDonough [a fellow *Globe* scribe] was there with his son Sean [now the television voice of the Boston Red Sox] and one of his friends. They had a car and, luckily, a couple of shovels to get the car out of a snowbank. I got behind the wheel on the Expressway while the other three pushed us down to the *Globe* exit [Morrisey Boulevard]. I was stuck at the office until Friday, when I finally was able to walk home to South Boston. The people who were stranded at the *Globe* were all doing different jobs in order to keep the paper going. I ate at the cafeteria for three and a half days straight. I haven't eaten there since."

Joe Bertagna, now Hockey East commissioner, was Harvard's assistant sports information director at the time:

"I ended up at my brother Bob's place in Watertown. His white van got us home from the game. I was coaching [the first] Harvard women's hockey team that year. The team actually skied over for a party that week. After five days, my brother and I were ready to kill each other. Being a doctor, he was able to drive his vehicle through checkpoints by showing his identification. He brought me back to Cambridge and I stayed with my assistant coach, John Christenson, back on campus."

For Steve Nazro, the FleetCenter's vice president and director of events and the director of the Beanpot tournament, "There was never a sense of danger. There were great poker games going on. It was a serene time.

"People were here because they wanted to be. Some of them could have left. They were all married. 'Hello, honey?' " he says, mimicking a typical blizzard phone call. "I'm sorry but I'm stuck here. You'll read about it in the paper.' "

What brought Billy Smith to the Garden Monday night?

"I told my wife this afternoon she had two choices. You know, she wanted to come down and see the Beanpot, too, but she's two days overdue with our second kid and she was worried about the weather.

"So I told her she could come down here to the games with me and, if she had to go to the hospital, we could go right from here. Or, if she wanted to stay home, I'd get my brother to stay with her and give me a call if she had to go."

It was shortly after 7 P.M. and Billy Smith of Somerville was among the early arrivals in a crowd of 11,666 that would eventually move into the Garden, despite the swirling storm outside. He said he wasn't worried about getting back home.

"I told the Garden people when I got here what the situation was so they gave me this beeper to wear," said Smith, fingering the telephonic beeper—like the ones doctors wear—attached to the front of his shirt.

"So if my brother calls, the beeper will go off. I'll walk home if I have to. But I don't know if I can make it in time. My wife was only in labor an hour with the first one. With my luck, she'll call right in the middle of the BC-BU game."

What brought Tommy McCarthy to the Boston Garden Monday night?

"My wife, Helen, told me not to come," said Tommy, the sixty-two-year-old press steward. "But I told her, Helen, come hell or high water, I have to go.

"You know, I started working here at the Garden forty-five years ago today. . . . Tim McCoy, the cowboy, was in here with the rodeo.

"In all those years I never missed an event here at the Garden. I've been here for every Beanpot since they started. . . . I told Helen I'd rather cut off my arm than not get to my job."

Tommy McCarthy doesn't drive a car. Never has. Last night he was counting on the MBTA to get him back to Quincy.

"I'll walk home if I have to. I remember I did once before, back in 1940. We had Sonja Henie in here with the ice show and a storm came in just like this one. Didn't get out of here until three in the morning. I walked home to East Cambridge and it took me four hours, even though it was just a couple of miles."

The same thing that brought Billy Smith and Tommy McCarthy through the snow and the wind also moved Tom Berry to make the trip. Tom Berry is blind. He works as a masseur at the Harvard Club on Commonwealth Avenue, but simply loves sports.

"This is some kind of guy," said Harvard coach Billy Cleary in a happy Harvard dressing room after the Crimson had beaten Northeastern 4–3 in overtime. "He comes to all the games—Bruins, Celtics. How'd you get here tonight?" Cleary asked Berry, who clutched his cane in one hand and carried a portable radio in the other.

"I came on the subway," said Berry, "but I'm worried about getting home. I've got to get to Randolph."

"No you're not," said Cleary. "You're staying at the Harvard Club. I'm getting you a room."

Bonnie Barrett and her husband, Tom, drove five of their nine kids from Southie to the Garden early in the evening. As they watched their oldest son Paul play for BC in a losing effort (12–5), the Barretts weren't worried about the storm.

They had waited a long time and sacrificed a lot for Monday night. Five years ago the Barretts sold the family car to raise money to send their son to prep school. Now he was the captain of the Boston College team in a Beanpot Tournament.

"He's a great kid," said Bonnie Barrett. "He's never given us a minute's trouble. I told him if he scored tonight, I'd give him a hundred bucks."

Just minutes after 11 P.M., at the end of the second period of the BC-BU contest, the Garden management announced to the crowd that they might be locked in for the night.

The roads were termed impassable. Most of the rapid-transit lines were inoperable.

There were still about 8,000 left in the stands at the time of the announcement, and most of them seemed to laugh off the thought of sleeping in the Garden for a night.

"We'll keep anyone that wants to stay," said Bruins president Paul Mooney. "We'll give them free coffee and try to find a place for them to sleep."

But somehow, the multitude vanished. An hour after the second game ended, less than 100 were still inside the building. A few went out onto the ice surface, running from one end and sliding headfirst into the nets. A few more huddled around three Harvard bandmembers in the lobby, belting out the Harvard fight song with two trumpets and a trombone.

But the rest simply vanished. The same defiance that brought them through the storm was now carrying them home. Did Mrs. Smith have her baby? Did Tommy McCarthy return safely to Helen? Did Tom Berry make it to the Harvard Club? For sure, Paul Barrett became richer for his experience Monday night. He did score a goal.

—Will McDonough

Beanpot, Olympus, and Back

A former Beanpot player who later won a gold medal with the 1980 U.S. Olympic team and played seven seasons in the NHL, Dave Silk was the guest speaker at the 1993 Beanpot Luncheon. The text of his address, which follows, gives some perspective on the flavor and emotion of the tournament:

I'm thrilled to be here. Absolutely thrilled to be here. When Jack Grinold called and asked if I'd talk about the passion of the Beanpot, I said, "Are you kidding? I'd be glad to.". . .

What the Beanpot means to me? Quite simply, there are two words that come to mind: *tradition* and *emotion*.

Dave Silk, Boston University forward (1976–79) and keynote speaker at the 1993 Beanpot luncheon
(Courtesy of Boston University)

The tradition of the Beanpot—anyone who has a pulse around here knows about the tradition of the Beanpot. I'm a local kid, I grew up in Scituate. I started coming to the Beanpot about the same time I started playing hockey. . . .

So I come to BU in '76 and I play in the Garden for the first time, my first Beanpot. I played at private schools, so I never played in the Boston Garden in the state tournament. This is it for me. I walk in, and I can remember walking by the Bruins' locker room. I was in shock. I was terrified.

I went out for warmup on the bad ice and I saw the Bruins crest at center ice. Oh my God! All of a sudden my skates weren't sharpened, my helmet doesn't fit, my gloves don't feel right. I was nervous. I was scared.

I went back into the room and all the Canadian kids—Rick Meagher, Bob Dudley and all these Canadian players—they're sitting there saying, "Hey guys, isn't this great?"

They're not nervous; they're just having fun. This is a ball for them. They're not playing for their parents, their girlfriends, their youth hockey coaches, their two hundred other close friends and relatives in the stands. They're having fun. For years, my theory was that one of the reasons why BU has done so well is that it's had a lot of guys who don't get uptight. . . . You know, these Canadian kids, and to an extent the guys who have played here a long time—like the Bavises, the Kevin O'Sullivans—they're used to play-ing here. This is like a second home to them. That's all part of the tradition too.

That was the first time I had ever played with Canadian guys. They didn't know about the Beanpot. They didn't know about Boston Garden. They didn't know about walk-ing from Durgin Park on Monday night over to watch the game. They were at ease and I learned from them. . . .

So I played in the Beanpot. And you know, I can't leave here without telling this story. We won the Beanpot in '78—we had a great team that year and won the national championship—but that's not why I remember the Beanpot.

In '78 we played Harvard in the finals of the Beanpot. In fact, in those days there wasn't a lot of USA Hockey, where guys played with guys from other teams, so we didn't really know each other that well. And the fact of the matter was that no one really liked each other from the other teams.

There was a lot of animosity, a lot of hatred. We took Harvard 7–1 that night, and near the end of the game it was starting to get ugly. Tempers were flaring and there was a lot of frustration. As happens, there turned out to be a fight down the stretch. Normally you can say that fights happen due to the competitive nature, this is just one of those things.

The fact of the matter was that the fight started because a particular BU guy and a par-ticular Harvard guy were going back and forth, and the benches were going back and forth, and it turned out there was a girl who might have been "seeing" both of the players. There was a lot of trash being talked on the ice, guys got kicked out, and that was it. I'll respect the privacy of the players involved, not so much because I respect them but because I respect lawsuits.

I talked to Jack [Parker] after the game and said, "I'm not that comfortable about get-ting thrown out of the Beanpot."

He said, "Oh, you shouldn't worry about it—Smitty [Ben Smith, later a BU assistant coach, now Northeastern's head coach] got thrown out."

The other thing I remember about that '78 game was the Blizzard of '78. The Boston Garden had turned into a quasi-shelter for fans who couldn't get out. By the time we had made it to Kenmore Square, going up Comm. Ave., it was obvious, to us at least, that we wouldn't be having classes the next morning. Our captain, Jack O'Callahan, as we're just crawling on Commonwealth Avenue, he went up to Jack and said, "Hey Coach, it's gonna be an awful long walk from Walter Brown Arena down to the Dugout Cafe, where we'd like to retire for a few 'coffees and cokes.' Would you mind if we just pulled the bus over and we just got out here?"

Well, obviously Coach Parker wasn't going to pull the bus over at the Dugout Cafe and let us out. So, in his infinite wisdom, he decided to tell the bus driver to pull another fifty yards up the road at the BU Chapel. He said to the guys, "Okay fellas, anyone who wants to go to Mass is welcome to go to Mass."

The guys filed out of the bus and one of the last guys out was Billy Cotter, a nice Irish Catholic kid from Charlestown. He turned to Carl James, our equipment man, and said, "Hey Carl, I'm as religious as the next guy, but we just beat Harvard in the Beanpot—I don't want to go to Mass!"

To which Carl had a reply. . . .

By the time we made it out of the Dugout, the snow was gone. Unfortunately, so were the '70s.

The other word that comes to mind here is *emotion*. The emotion that comes from the Beanpot is unbelievable. You can feel it.

The Beanpot's special that way. It's really special. When you go in and walk past the Bruins' locker room, all the hoopla's over, all the tickets are gone, there's nothing more you can do about making sure that your girlfriend and your youth hockey coaches and your parents are taken care of. All that's behind you, then you get into The Room, and The Room becomes your family. They're all brothers for you. It's the greatest feeling in the world.

One of the things that's special about the '78 team is that it didn't matter what we did away from the rink. When we came to the rink and played in that game, we were family. We were all brothers. We had something special. When we won that Beanpot, and skated around the ice, I'll never ever forget being handed the Beanpot and being able to show it to my family and friends and all those other people up in the stands, maybe taunting the other team's band. I'll never forget that.

It didn't matter if you were from Gloucester, Mass., or Gloucester, Ontario; we were all brothers. We were all family, and to me, that's the emotion of the Beanpot. . . .

There's another great thing about the Beanpot, too. I was fortunate enough to play in Lake Placid on that 1980 [Olympics] team, the gold-medal team. I don't want to compare the two experiences, but when you win the Beanpot, you can't wait to meet someone from Harvard at Fenway Park or wherever, and say, "Hey, better luck next time." It's tough to walk up to Krutov or Makarov or Fedorov and say, "Hey, sorry about that." The bragging rights for the Beanpot are incredible. . . .

To be part of this, to be part of the Beanpot, to be part of the great people associated with it is great. We kid our guys on our team. Someone asks, "What time is it?" Someone will answer, "It's the time of your life—enjoy it."

To the writers, coaches, and staff—this is special. Watch the enthusiasm, the emotion, the passion these guys bring to the game. It's contagious—let's all try to catch some of it. This *is* the time of our lives, and I hope we all enjoy it.

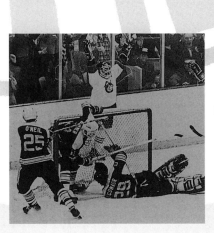

NEXT YEAR COMES
TO HUNTINGTON AVENUE

1979–1980

C H A P T E R
S I X

1980 wasn't supposed to be next year. On the contrary, the arrival of the first Monday in February, the twenty-eighth renewal of the Beanpot Hockey Tournament, appeared to promise another dose of disappointment for the beleaguered Northeastern University hockey team and its followers.

"There was an annual move to get out of the Beanpot altogether, supported by members of our varsity club," recalls Jack Grinold, Northeastern's associate athletic director for sports information. "The idea of us sparing ourselves the annual embarrassment was gathering momentum."

In fact, the twenty-seven years of Husky frustration had been compounded by the previous two Februarys' results. The first post-blizzard Beanpot posed a familiar question: had the year of the Husky finally arrived?

Jack Grinold, Northeastern's
associate athletic director
(Courtesy of Northeastern University)

A youthful Northeastern squad was streaking toward February. A record of 9-8 placed Fern Flaman's pups fourth in the ECAC. The Huskies' level of confidence had been raised by their first win over BU since the 1963–64 season.

Boston College, the reigning ECAC champion team and NCAA runner-up the previous season, was at 10-11. On opening night, the Huskies were in the unfamiliar role of favorite over the Eagles.

1979 The largest first-round crowd in almost a decade (14,679) turned out for the contest, the majority hoping to witness history in the form of Northeastern's first advance to a championship game since 1967. History would be placed on hold.

Courtesy of three goals in two minutes, Boston College stormed to a 6–0 lead early in the third period and displayed total domination en route to their 7–2 win. The loss of NU defensive-stalwart Jim Walsh proved to be a significant one, as a depleted Husky blue-line corps struggled in front of twenty-five-year-old Northeastern goalie Ed Arrington, a former garage mechanic and a fan favorite. In the other goal, Boston College's returning all-American netminder, Paul Skidmore, handled twenty-eight of thirty NU shots.

The *Boston Globe*'s John Powers suggested a new country-western song for Grinold and his despondent dogs: "My Hound Dawg's Singin' Those 6:15 Blues Agin."

"The Beanpot is like a looooonnngggg Bela Lugosi movie with just a lot of baying in the darkness at the end," commented Grinold after the Eagles' fifth goal. From the prospect of history to the familiar horror-movie protagonist, such was the plight of the Huskies on another first Monday in February. Northeastern would finish their season 12-15, missing a coveted berth in the ECAC play-offs by virtue of an overtime loss to Providence in the season's final game.

The other first-round game held far more suspense. Boston University, the East's number-one team, faced a vagabond Harvard team that had been forced to play their entire schedule on the road while awaiting the construction of a new arena. Though the Terriers were a prohibitive favorite over the Crimson team, which had won but a single Division I game in two months, BU trailed early in the third period, until a salvo of three goals in four minutes propelled the Terriers to their sixteenth straight Beanpot final—the eighth between the Terriers and the Eagles.

Boston College had last defeated Boston University in the epic 1976 Beanpot final. Since that fateful February evening, BU's record for the previous ten games in this fiercest of all local collegiate rivalries was 9-0-1. Another BU win would keep the Green Line's B trolley following the same track.

An unlikely Terrier hero, sophomore forward and tourney MVP Daryl MacLeod, converted a rebound of a shot by linemate Bill Cotter, with 7:45 left, to give the Terriers a 4-3 victory and their eleventh Beanpot title. Boston University goalie and future Olympics hero Jim Craig made twenty-seven saves but could not prevent BC's Skidmore from capturing a second Eberly Award.

Huskies defenseman Jim Walsh was one of several members of the 1978–79 team who did not return to the team the following year.
(Courtesy of Northeastern University)

"We're due, maybe overdue," said Skidmore, referring to BU's mastery.

"Maybe our day will come to get even or one-third or one-quarter even," added frustrated Eagles coach Len Ceglarski. What of the day of the Husky?

1980   Northeastern's 1979–80 preseason prospectus boasted the return of sixteen lettermen and the loss of just four from the previous year's squad. By the time Fernie Flaman blew the whistle for the team's first practice, the number of departed Huskies had doubled. Dependable returning forwards Chris Nilan, Dave Wilkens, and Mark Simmons, along with hard-nosed defenseman Jim Walsh—a two-sport standout— had all signed professional contracts. Left without an experienced goaltender after the unexpected departure of Ed Arrington, who had been the starter for two seasons, the Huskies' fortunes took a dramatic fall.

"It's been a disaster," commented Coach Flaman. "We haven't been getting blown out by any team, even with all the problems we've had. We're better than what our record shows. It's just that we have a lot of new kids on the team, you can't expect them to jump in and do the job right away."

The goaltending situation the coach faced was typical of the team's overall struggles, as freshman netminders Mark Davidner and George Demetroulakos had both been pressed into immediate service.

George Demetroulakos, Northeastern University's goaltender in the 1980 tournament

(Courtesy of Northeastern University)

"They had some big shoes to fill when we found that Arrington wouldn't be back. This game of college hockey is quite a big step up from the kind of competition they've been facing," said Flaman prior to the Beanpot. "I'm alternating them, pretty much, because they're very young."

In Northeastern's final game before the 1980 Beanpot, the Huskies ended a six-game losing streak with a 9–3 win over Maine for Flaman's one-hundredth career win. The recently formed forward line of co-captain Wayne Turner centering Jerry Dwyer and Dale Ferdinandi combined for five goals. It was the Huskies' first Division I win since December 7, when rookie netminder Demetroulakos stopped twenty-nine Black Bear shots.

"We start a new season with the Beanpot," observed defenseman Paul Filipe.

On Chestnut Hill, meanwhile, the Eagles' fortunes were rising. Boston College, number-one ranked team in the ECAC, arrived at the Garden having won nine of their last ten games. The Eagles had recently earned their first-ever win at Boston University's Walter Brown Arena, in overtime, avenging a defeat in the previous year's Beanpot title game. A deep, experienced, and talented team, the Eagles entered the 1980 Beanpot as the tournament favorite.

"I don't think our past record matters," said Northeastern's Wayne Turner at that year's Beanpot luncheon. "If we haven't won it in twenty-seven years, that isn't going to bother me. I haven't been here for twenty-seven years."

The two-time defending-champion Boston University Terriers were Northeastern's first-round opponent. Despite an overall record of only 9-8, BU was a clear-cut favorite over the lowly Huskies (3-11). In a series that spanned a half-century, BU had dominated Northeastern with sixty-seven wins in eighty-six meetings. Most important, it was the first Monday in February, traditionally the Terriers' time.

 John Montgomery, a 5-foot-6, 160-pound winger from Gloucester, ripped home a 45-foot slap shot at 5:09 of sudden-death overtime to give Northeastern—that's right, Northeastern—a stunning 6–5 victory over Boston University last night in the opening round of the 28th annual Beanpot Hockey Tournament at Boston Garden.

"Biggest thrill in my life," said Montgomery with a grin as he sipped a Coke and cooled off. "Once I got over the blue line and looked, I didn't see anyone to pass to. So I just cut loose with my best shot.

John Montgomery celebrates his winning overtime goal that clinched Northeastern's first-round defeat of Boston University.

(Courtesy of Northeastern University)

"No, I wasn't shooting for any part of the net. I just was hoping that maybe the shot would be on net and we'd have a chance to get another shot on a rebound. But it went in [past BU goalie Bob Barich], and am I ever happy. I can't explain what this means.

"I was tired at the start of the third period. Really tired. But the coach [Ferny Flaman] just kept telling us to put out as much as we could. He told us we had more in us than we thought we did. Well, I guess he was right."

After Montgomery got the winner, the entire club and coaching staff gathered around goaltender George Demetroulakos, who only had to make 19 saves but came up with 5 on extremely difficult shots.

Demetroulakos, a freshman from Chelmsford, wandered a bit too much and did allow two goals that could have been avoided. And he benefited from a good two-way performance by his teammates.

BU scored at 5:03 of the first period when Billy Cotter soloed in and fired a shot that was deflected into the NU goal by a sliding defender.

NU then scored three in a row. Mark Derby finished off a 3-on-2 break with a shot from the crease at 14:09, Sandy Beadle blasted home a 25-footer from the left side at 15:03, and hustling Wayne Turner connected on a 40-footer at 19:36.

BU's Grant Goegan scored the only goal of the second period at 17:46, converting a Daryl MacLeod pass from right out front.

In the third period, Goegan struck again at 0:10 on a 10-foot backhander, but NU's Gerry Cowie countered with a 10-footer after taking a fine passout from Paul McDougall.

BU then went ahead, 5–4, with a pair of goals. Goegan completed his hat trick at 4:08 and Paul Fenton scored at 13:27. It stayed that way until 17:04, when Turner deflected in a hard shot by Ferdinandi—perhaps the scoring play of the night.

—Bob Monahan, *Boston Globe,* February 5, 1980

In the other first-round match heavily favored Boston College (17-4-1) rallied back from a 3–0 deficit to defeat 4-11 Harvard 4–3, on a Gary Sampson third-period goal, setting the stage for an unlikely Beanpot final.

A week of unbridled Beanpot mania engulfed the Northeastern campus in anticipation of the championship game. In between answering the phone and opening telegrams from fans, alumni, former players, and assorted luminaries, "6:15 Grinold" was being interviewed by every sportswriter in the region and enjoying his Warholian fifteen minutes.

 Jack Grinold has earned the right to gloat. He is the popular—no, make that beloved—sports information director at Northeastern, and it's been 13 years since Northeastern has been in the Beanpot final. When people talk about the aura of the Beanpot Hockey Tournament, they are never thinking of Northeastern. Rooting for the Huskies on the first Monday evening of each February has been like rooting for the Washington Generals against the Harlem Globetrotters. Northeastern's history in the Beanpot has enabled Grinold to live an ordered life. If someone were to ask him on any given July 4 where he would be at 6:15 P.M. on the second Monday of the following February, he could safely reply, "Standing in the press box at the Boston Garden handing out Northeastern press notes and waiting for us to play the consolation game of the Beanpot."

No longer. On Monday, February 11, 1980, Jack Grinold can arrive late for the Beanpot. "There are people," he says, "who want to be with me all day. They want to see where I will go, what I will do when Monday comes. They want to know where I will be at 6:15. They want to see if I will come into the Garden early and head like some lemming directly to the press box. And I really don't know what I'm going to do yet.

"Two years ago really hurt," reminds Grinold. "We had beaten Harvard something like 14–5 a couple of weeks earlier. We came into the game heavily favored, and they beat us in overtime, 3–2. Our last two teams have been decent, in fact. We came in favored slightly over BC last year, and they had us down, 4–0, in five minutes. There were other years when BU was so dominant that we drew BC or Harvard first and could have won a game. We lost all of them."

The game was played on Monday, but Tuesday is the day Grinold will never forget. "Our office," explains Grinold, "Fernie's office at the Arena and [athletic director] Joe Zabilski's office were all paralyzed as far as work was concerned. There were phone calls from all over. I heard from one Bowdoin guy I haven't seen in 25 years.

"I probably shouldn't admit this," he says, "but I felt like Charlie Brown when Lucy is holding the football for him to kick. All those years, the football has been pulled away.

"But this time I got to kick the football."

—Bob Ryan, *Boston Globe*, February 8, 1980

As always, there were games to be played in between deciding Beanpot bragging rights for another year. Boston College hung on to defeat New Hampshire at home, 4–3, as little-used freshman goalie Bob O'Connor played the first two periods despite a nagging knee problem. Sophomore netminder Doug Ellis finished the game. Northeastern traveled to Brunswick, Maine, and fell to Division II Bowdoin (Grinold's alma mater), 4–3, on a disputed last-second goal. All would be forgotten come Monday.

For just the third time in the tournament's twenty-eight-year history, Northeastern would play for the Beanpot. The soaring Eagles, number-one in the East and number-three in the nation, led the all-time series between the two schools 78-13-4. The local game-day advance buzz placed the prospects of a Huskies Beanpot victory on the level of two of sports' all-time monumental upsets: the New York Jets' Super Bowl III win over the Baltimore Colts; and, just four months prior to the Beanpot showdown, the Pittsburgh Pirates' World Series comeback from a 3–1 deficit to defeat the Baltimore Orioles. Another hockey upset of epic proportions—the USA's "Miracle on Ice" triumph over the USSR at the Lake Placid Olympic Games—was still eleven days away.

"Yes, we have a secret weapon for the game. Score more goals than they do," commented Coach Flaman. "We'll need a lot of luck to have a chance at beating a good Boston College team. They're probably the better team but, God, if our kids can get up for them and play like they did against BU, they have a chance."

 It came just 2:47 into overtime in the championship game of the Beanpot hockey tournament last night before 14,456 roaring fans at the Garden. It lifted the beloved underdogs from Huntington Avenue to a 5–4 win over Boston College—and their first title in the 28-year history of the tournament. And it served as the climax to a performance that was charged with drama.

Make no mistake about it; this was no fluke. The Huskies came back from a 4–3 deficit to tie it on a goal by Paul McDougall with 3:36 left in the third period and then all but won it when Turner went in alone as time ran out in regulation.

The Goal!

Wayne Turner's "shot heard 'round the Beanpot" slips past BC goalie Bob O'Connor.

(Courtesy of Northeastern University)

On that one, Ferdinandi slid the puck to Turner as he broke into the clear. Turner went in on surprise-starter Bob O'Connor in the BC nets but came up empty. "If I had made a good shot," said Turner, "I had it. I was half on my backhand. He [O'Connor] forced it. I just couldn't lift it."

So they teamed up again in overtime, two seniors who have endured indignities for four years, and this time they connected. Ferdinandi was tripped and fell, but he managed to throw the puck over in the direction of Larry Parks. It wound up on Turner's stick, and he put it away.

"I was trying to get it to Parks," said Ferdinandi.

"He overskated it," said Turner. "I just put it up high over his [O'Connor's] glove. He was leaning."

It touched off a turbulent celebration as the NU players engulfed Turner at one end of the ice and NU coach Fern Flaman quietly hugged freshman goaltender George Demetroulakos at center ice. On a night when there were all sorts of heroic NU performances, few outstripped that of the freshman from Chelmsford.

Not to be overlooked was defenseman Dave Archambault, whose enormous presence in an ironman role was recognized with the MVP award. It was the ninth Beanpot for a member of the Scarborough, Ontario, Archambaults. Brother Gene had played in four, brother Mike in two, and this was the third for Dave.

If he and his teammates left a legacy, it was simply put as he sat in a corner of the frenzied NU locker room. "People don't take too kindly to being the constant underdog. It was tough to take. This'll break the ice for the future. Hopefully, they won't be such underdogs."

Perhaps it was appropriate that Turner won it. Certainly nobody traveled any farther to get to this night. He is from Kitimat, B.C., a town some 700 miles north of Vancouver on the Pacific Ocean. For the first time in his four years at NU, his parents were able to see him play in the Beanpot. In game one, NU beat Boston University, 6–5, at 5:09 of an overtime session and, well, last night speaks for itself.

"We didn't deserve to win," said BC coach Len Ceglarski, who started O'Connorl in place of regular Doug Ellis because Ellis reportedly showed up late for a team meeting. The BC players filed out of the Garden quietly, leaving NU to bask in the sun.

"I'm drained," said Ferdinandi. "I'm just drained."

—Joe Concannon, *Boston Globe*, February 12, 1980

Jubilant Huskies carry away head coach Fernie Flaman.
(Courtesy of Northeastern University)

The celebration following Turner's goal lasted for days. At Matthews Arena, Coach Flaman let the players cover the phones. "Home of the Beanpot champions," answered defenseman Paul Filipe in response to the nonstop ringing in the hockey office.

Virtually everyone in the hockey world checked in to congratulate Fernie Flaman, the former Boston Bruins captain, and his Cinderella team, including Bruins legend Bobby Orr. Most seasoned hockey observers agreed that Turner's goal had joined Orr's Stanley Cup game-winner of a decade earlier in the pantheon of the aging Boston Garden's most emotional moments on ice.

Up the street, at Punter's Pub on Huntington Avenue, Northeastern hockey's favored hangout, the afterglow of the raucous Monday night lingered on.

"It's a great day to be a Husky," said bartender Phil Smith. "It's the team of the eighties." Mr. Smith's prognostication would prove to be accurate.

The Husky momentum continued through their next game, an 8–7 win over Clarkson, but after that came a 9–1 loss at Boston College. Despite their Beanpot victory, the Huskies failed to make the ECAC play-offs. In fact, Northeastern's 1980 victory began a four-year stretch during which each of the four schools would earn a Beanpot title, then fail to qualify for the ECAC play-offs in the same season. A two-game season, indeed. And now a four-horse race.

Despite players lost to the pros, academics, and injuries, the Hounds of Huntington Avenue were, for the first time, the dogs barking loudest.

Arch, Go!

Dave Archambault was the exception to one of the Beanpot's most often recounted stories: the kid from Canada who comes to Boston and discovers the significance of our parochial hockey festival.

Instead, Archambault, a native of Scarborough, Ontario, was all too familiar not only with the tournament's importance but also Northeastern's well-documented February struggles on Causeway Street. Archambault had been preceded on the Huskies' ice by his older brothers, Gene and Mike.

"I was fifteen and remember the whole experience of coming down and watching my brothers play in the Beanpot," Archambault recently recalled. "I knew how big it was to the four Boston schools."

Archambault's road to Northeastern was far from a conventional one. Unlike the typical Canadian product, who comes to the United States to play college hockey after playing junior hockey, Archambault had only played at the prep level. In fact, before matriculating at Northeastern as a freshman, in the fall of 1976, Archambault had been out of hockey completely for two years.

If not for the encouragement from his brothers to get back in the game and the tutelage of coach Fernie Flaman upon his arrival on Huntington Avenue, Archambault would never have had the opportunity to excel as a Husky.

After spending a year with the j.v. program, then-sophomore Archambault began to take a regular shift on defense with the 1977–78 team. "I had a good sense of discipline on the ice," Archambault observed. "From a young age I was always defensively minded."

The early training would lead to an increased level of confidence on the part of Coach Flaman.

Archambault's first two on-ice opening-round Beanpot games, in 1978 and 1979, were continuations of the Huskies' disappointments. A 4–3 loss to Harvard in the first game of the infamous "Blizzard of '78" doubleheader was particularly painful. The following year Boston College decisively denied Northeastern a ticket to the title game, by a score of 6–2.

As the 3-11 Northeastern hockey team approached the 1980 Beanpot, co-captain Dave Archambault and his fellow seniors began to reflect on their final opportunity to accomplish what no Northeastern team had before.

"We didn't care who we played. All we knew was it was our last chance," said Archambault.

In the aftermath of the Huskies' monumental Beanpot victory, Archambault remembered feeling "relief, the mission was completed, everything was happening in slow motion. I looked in the stands and just felt so proud of what we had accomplished."

Archambault's personal contribution to the Northeastern victory went well beyond his one assist on the scoresheet and thankfully was not lost on the tournament's MVP selection committee. Archambault was simply everywhere: protecting in front of his own net, clearing rebounds, working the corners, blocking shots, and keeping the puck in on the offensive blue line. Archambault and his defense partner, Paul Iskyan, played an amazing fifty of the nearly sixty-three minutes of game time.

"He was our top defensive defenseman," said Coach Flaman. "He positioned himself perfectly in the zone and had natural instinct when it came to playing the opponent when he had the puck. He concentrated on his job and that was important. In the Beanpot, he was a tower of strength."

When asked how much time he spent on the ice some twenty years removed from that magical February night, Archambault remembered vividly two simple words from his coach. "'Arch, Go!' he kept shouting," recalledthe NU blue liner. "Everytime I got off the ice it seemed like Coach Flaman was calling me to go back out there."

In the Northeastern locker-room pandemonium, the captain spoke for his entire jubilant team. "Winning the Beanpot was a dream come true," said Archambault. "It's something we worked real hard to get. The Beanpot games were the two biggest games I ever played in. We were ready, wouldn't quit, and we're the champions. It's something I'll never ever forget."

After playing seventy-eight consecutive games over three years for the Huskies and being named team MVP as both a junior and senior, Archambault signed a professional contract with the Edmonton Oilers of the World Hockey Association. After an injury-plagued minor-league season, Archambault moved on to a ten-year career playing and coaching in France.

Archambault settled down in the village of Marzine, in the French Alps, where he and his wife, who is a native of the area, have two children. The Archambault family owns the Hôtel Fleur de Neige ski chalet.

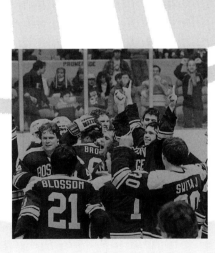

A FOUR-HORSE RACE

1981–1983

The Huskies' historic triumph of 1980 for the first time made the Beanpot a four-team tournament in reality, not just in name.

Northeastern's Beanpot success served as a springboard to its best start in history as, the following year, the Huskies rang up twelve straight victories to open the 1980–81 campaign. Even consecutive defeats at Cornell and to Boston College (on home ice) could not curb the enthusiasm surrounding the rejuvenated Northeastern hockey program.

Across the ice, awaiting the defending champions in the first match on opening night, was a Harvard team that had dropped nine of their last ten contests. The Crimson had been uncharacteristically sub-.500 for the past three seasons and out of the ECAC play-offs for four long years. An earlier meeting between the two schools had resulted in an 11–5 Northeastern win. Northeastern was a huge favorite in the early game. How would the Huskies, already assured of their first ECAC play-off appearance in fifteen years, handle the role of favorite? Harvard had a resounding answer.

1981   In one of the tournament's most stunning upsets, the Crimson humiliated Northeastern. Harvard surged to a 4–0 first-period lead before Huskies' defenseman Paul Filipe answered with a missile from the point to cut the margin to three. Northeastern would draw no closer, buried under a five-goal second-period Crimson blitzkrieg. When all the upstate returns had been tabulated, the final score was Harvard 10, Northeastern 2.

The tourney's co-favorites from Chestnut Hill would fare much better. On a 7-0-1 streak since the first of the year, Len Ceglarski's club was determined to erase the painful memories of the 1980 overtime defeat.

Boston College's co-captain, left wing Mike Ewanouski, took note of the improbable first-game upset, then took matters firmly in his own hands, scoring a power-play goal versus Boston University with 1:23 left in the third period. The goal extended the BC advantage to 4–2 in an eventual 5–2 victory. It was the fifth straight win for the Eagles over their Commonwealth Avenue neighbors.

"We don't look at BU as the power it used to be," observed Ewanouski. "When we were freshmen we lost to them four times. We beat them at the end of our sophomore year and that carried us through the summer. They're not a power team in the ECAC. They're just another team. Now they have to struggle to stay in the game with us."

A group of five Boston College seniors led by Ewanouski now had one final opportunity for Beanpot glory.

The goaltending opponents for the 1981 championship game were both haunted by ghosts from Beanpots past. Boston College's sophomore netminder, Bob O'Connor, had established himself as a solid, number-one goaltender, with a record of 11-2-2. But, in recently minted Beanpot lore, O'Connor was the eleventh-hour replacement who had lost the 1980 championship game in overtime to the miracle Huskies. O'Connor was also the unwilling centerpiece of "The Picture" that immortalized Northeast-

Wade Lau, Harvard goalie, 1981
MVP, and Eberly Award–winner

(Courtesy of Harvard University)

ern captain Wayne Turner's game-winning goal. All of the Northeastern publications—even the Beanpot program itself—featured a cover photo of the BC netminder on his side looking at the puck nestled in the Eagle net. The Billerica native had known Garden success as a schoolboy, winning a pair of Division II state titles for Billerica High School, but as a collegian the Garden now represented bitter disappointment.

At the other end of the ice, Harvard netminder Wade Lau, a Minnesotan, couldn't draw on any positive Causeway Street memories. Lau had been guarding the Crimson net versus Boston College in the 1980 opening round. Harvard had jumped to a 3–0 advantage that fateful night only to see their lead disappear in a 4–3 loss. Despite the Crimson's woes, Lau had allowed no more than three goals in his last five outings. Two goalies motivated to exorcise their personal demons were primed for the challenge.

 When time finally ran out on a glorious championship game in the 29th Beanpot Hockey Tournament last night at the steamy Boston Garden, the puck appropriately wound up on the stick of Harvard captain Tom Murray, who calmly poked it into a corner, reached over to pick it up and proceeded to skate off with it in a wildly emotional reception.

Before this entire parochial festival of college hockey began, Murray looked back over four seasons of frustration in a Crimson uniform, talked of the feeling of emptiness that went with it and surveyed the upcoming Beanpot. "I can't imagine playing four years and not winning one of these," he said. "There's an empty slot."

He sat later amid the bedlam of the Harvard locker room, the Beanpot trophy resting on his lap. "The empty slot's been filled," said this product of Natick, who had grown up watching it and dreamed of someday winning it. "I don't have to do another thing as long as I live. It's all downhill. The Beanpot. It's sitting in my lap."

In a textbook exhibition of the college game played out in front of a roaring capacity crowd of 14,456, unheralded Harvard beat Boston College, 2–0. In effect, Harvard took a page out of its rich hockey past, dusted it off with feeling and gave it a 1980s revival.

Had it not been for the goaltending heroics of Bob O'Connor (21 saves) who kept the margin at Harvard 1, BC 0, until David Burke put a high shot over his shoulder with 1:55 to go, the issue might have been settled earlier. Instead it evolved into an enthralling expression of the college game, two teams at each other's jugulars in what should be a bonanza for the two cable-TV networks who showed it. . . .

Wade Lau, who was credited with just 15 saves in the game and was named tournament MVP, authored this shutout with the help of a defense that seemingly grew up overnight for the Beanpot. Just a week earlier, Harvard had stunned Northeastern 10–2. For Lau, two goals allowed in two Beanpot games. For Harvard, wins over the East's No. 1 team (Northeastern) and its No. 3 team (BC).

Crimson forward David Burke

(Courtesy of Harvard University)

In the early stages, the initiative was all BC. In fact, Harvard failed on an early power play. When Harvard did get its first shot on goal at 12:41 of the period, it went in for that 1–0 lead that had to hold up for what seemed an eternity.

Jim Turner went in deep to retrieve the puck in the corner. He fed it out to the slot. It went past the stick of an attacking Burke. Bill Larson picked it up and shot it past O'Connor. "There was nothing else to do except shoot," said Larson, a sophomore whose previous varsity goal production added up to 1 since he was added to the roster in December. . . .

So it became the Bob O'Connor show, a magnificent performance that earned him more than a few MVP votes. In a second period that saw Harvard outshoot BC 10–2, O'Connor blunted a solo bid by Greg Olson, smothered one Harvard rush in the crease, made a quick glove save on a Phil Falcone blast and was there to frustrate Turner twice on a shorthanded blitz at the end of the period.

The Beanpot: Fifty Years of Thrills, Spills, and Chills

"It was a great game, an exciting game to watch," said BC coach Len Ceglarski in the stony silence of the locker room up the corridor. "We played about as well as we can play. They played every facet of the game about as well as they can play. Their defense handled the puck as well as any team we've played."

This was the eighth Beanpot title for Harvard, its first since 1977. Even if the game does not count in the ECAC play-off picture, Harvard still has some faint hopes of making it into the Final Eight. "This team believes," said Murray, the Beanpot still in his lap. Watching this Harvard team on two Monday nights in February, one can only wonder where it's been hiding for so long.

—Joe Concannon, *Boston Globe*, February 10, 1981

1982   For two straight years the team with the worst record entering the tournament had finished first, securing the coveted Beanpot trophy. Once again, Boston College, with a record of 15-5, loomed as the pretourney favorite. The Eagles would face Northeastern (11-5-1) for the first time in Beanpot play since the 1980 final.

Boston College exhibited great resiliency, watching a two-goal lead disappear only to rally for a 3–2 overtime victory. Another in the long run of unlikely Beanpot heroes was Eagle freshman Chris Delaney from West Roxbury, who scored the winning goal off a third-chance rebound in front of Northeastern goalie Mark Davidner. It was the rookie's third goal of the season.

The game had remained tied from the halfway point through a third period dominated by the Huskies, who thought they had taken the lead, with 2:32 left, only to have the officials rule a no-goal on a wild scramble around BC goalie Bob O'Connor. For O'Connor, the victory went halfway to erasing the painful memories of the previous two years, but only a Beanpot championship would bring him all the way. He and the Eagles would get another opportunity to capture the elusive Beanpot.

An improving but still-.500 BU team (8-8-2) was looking to wake up the echoes of past glory. After playing in the finals every year from 1963 to 1979, the Terriers incredibly had missed the feature game for two consecutive years. A Harvard team that entered the Beanpot on a six-game losing streak stood between the Terriers and their return to the finals.

A hat trick by forward Bob Darling and a twenty-six-save performance from goalie Bob Barich were the key elements that sent BU back to the finals. The 5–1 victory was particularly meaningful for Barich, who had been the losing goalie the night Northeastern's historic Beanpot run began two years earlier. "During my freshman year Coach Parker started me against Northeastern in the Beanpot and we lost 6–5 in overtime. I sort of feel I helped make up for that loss," said Barich, in the Terriers' happy postgame locker room.

The thirtieth renewal of Boston's midwinter rite of passage was the tenth Commonwealth Avenue Beanpot battle, with BC holding a slim 5–4 edge in the previous clashes.

A BU squad that stood at 5-8-3 in the ECAC, after a crushing loss at Colgate the previous Friday, was in a similar position to the two previous champions. The Beanpot presented an opportunity to redeem a season that appeared to be lost.

 Even before the siren sounded to end a wondrous Beanpot Hockey Tournament, the Boston University hockey players were starting out over the Garden boards and, for the next several minutes, the ice at one end of the building was littered with gloves and sticks and bodies, the litter of a celebration that would last well into this night.

At the opposite end of the Garden, the Boston College players just stood, stunned in disbelief. Some simply stayed and sat on the bench, staring into space. For the fourth straight year in the championship game of Boston's parochial collegiate hockey tournament, BC had come up empty and, for the seniors, this one was almost too much to take.

This was the closing Beanpot tableau in the aftermath of a marvelous game that saw a BU team that many have written out of the ECAC Division I play-offs take it to a BC team that occupies the No. 3 spot in the present standings. And BU's 12th Beanpot title came on a 3–1 victory played out in the 30th edition of the tournament before a capacity Garden crowd of 14,673.

In its unraveling, it also became a night when a BU goaltender from Canton named Cleon Daskalakis skated onto the Garden ice for the very first time, took the ice for his

In the 1982 Beanpot final, Boston University goalie Cleon Daskalakis posted forty saves.

(Courtesy of Boston University)

first game against BC and, after giving up a goal to Jim Herlihy 3:51 into the game, came up with a 40-save performance that may have been the difference between victory and defeat.

This was, as well, a game set off by the unrelenting persistence of tournament-MVP Tom O'Regan of Cambridge and Matignon High. He scored the first BU goal, and set up the second by Mark Pierog that enabled BU to take a 2–1 lead out of the first period.

Then, with 4:45 remaining, O'Regan knifed his way through the slot and was perfectly positioned to lift an on-target Bruce Milton shot into the net to wrap everything up. . . .

"I haven't felt anything like this in my life," said BU captain Paul Fenton, who picked up the Beanpot trophy and kissed it. "We're drinking out of this thing tonight. It's the greatest feeling. You've got to love it. We clipped the wings off the Eagles.". . .

"We just couldn't put the puck in the net," said BC coach Len Ceglarski amid the sustained silence of the BC locker room. "We had our chances. In our last two games, Billy O'Dwyer had five breakaways, five perfect chances. He doesn't score. When a kid like O'Dwyer can't score, maybe there's something to it."

—Joe Concannon, *Boston Globe*, February 9, 1982

1983   As Beanpot 1983 approached, the only certainty was that no one wanted to be the favorite, especially Boston College. The Eagles' three consecutive championship-game defeats had one thing in common: each time, the team with the worst record entering the venerated Garden on the first Monday in February had exited a champion on the second Monday.

It appeared to be in the Eagles' favor that, for the first time in a decade, all four teams would come to Causeway Street with winning records. Boston College's overall 'Pot-less drought extended back seven years, the longest among the four participants. The Eagle co-captains, Lee Blossom and Mike O'Neil, were acutely aware of the February pall that had engulfed Chestnut Hill. Both had played as freshmen in the devastating 1980 loss to Northeastern. O'Neil had the dubious distinction of being prominently depicted in the same photo that included Eagle goalie Bob O'Connor, the one that adorned the cover of the 1981 tournament program. The Eagles' motivation to win was unparalleled.

The Terriers take their 1982 victory lap.
(Courtesy of Boston University)

In one of his final State of the Beanpot addresses, Snooks Kelley, the ancient and honorable Eagle for all time, invoked a higher authority: "You have to know the Pope to get a [Beanpot] ticket," he said. "And you have to know Lennie [Ceglarski] to get to the Pope." Coach Kelley also offered, "I wouldn't be surprised if President Reagan showed up at the Iron Horse and had a beer." But would the Gipper be rooting for the Eagles? If the Snooker was buying, you could bet on it.

An opening-night sellout crowd of 14,523 was treated to a compelling night of Beanpot hockey that meshed with the perceived parity of the competitors. The first match, between the defending Beanpot champions from Boston University and the reigning ECAC champions from Northeastern—in 1982, the Huskies had become the sixth team in Beanpot history to lose the Beanpot and win the Eastern crown—was a tale of

Boston College goalie Billy Switaj won the 1983 Eberly Award.

(Courtesy of Boston College)

two games. A 3–0 BU lead early in the second period proved to be far from safe, as Northeastern rallied to tie the game on a shorthanded goal by Randy Bucyk, nephew of Bruins hall-of-famer John Bucyk, early in the third period. Northeastern's Greg Neary then completed the comeback, with 6:47 remaining in regulation, giving the Huskies a 4–3 victory.

The late show was no less suspenseful. The Boston College–Harvard match was similar to the earlier game, with significant momentum swings playing a starring role. Trailing 3–2, with 3:54 left in the third period, Eagle co-captain Lee Blossom took a feed from freshman Bob Sweeney and deposited the puck to tie the game. Then, with a second overtime imminent, Boston College forward Ed Rauseo finished a play started with a poke check by linemate Bob Sweeney, sending the Eagles to a fourth straight championship-game appearance.

The Eagle seniors hoped that their fourth and final journey to the Beanpot summit would be the charm. They were now joined by a seldom-used netminder named Billy Switaj. The Ohio native, younger brother of BC center Mark Switaj, probably would have been red-shirted had Bob O'Connor not turned pro after the 1981–82 campaign. Instead, Switaj was right at home in the Garden spotlight, coming up with a combined fifteen saves in the third period and overtime, none bigger than a stop of a shot by Harvard's all-American defenseman—and future Hobey Baker Award recipient—Mark Fusco, with 2:22 to go in the third period.

The Boston College seniors were thus presented a unique opportunity at redemption: a chance to break their three-game Beanpot finals losing streak against the school that had commenced it on that fateful night in 1980. The two most February-cursed schools of recent vintage—only two titles between them in eighteen years—would play for all the beans.

 With 5:28 remaining in the second period of the 31st Beanpot Tournament's championship game last night in the steamy Boston Garden, Boston College's Bill McDonough fielded a little poke pass from Lee Blossom, turned it on as he swept through center ice and went in alone to beat Northeastern's Mark Davidner.

When the puck went in the net, everybody on the BC bench started warming up to what now seemed inevitable. There was Blossom, kneeling and alone, throwing both arms into the air, his stick clenched tightly in one hand in this solitary tableau, the story of the 31st Beanpot was symbolically spelled out.

The score, at that juncture, was BC 6, NU 1, and for all practical purposes, the count-down had begun. The Eagles went buoyantly on their way to an 8–2 win before a capacity crowd of 14,523 to win their first Beanpot since 1976 and put to rest the legacy of recent seasons, when the word was they simply couldn't win the big game. . . .

From the opening moments, when tournament-MVP Bob Sweeney scored a power-play goal just 40 seconds into the game, until the closing minute when the BC bench became a festive Garden party, this was the night to be an Eagle.

"We did it, we finally did it," said co-captain Blossom. "The big thing, unfortunately, is the pressure that was put on us by our own people. We won this for the school, for the athletic program, for everyone involved with BC athletics. I think we got a lot of people off our backs."

Mike O'Neil, the other BC co-captain, has had to live with the memories of his picture on the Beanpot program after NU's Wayne Turner scored the overtime goal in 1980 that gave the Huskies their only Beanpot. "I've heard a lot about that picture," said O'Neil, "so this is nice. I can't explain what it really meant. Three years of losing in the finals. It's so frustrating. It's a beautiful way to go out."

BC forward Bob Sweeney, the 1983 Beanpot MVP

(Courtesy of Boston College)

There is also quiet, gentlemanly Len Ceglarski, the coach who won his second Bean-pot in 11 trips to the tournament. He'd heard the gripes, the voices of the syndrome after three ECAC quarterfinal defeats and the four straight Beanpot defeats on the second Monday. "We know there's an awful lot of pressure on the coach," said O'Neil. "He's always the first guy to take the blame for the loss. I think it'll quiet a few of our critics for a while."

Sweeney, who poked the puck away from Harvard's Mitch Olson in the opening round to set up Ed Rauseo's over-time goal that put the Eagles in the championship game, pounced on a loose puck for the 1–0 lead (after Bob Averill's high-sticking penalty 0:12 into the game), and Dave Livingston made it 2–0 when he stole the puck from NU's Craig Frank, went in through the face-off circle and shot the puck between Davidner's legs at 8:33.

NU's Mike O'Brien scored at 10:01 of the opening period, but BC's Doug Brown finished off a 2-on-1 with Robin Monleon with a low shot from the top of the circle into the far corner to create a 3–1 lead as the teams left the ice after the first period.

The game turned decisively in two segments of the second period. After Sweeney had picked up Livingston's rebound for a 4–1 lead 2:08 into the second period, the Huskies had a power play and they were all over the Eagles. Ken Manchurek mirrored the frustration of the night as one shot went wide of the net and another bid was muffled by Switaj.

Neil Shea picked up a gift goal that trickled past Davidner for a 5–1 lead at the 12:54 mark, and then Blossom and McDonough teamed up for the sixth goal at 14:32. "He [Blossom] poked it across to me," said McDonough. "I was curling in behind him. It became a foot race. I had a head of steam [on the NU defender] and I saw Davidner start to drift into the net. I went to the right and. . . ."

The Eagles celebrate their 1983 Beanpot championship.

(Courtesy of Sports Museum of New England)

Livingston's second goal, at 14:32, gave the Eagles three within a 2:08 span and many of the 14,523 started heading for the exits. O'Neil finished off a set-up from freshman Scott Harlow at 17:51 to give BC its fifth unanswered goal in the second period. "We let in too many easy goals," said NU coach Fern Flaman. "Our goaltender [Davidner] had a bad night, but he got us where we were. There were 19 others who contributed or didn't contribute tonight."

"I have a feeling that this is our night," BC assistant Paul Barrett had said before the game. He'd played on the 1976 Beanpot team, and he took a reading on the emotion in the pregame locker room. "In other years," Barrett said, "it seemed there was a fog coming down on our shoulders. [This year] you could sense we were relaxed." He then relaxed in the press box and watched the team he works with fulfill its Midwinter Night's Dream.

—Joe Concannon, *Boston Globe,* **February 15, 1983**

The 1983 tournament completed an unprecedented cycle in Beanpot history, as the trophy was passed between the four schools in four consecutive years. Almost twenty years later, it remains the only time this has occurred: a four-horse race with the fourth horse from Huntington Avenue charging hard on the rail.

My Boston, My Beanpot

Tom Burke has covered the Beanpot as both a writer and a broadcaster, beginning in his undergraduate days at BC almost five decades ago. His uncle, Walter Brown, was the founder of the tournament. In 1995, Tom was guest speaker at the last Beanpot luncheon held at the Boston Garden's Blades & Boards Club.

I'm honored to be allowed to address you today. This is the last time we'll be gathered for our Beanpot luncheon in the House of Magic, as Eddie Powers used to say. We all have so many memories from this building. . . .

There are people in Boston who come to the Beanpot who never attend another sporting event. They've just got to be here. I think I know why that happens. . . . That's my message.

When I was growing up here, Boston to me was its sporting life. Sport is as old as humanity. Sport identified with cities is as old as civilization. Every city has its sporting life. But here in my Boston, we're truly blessed. We of my generation have four matchless traditions. They're really not traditions, they're more like defining events. They remind us who we are. They make our city a small town. They bring us together. These four traditions are:

Fenway and the Sox,
the Boston Marathon,
Celtic Pride, and
the Beanpot Tournament.

And the greatest of these is the Beanpot Tournament. . . .

All of the people who built this city, who made it the world-class metropolis it is, . . . not only come to the Beanpot. They play in the Beanpot. And who are they?

The men of Harvard are here. The people who came to these very shores first. The people who defined our American way of life. Boston is the education capital of the world. That's because Harvard is here. Oh, there are others, but they all stand in line behind John Harvard's school. Since 1636, the best and the brightest have gone to Harvard. They go there still. Wasn't it only fitting that the first Beanpot champions were the men of Harvard?

The Catholics are here. Boston College. My school. There is no group of people who have done more to shape and mold our city of Boston, since its founding, than the Catholics. In wave after wave the Catholic immigrants came to Boston. Uneducated, but devout and hardworking. And when there was nobody else around to educate them, Boston College was here.

Then there's Northeastern. I like to call them the kids of the American dream. Because they do it on their own. The hard way. It takes an extra year to put yourself through Northeastern. You study. You work. Then you study some more. And you work some more. And by the time you're through with the co-op program, you're ready for anything that life could ever throw at you. Northeastern University has given to Boston many thousands of graduates in all sorts of professions. But more than that, Northeastern has given Boston an outstanding work ethic. That's Northeastern's enduring gift to Boston.

And there's Boston University. And because this is the Beanpot luncheon, after all, we always save the best for last. And friends, I must confess that I couldn't find a way to capture, in a capsule, the educational essence of BU. It's a big, sprawling place. They've got everything there. All range and manner of grad and undergrad schools and programs. And maybe, just maybe, the educational character of BU has been eclipsed, from where I stand, by the incandescent personality of the man who runs the place [John Silber]. If you've got a question, the man who runs BU has your answer. And it's always a good answer.

And I want my friends from BU to know how very special they are. They're special to me. I've been a student in the Metropolitan College. My grandfather, George V. Brown, was your first athletic director. And you play your superb brand of hockey— the pride of the East—in Walter Brown Arena. . . .

And every time I see Boston University skate out onto the Boston Garden ice, the Boston College man in me says "Oh, God. Here they come again!" But the Beanpot man in me, the Bostonian in me, just tingles with anticipation. I'm seldom disappointed. I know I'm going to see something grand. And so does everyone else in Boston, no matter where their allegiances lie.

That's what the Beanpot means to me, my friends. That's what it does to me. That's what it does to my city.

Boston is indeed many things. The poetry of its street names. The education capitol of the world. The sporting life. And Boston is the Beanpot. And the Beanpot is Boston. That's why it's a social must. That's its mystique. That's why it's irresistible. That's why we've all got to be there.

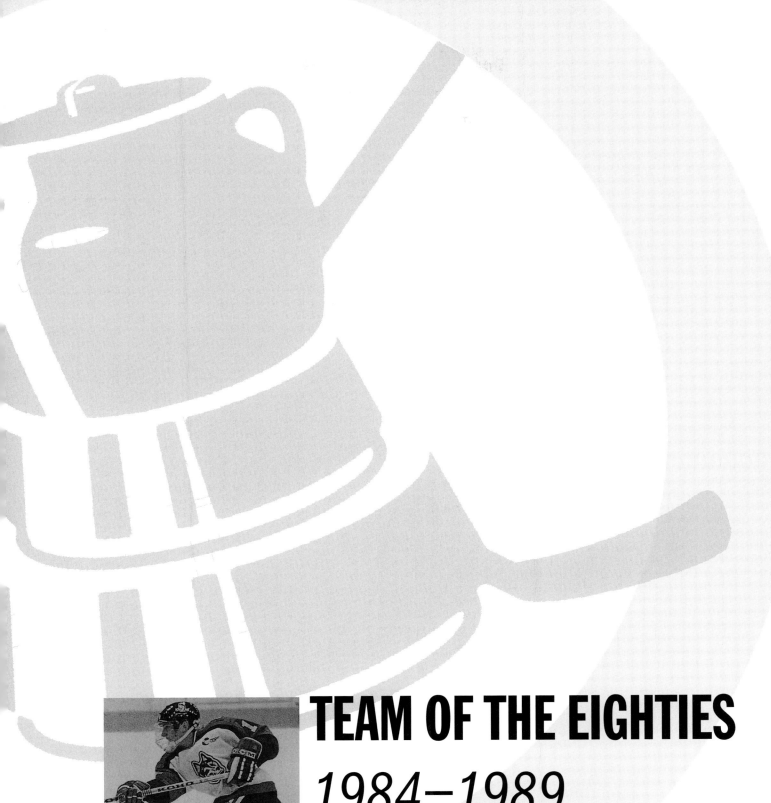

TEAM OF THE EIGHTIES

1984–1989

On paper, the 1984 Beanpot balance of power resided in the opening round's feature game between BU and BC, both with 20-5 season records. The early contest between Northeastern (12-9-1) and Harvard (7-9-1) seemed to hold less potential impact.

The Huskies, now four years removed from their first Beanpot, showed requisite hunger, pouncing on the Crimson by taking a 4–0 first-period lead en route to a 7–3 victory. Sophomore center Jay Heinbuck spearheaded the Hounds' attack with four assists. "I sort of think that the small Garden surface helped us," observed Heinbuck. "Our rink [Matthews, formerly Boston, Arena] also has a small surface and that's probably why we have an 8-1 record on home ice."

The second game pitted the two previous years' champions, BU and BC, against each other. A 4–1 Terrier lead at the outset of the third period was far from safe as the Eagles crept within a goal at 6–5 in the waning moments. Two men down for all but eight seconds of the game's final 2:09, BU defenseman and captain T. J. Connolly, partner Joe Delorey, center Mark Pierog, and all-American goaltender Cleon Daskalakis dug their skates in to protect the one-goal lead. Daskalakis's forty-two-save performance, highlighted by twenty in the third period alone, ranked with the Beanpot's best.

For the first time since 1967, it would be a true dogfight: the Terriers versus the Huskies for the Beanpot. The game itself, however, was transcended by the most poignant single moment in the tournament's history.

 Emotional. That's the only word to describe what happened at Boston Garden last night after Northeastern beat Boston University in the Beanpot finals.

It was a flood of emotion that started when the final buzzer said that NU had defeated BU, 5–2, before a packed house.

When the NU players were given the prized trophy, they skated it around the ice and singled out a special section to acknowledge two fine people, who were in wheelchairs. They were coach Fern Flaman's son, Terry, who has a kidney disorder, and his wife Jean, who is recovering from a broken knee.

Flaman was crying as he left the Garden bench and headed for the dressing room. Fern Flaman, the former Bruin defenseman who made No. 14 one to be feared in the National Hockey League.

Flaman pulled himself together and talked with his players for a short while. He thanked them all for the great wins they had given Northeastern.

Then Flaman grinned as he opened a bottle of champagne, and he laughed when the cork hit the ceiling and the bubbly stuff spilled on the floor. He was relaxed for a moment and talked with scores of media people. . . .

Flaman was composing himself when his son, Terry, was wheeled into the crowded locker room.

Terry Flaman during his Harvard hockey career, 1966–69

(Courtesy of Harvard University)

Flaman took a hard look at the former Harvard defenseman, and he started to cry again. He hugged his son and thanked him.

Terry said, "I told you guys I'd be here. And by here, I mean not just in the Garden, but in the locker room with you. You guys did a terrific job all night. I just want to congratulate you. Thanks."

Terry then acknowledged every player and after a very brief lull, the entire team gave Terry a tremendous applause. . . .

Northeastern players shook Terry's hand and patted him on the back. They smiled and grinned, but when most of them left, they had tears in their eyes. Tears that were shed without shame.

They knew they had played their hearts out for some very good people. And seeing Terry, who was indeed a profile of courage, right in the thick of things, seemed to make them appreciate the victory all the more.

—Bob Monahan, *Boston Globe*, February 14, 1984

 In his initial visit to the Garden as a recruit out of Windsor, Ontario, Ken Manchurek sat in the loge in one corner of the building and watched as Wayne Turner scored in overtime to wrap up Northeastern's first Beanpot against Boston College in 1980. "I was there with a beer in my hand," said Manchurek last night. "I'd never seen anything like that."

In what may be his final visit to the Garden as a player and the tricaptain of the NU team, Manchurek took off with the puck on his stick in the championship game of the 32nd Beanpot Hockey Tournament last night and shot it into an open net to all but wrap up the game. Moments later, when Randy Bucyk found another open net, NU had put the lid on a 5–3 victory over Boston University.

"The defenseman [BU captain T. J. Connolly] came in and misplayed it," said Manchurek. "I saw there was nothing in front of me but that four-by-six cage. I wasn't stopping. I was going to go right through the net. I was just scared they were going to call me for being in the crease."

In a poignant and heart-wrenching aftermath to this emotional night, the NU players skated the Beanpot over to a corner of the Garden where Terry Flaman—the son of their coach, Fernie—sat in a wheelchair. He later came to the locker room, Manchurek put the Beanpot trophy in his lap, and he told the team, "You played your hearts out."

Terry, who was a teammate of BU assistant coach Ben Smith at Harvard and a Beanpot participant in the late 1960s, became gravely ill last month and has been waging a personal fight against some critical odds. "I've been working hard for two weeks," he said later as he and his father shared a private moment together apart from the

tumult of the locker room. "I wanted to make it to the game. I wanted to see them win. They've worked hard.". . .

This was also a victory set off by the glittering performance of tournament Most Valuable Player Tim Marshall in the NU goal. He came up with 34 saves, but none will linger any longer than the two he made on namesake—but no relation—Peter Marshall, with less than six minutes to play and the Huntington Avenue Hounds clinging tenaciously to a 3–2 lead. Backed into the net on the first one, [Tim] Marshall recovered and regained his balance just in time to blunt [Peter] Marshall's follow-up bid.

This was the way it went for the Terriers, a team of considerable talent that has its problems converting shots into goals. "It's not that we lost it," said Connolly. "We played pretty well. They played well." BU coach Jack Parker agreed. "We held them to 24 shots," he said, "but we couldn't get going offensively."

The first period sort of set the tempo. NU had to come out of it even up, and the score was 0–0. BU had exactly zero shots on its only power play, a tip-off perhaps. But the Terriers jumped on top, 1–0, just 11 seconds into the second period when Joe Cappellano swooped in to the goalpost to flip a rebound of a Tony Majkozak shot past Marshall.

Bucyk, whose uncle, John, enjoyed a few moments of glory with the Bruins in the Garden, tied it on an unassisted shorthanded goal that was a thing of beauty. He'd been stopped by BU goaltender Cleon Daskalakis on two bids just before the penalty to teammate Craig Frank (hooking, 10:42), so he showed the poise of a senior when he weaved in front, waited until Daskalakis sprawled in an attempt to poke the puck away and put it past Connolly as he tried to guard the vacant net at 11:49 of the period.

Kevin Mutch came right back and broke an 0-for-16 power-play run for the Terriers, when he picked up Scott Shaunessy's rebound just 16 seconds later and lifted BU into a 2–1 lead. Jay Heinbuck tied the game when he picked up a drop pass from Brian Fahringer and beat Daskalakis to the stick side at the 16:33 mark.

"I got a pass from [Craig] Frank," said Fahringer, who was in the Garden seats with Manchurek on that night when the Hounds won the Beanpot four years ago, the other recruit out of Windsor. "I went as hard as I could and laid it off to him. It took us four years, but we did it. I've never seen anything like that night four years ago. Well, maybe tonight."

The momentum had swung clearly and decisively. Just six seconds after Cappellano went off for a tripping call, Bob Averill took a pass from [his] brother, Jim, and shot it into the net from the left point for a 3–2 lead at 17:34 of a wondrous period of hockey. NU 3, BU 2, and the feeling began to grow that this was the night to be a Husky. . . .

So the 32nd Beanpot was an emotionally gratifying night for the Flamans, for Fernie the coach and son Terry. It was a night for the seniors, Manchurek, Bucyk, Fahringer, Frank, Bob Averill, Maurizio Pasinato and Bill Kessler. If Manchurek's dash to the net wasn't quite as electrifying as the one by Turner that he saw four years ago, it sure ranks pretty close to it on the spectrum of Beanpot moments.

—Joe Concannon, *Boston Globe*, February 14, 1984

1985 The 1985 tournament was the first following the reformation of Eastern college hockey. For the first time, the four Beanpot schools would not all enter the tournament as members of the ECAC. The formation of the Hockey East Association for the 1984–85 season, with Boston University, Boston College, and Northeastern among the league's charter members, isolated Harvard as the only Beanpot school remaining in the old ECAC. The realignment allowed for the virtual retirement of two distinctive Beanpot facts:

1. the last five Beanpot champions had failed to qualify for the ECAC playoffs; and
2. an amazing seven times since 1962, the team defeated in the Beanpot went on to win that year's ECAC tournament.

As a result of the new order, first-game first-round opponents Boston University (16-11-2) and Harvard (13-2-2) had not met during the regular season. BU surged to a 4–0 second-period lead, checked diligently, and skated off with a 5–3 win. The Crimson were unable to solve the mystery of Bob Deraney, a rookie Terrier goalie from West Roxbury via Catholic Memorial.

The six-foot, 190-pound sophomore wasn't awed, only inspired, by the Garden's visceral power. "It was dark and it was beautiful," Deraney said in reference to the empty pregame arena. "And I knew I'd be on that ice in just a short time. It was going to be my first appearance on the Garden ice and that's a feeling that Boston-bred kids dream about. My dream was going to become a reality."

Due to injuries, Deraney, the number-three netminder on the Terrier preseason depth chart, got the opportunity and had now won his seventh straight start. In the Beanpot. On the Garden ice. The dream of generations of Greater Boston rink rats personified.

The second semifinal featured Hockey East's number-one team, Boston College (22-7-1), and a Northeastern team (11-19) that had won just twice in its last eleven outings. The last meeting between the two first-round opponents read BC 10, NU 5; but this was the Beanpot. Huskies freshman defenseman Joe MacInnis's goal, with 5:02 left, snapped a 2–2 tie, and a Jim Averill empty-net tally, with seven seconds remaining, completed a 4–2 NU upset.

"This is a whole new season," said MacInnis, the pride of Watertown. "There's so much emotion in this game. It's a great feeling. Against BC, especially. Growing up, the Beanpot is something you dream about just playing in. I never dreamed I'd someday score a winning goal in it."

Another Beanpot dream also came true. Tournament aficionados noted a thirty-one-save performance by a freshman goalie named Bruce Racine.

A revenge-minded BU squad would have a chance to get even for the previous year's verdict. Meanwhile, Northeastern was in position to repeat for the first time, having failed to make it back to the 1981 title game. Let the dogfight resume.

 They used to be the Beanpot's beloved underdogs, the city's rank outsiders on these two Monday nights in February. They had been the perennial also-rans through 27 years of the Beanpot until Wayne Turner ended the era of embarrassment with a wondrous overtime goal five years ago.

What that did for hockey at Northeastern was immeasurable, but what it did for the Huskies in terms of the Beanpot was even more compelling. Those underdogs from Huntington Avenue have become the unquestioned class of the Beanpot, the team to beat in the Eighties.

In the latest of these Beanpot curtain calls in front of the tournament's 15th straight sell-out crowd—which numbered 14,451 last night in steamy Boston Garden—Northeastern rode the goaltending acrobatics of freshman Bruce Racine and two third-period goals by Mark Lori to a rousing 4–2 victory over Boston University.

The Huskies became the first team to successfully defend a Beanpot title since BU did it in 1979. And after going 27 years without a Beanpot, NU has won three out of the last six. . . .

A shot that didn't go in was the tip-off that the Huntington Hounds were knocking on the door and about to kick it down. Lori, from Windsor, Ontario, the latest member of NU's underground railroad in reverse that has included Ken Manchurek and linemate Rod Isbister, had put a point-blank shot on BU goaltender Bob Deraney in a 2–2 game early in the third period. "I was getting frustrated," Lori said, "but my time would come."

Indeed, Isbister created the go-ahead goal when he forechecked BU's Jay Octeau and Octeau's pass was intercepted by Lori. He cut in front and put a backhander past Deraney at 10 minutes, 28 seconds of the period. "Izzie forced him to make a bad pass," said Lori. "He picked a defenseman. I was one-on-one with the goalie. I shot it low and got it through."

Just over 5 minutes later, the persistent Isbister sent his big right wing in again. "He [Isbister] did all the work," said Lori. "He's so shifty. He made a couple of moves."

Lori took it from there, went in on Deraney and shot the puck in with 4:24 to go to send the faithful in the direction of the postgame celebration at Punter's Pub.

Huskies forward Mark Lori

(Courtesy of Northeastern University)

Greg Neary had started 13-19 NU on its way when a pass by Claude Lodin sprung him between two BU defensemen and sent him on his way to a 1–0 lead at 7:43 of the first period, and it would eventually define their victory.

All of BU's scoring came in a 112-second blitz in the second period. Ed Lowney tied it when he took John Cullen's face-off-winning pass and beat Racine with a rocket at 4:44 of the period. Tom Ryan sent Chuck Sullivan in for the 2–1 lead at 6:36 and the Terriers were threatening to seize control.

The goal that swung the momentum back to NU was Kevin Heffernan's tying score at 10:21 of the period. "It was a three-on-two," said Heffernan, who credited Scott Marshall with a shot on Deraney. Actually, a BU defenseman helped it along and Heffernan swooped in to pick up the rebound that Deraney had kicked out. He found plenty of room for the goal.

The Huskies entered this tournament with the weakest record of the four teams, but disposed of Hockey East–leader Boston College last Monday night and Hockey East's No. 2, BU, last night. . . . BU coach Jack Parker wasn't as disappointed as he was angry, and he talked of the contrast between BU's two Beanpot losses to NU in the title game.

"It's tough to take because we didn't play well," said Parker. "Last year we did, and things just didn't go our way. Northeastern played terrific. They played real smart defense. It's always a problem, no question, after losing in the Beanpot final. We'll have to dig down deep character-wise."

The Terriers (17-12-3) had been on a 7-0-1 run since the unheralded Deraney entered the picture out of the ashes of a 10–1 loss to BC on January 8. This was the night of the Husky, however. Yes, hockey's hockey, as Averill said, and a victory in any sport smells just as sweet. Yankee (Conference), go home.

—Joe Concannon, *Boston Globe,* February 12, 1985

1986 The 1986 tournament renewal featured all four teams with winning records for just the second time in thirteen years. If there was any doubt regarding the season-making mystique of this uniquely parochial exercise, then consider the fact that the previous three champions had finished their respective seasons a combined 2-13-1.

Northeastern (17-10-1) and Boston University (15-11-2), the finalists the previous two seasons, clashed in the early first-round match. The Terriers promptly fell behind the two-time defending champions after the first period. A four-goal second-period deluge, however, carried BU to an 8–5 victory and their seventeenth appearance in the finals in twenty years.

The main attraction on opening night showcased the first-place team in Hockey East, Boston College (18-9-1), and the leader in the ECAC, Harvard (12-4-1). Although the teams had played to a 4–4 overtime stalemate early in the season, the Eagles dominated this game from the outset. Eagle netminder Scott Gordon successfully protected a 4–0 first-period lead until Harvard all-American Scott Fusco converted twice late in the game. But it was far too late for the Crimson. The Eagles would face BU for the Beanpot.

Just a little over one year ago, Terry Taillefer's career as a goaltender at Boston University was in doubt. Bothered by a persistent hip problem that wasn't fully diagnosed, he went home to Edmonton, Alberta, uncertain about his future. "It was something," he said earlier this year, "that just got progressively worse."

If there had been doubts about Taillefer's future in the college game, they were soon dispelled during the season, and if there were doubts about his ability to pull off the big-game victory, they were certainly dispelled last night in the 34th Beanpot-championship game before 14,451 at Boston Garden last night.

Terry Taillefer, Boston University goalie, was named Beanpot MVP for 1986.

(Courtesy of Boston University)

The Terriers responded in kind with a clinical exhibition of hockey and skated to a 4–1 victory over Boston College to win this championship for the first time since 1982 and [their] 13th time overall. Taillefer was named the tournament MVP as he came up with a save on virtually every one of the talented BC forwards. . . .

The Terriers were pumped up and came out flying. BU coach Jack Parker put his normal second line of center Peter Marshall and wings Chris Matchett and Paul Gerlitz on against BC's potent line of center Ken Hodge and wings Scott Harlow and Doug Brown. A checking line? Hardly.

Gerlitz was sent on his way up the left wing by Marshall just 20 seconds into the game. Gerlitz turned the BC defense and put a backhander on goaltender Scott Gordon. The Eagles came back and almost scored when Michael Barron's shot from the right point was nearly put into the BU net by BU defenseman Tom Ryan.

Taillefer, who was sharp in the opening 20 minutes, tipped Chris Stapleton's shot over the net. BU's Scott Shaunessy wound up in the BC net and came out mixing it up with Barron. They drew matching penalties at the 3:29 mark. BC's John McNamara was called for holding at 3:52, giving the Terriers a man advantage for 1:28.

They capitalized at the 4:30 mark when Clark Donatelli took a goal-mouth feed from John Cullen and shot it into the open side of the net for a 1–0 lead. Jay Octeau had put the initial shot on net and Cullen picked it up and danced through the defense to set up Donatelli. Referee Frank Cole had already signaled a penalty on BC's John McLean, so the Terriers still had a four-on-three situation.

Octeau drew a hooking penalty at 5:39, however, and the Eagles wound up on a power play. Scott Harlow tied it with 10 seconds left in the penalty to Octeau. Bob Sweeney had won a face-off in the BU zone and slid the puck out to Hodge. He put a shot on Taillefer who gloved it momentarily. When it fell to the ice, Harlow was there to score his 32nd goal of the season.

Donatelli lifted BU into a 2–1 lead on a goal created by Shaunessy. Shaunessy forced his way through the BC defense, Donatelli took the puck and lifted it over Gordon's shoulder at the 8:12 mark.

Marshall dropped off a pass to Scott Young, but Gordon blunted that bid.

Tony Majkozak, who was inserted in place of Eric Labrosse as fourth-line wing, made it 3–1 when he took a pass from Jeff Sveen in front and tipped it between Gordon's legs at the 11:20 juncture.

—Joe Concannon, *Boston Globe*, February 11, 1986

The message Scott Shaunessy received from his coach was simple and to the point. Especially for a Terrier.

**Boston University defenseman
Scott Shaunessy**

(Courtesy of Boston University)

"Sic 'em."   *Sic 'em?*   "Sic 'em."

"I was talking with my brother [Sunday] night and we were wondering if Scott was aware of the difference between 'Come here' and 'Sic 'em,'" said Jack Parker, the Boston University hockey coach, the most exhilarated Boston University hockey coach. "I just wanted to make sure Scott knew the difference."

Inspired by his coach's grandiloquent oration, Shaunessy stepped onto the Boston Garden ice and promptly, if not sooner, crashed into each maroon-and-gold sweater in sight. And, in fact, it was a sight.

"The coach came up to me before the game and he said just those two words to me," said Shaunessy, a defenseman out of Reading and St. John's Prep. "He told me to 'sic 'em.' I knew what he meant."

So Shaunessy crushed Boston College's Paul Marshall within five seconds of the opening face-off and then crashed into the Eagles' Doug Brown and the tone of this magical Beanpot night was set. Boston University took the hitting to the hitters of BC, the Terriers controlled the opening period and, as the crunches turned to bunches, the game and the Beanpot championship. Sic 'em.

"They were talking before the game that they were going to play physical with us," said Shaunessy, "but we wanted to go out and bring the tempo to them. We wanted to show we could be as physical as they were."

This night of BU's sweet return to the hockey championship of Boston mostly will revolve around Terrier goalie Terry Taillefer, he of the 43 saves and the MVP trophy. Yet, this was just as much a night of solid defense—BU barring the Eagles from any errant rebounds—and a tad of good fortune.

Each pass to the possible breakaway for BC seemed just a tad too long. Each bounce of the puck went that way for the Eagles instead of this. Each chance loomed but quieted back into precisely that—only a chance. It was all just a step away for Boston College.

Yet it was such a fine combination of force and finesse because BU also was fashioning plays of precision, especially the nifty John Cullen. Twice Cullen made superb plays in that deciding opening period and twice BU scored—the first when Cullen collected a loose puck and stickhandled in the slot until BC goalie Scott Gordon was down and all Clark Donatelli had to do was steer the puck into an open net. Cullen's second play again came in the slot, but this time it was a slick drop pass that Donatelli again brought home.

So it went, the Terriers a bark and a buzz. So dominant was BU in those opening 20 minutes that BC was unable to get the puck from its own end, this when the Eagles were on a power play. And when the period ended it was so fitting, Shaunessy poking the puck off the stick of BC's Ken Hodge as Hodge was about to go in alone on Taillefer.

"Oh, that play," laughed Shaunessy. "I know Kenny because we went to school together at St. John's Prep and I know his inside-out move pretty well. When he started to make the play, I saw the old 'inside-out move' and I was able to poke the puck away from him."

So it went, the second period scoreless as BC stormed Taillefer, but with few of the Eagles' 15 shots on net dangerous to the Terriers. They were coming from the right point, they were coming from the left and they were coming from the blue line, but few were coming from the danger zone, few from the slot.

"That's what we wanted to do," said Shaunessy. "Let them shoot from out there. I've been saying all along that Terry's the best goalie in the country on the first shot, so those first shots weren't worrying us. But they weren't getting the rebounds; every time that rubber hit the ice a white jersey [BU] was right on top of a maroon jersey so there would be no second shots."

There weren't. BC's last charge in the third period brought on 15 more shots to the pipes, leveled Taillefer when Sweeney's blast from the left circle struck Taillefer in the Adam's apple. But it all ended—so symbolically—when BC pulled its outstanding goalie, Scott Gordon, for the final 6-on-5 rush and Peter Marshall blasted away. . . only to have his stick break into pieces and the shot dribble in.

It meant so much to BU, this Beanpot victory, to Parker whose team was so well-prepared and motivated, to Taillefer whose bursitis in the hips a year ago left him barely able to walk and unsure if he could again play hockey.

Yet it meant as much to Shaunessy as any of them. For the last week, he had been thinking every day of one goal, winning a big game in the Boston Garden. Four times he had tried and four times he had failed.

"The first time was when I was in high school and St. John's lost to Matignon in the Eastern Massachusetts final," said Shaunessy, "and then my freshman year we lost in the Beanpot finals and we lost in the ECACs and last year we lost in the Beanpot again. I spent the whole week thinking, 'I've got to win a big game in the Garden.'"

Shaunessy, Parker, and the Terriers now have it all for another year because last night they had a buzz and a bark. Sic 'em.

—Michael Madden, *Boston Globe*, February 11, 1986

1987   The 1987 tournament placed Harvard and Boston College, the two teams in the throes of the longest Beanpot drought, as the co-favorites.

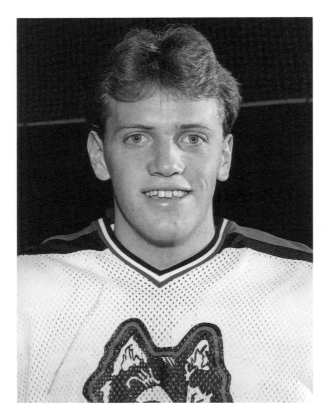

The Crimson, a gaudy 15-1 entering the tournament, had not played any of the other schools prior to the tournament. Their first-round opponent, Northeastern, may have been struggling at 6-16-3, but they did have 1985 Beanpot MVP Bruce Racine in the net. The Huskies allowed a two-goal lead to evaporate in the third period, only to recover for a 5–4 overtime victory. A spectacular thirty-two-save night's work from Racine surprised nobody. The presence of "stay-at-home" defenseman Brian Dowd in front of the Harvard net, pushing home the winning goal, was another matter entirely. NU coach Fern Flaman, a classic, old-school NHL defenseman during his playing days, described Dowd's positioning on the play as "a beautiful error; a great mistake." The Huskies would be making their fifth finals appearance of the decade.

Boston College coach Len Ceglarski had a chance to make history in the second game of the first round versus Boston University. At 555 career victories, Ceglarski was tied with Michigan Tech's legendary coach, the late John MacInnes, for first all-time among college coaches. Ceglarski would have liked nothing better than to become the college game's all-time winningest coach and deliver his Eagles to the Beanpot final. The Terriers, winless in their last twelve regular-season games (0-10-2) versus BC, had other plans. BU got control of the game early and led 3–0 just beyond the halfway mark on the way to a 6–3 triumph. The match between Boston College and Harvard was "moved up" to 5 P.M., courtesy of the underdogs from BU and NU who didn't get the memo.

Two past Eberly Award/MVP recipients would guard the nets to decide the thirty-fifth Beanpot. Northeastern goalie Bruce Racine pointed out how his Beanpot perspective had changed since his freshman heroics in 1985. "Now that I know the magnitude of the Beanpot, it isn't as easy to relax," he said. The previous year's MVP, BU goalie Terry Taillefer (a draft selection of the Boston Bruins), referred to the special feelings associated with the Garden: "It's a thrill for all of us. You'd be surprised how many players just can't wait to skate on that big letter B at mid-ice. The Garden is the place to play."

The Garden would also be the place for an unusual consolation game, which featured Harvard versus Boston College, the number-two- and number-four-ranked teams in the nation, respectively. The Ceglarski record watch had carried over from the previous week, adding another twist to the plot of the early match.

 Ken Hodge scored on a 65-foot shot during a power play with one second left in sudden death last night to give Boston College a controversial 7–6 victory over Harvard in the consolation game of the 35th Beanpot at steamy Boston Garden.

The win gave BC coach Len Ceglarski his 556th career victory, making him the winningest coach in college hockey history. He had been tied with the late John MacInnes of Michigan Tech.

Most onlookers thought the winning goal didn't go in until after the final buzzer. Harvard coach Bill Cleary was extremely upset when the goal was allowed, and most of the house appeared to be on Cleary's side.

That the extra session itself was played was the cause of controversy, because most media people had been told that, if the game ended in a tie in regulation, there would be no overtime so that the championship game could start at 8 as scheduled. . . .

Hodge, who also scored BC's fifth and sixth goals, said, "We all wanted to win the game for Lenny. There was a lot written about it and I think that we took a big monkey off his back.

"Maybe we were trying too hard in our last three games."

On the winning goal, a slap shot from outside the blue line, Hodge said, "I just wound up and let it fly. I didn't see it go in. But it did and we won—that's what it's all about. Now the coach can relax and we can play better hockey for him.". . .

"Give all the kids credit," said Ceglarski. "We did it as a team, and doing it at the Garden means all the more.

"And please don't forget David Littman. He played a great game in goal, making those 38 saves. He did more than his share.

"Hodge? Terrific. His sixth goal was really classic and the winner was something else. He's some player."

Harvard led, 3–1, after a period. Tim Barakett scored on the power play at 1:29 from in tight, and Alan Bourbeau scored another power play at 10:55 on a 5-footer.

BC got one back at 19:39 on a Brian Leetch shot that deflected home, and Harvard's Steve Armstrong connected at 19:47 when he popped in a Barakett rebound.

BC came out smoking in the second period and Steve Scheifele completed a two-on-one break at 46 seconds with an 8-footer high to the glove side of Dickey McEvoy, and Craig Janney sank a neat backhander at 4:07 while BC had the man advantage to tie it.

Harvard went up 4–3 at 9:47 when Lane MacDonald tipped in a blast by Randy Taylor.

In the 1988 tournament final— BC versus Harvard—forward Ken Hodge's overtime goal for the Eagles gave coach Len Ceglarski his 556th career win.

(Courtesy of Boston College)

Harvard's C. J. Young hit at 5:00 of the third on a rebound, and then BC took over, scoring three in a row. Tim Sweeney hit at 7:34 and Hodge potted a pair, hitting at 16:39 and 17:17. That gave BC a 6–5 edge.

Cleary pulled McEvoy for an extra skater and Barakett, with assists going to Young and Bourbeau, scored at 18:53 to make it 6–6.

—Bob Monahan, *Boston Globe,* February 10, 1987

 Mike Kelfer scored his first goal of what had developed into a wondrous Beanpot Hockey Tournament at 5:28 of overtime in the championship game to lift Boston University to a 4–3 victory over Northeastern last night before 14,451 in the Boston Garden. . . .

The Terriers seized a 1–0 lead when Lowney picked up a puck poked to him by the fallen Sullivan, busted in on Kiley and put a blistering wrist shot past Racine at 15:57 of the period. The Terriers were aroused, and Racine had to come up with big saves on Lowney, Eric Labrosse, and Tom Ryan as the Terriers stormed the NU cage.

Dale Thiesing, who had scored only four goals in his previous three seasons, scored his first of this season and biggest of his career with a slap shot from the right point, with 15 seconds left in the period, to give the Terriers a 2–0 lead. Racine had come up with a save on Clark Donatelli's bid, but he picked up the rebound to the side of the cage and fed the puck out to Thiesing.

Forward Mike Kelfer scored the Terriers' Beanpot-winning overtime goal in 1987.

(Courtesy of Boston University)

Taillefer was credited with 13 saves to 11 for Racine in a wide-open second period.

The Huskies came out of a third period melee with a man-advantage situation. Taillefer fell on a loose puck after Dave Buda had put a shot on net and, when Buda came out to try to poke the puck loose, the mini-brawl broke out. Donatelli and NU's Harry Mews drew four-minute matching penalties for roughing. BU's Scott Young and [David] Quinn were each given two minutes for roughing and Buda joined them with two minutes.

Dowd followed up his lead pass to Heffernan and rerouted the puck past Taillefer to bring the Huskies within one at 10:59. The Huskies then jumped on a four-on-three situation as Dowd took a pass from Claude Lodin on the left point and rifled a shot past the screened Taillefer to tie the game at 12:57 of the period.

Cullen, who has scored so many big goals before in his career, took a lead pass from Lowney and scored with 6:20 left in a tumultuous third period to stake the Terriers to a 3–2 lead. Lowney, who has sometimes played in Cullen's shadow, created this goal when he put a move on an NU defenseman and slid the puck ahead to his linemate.

Just as NU coach Fern Flaman was about to pull Racine and get the extra man on ice, [David] O'Brien, a one-time walk-on from Brookline who has blossomed into a complete player in his three years on Huntington Avenue, wound up and shot the puck past Taillefer, with one minute left in regulation to put the game into overtime.

—Joe Concannon, *Boston Globe,* February 10, 1987

1988 Boston University and Boston College both were below .500 prior to the 1988 tournament. The Olympics had a profound effect on both squads, resulting in the absence of several key performers.

A return to the finals for BC was contingent upon a reversal of fortune versus Northeastern. Earlier in the season, a solid Huskies team had beaten the Eagles twice, both times by identical 6–3 scores, and had recorded an impressive 6-2 mark against the Western College Hockey Association. Perhaps most important, Northeastern still had Bruce Racine guarding the net. The senior goalie from Ottawa, Ontario, was at his finest, fashioning a shutout (4–0) in the opening game of the first round. It was the first time in 188 games that the Eagles had been shut out. Racine was very hungry, not only for the win, but also for the shutout. "I wanted it badly. I only had about five tough shots of the twenty-five they put on me," he said humbly. "But you saw the way my defense played. These guys were terrific. I'd make the stop and they cleared so fast it was great."

Coach Fern Flaman, a gentleman who had certainly seen his share of hockey, was impressed with his team's overall effort. "That was one well-played game and I'm very pleased," said Flaman. "Bruce got his shutout, the team reached the finals of the Beanpot, and the seniors were just great. Now don't get me wrong, the younger kids played great, too. They played as a team and it was only the second time this year that we played solid hockey for sixty minutes. It was beautiful."

Based on pregame analysis, BU (8-12-3) seemed to have an even tougher task facing them in the first round. The two-time defending champions, who hadn't missed the finals since 1983, would have to defeat Harvard (12-4), the ECAC's top-rated team. In a patented "the Garden is our second home" performance by the Terriers, BU erased a 3–1 early second period Crimson lead on a Peter Headon goal with only twelve seconds left before the second intermission. Headon perfectly fit the now-familiar profile of most-unexpected player on the ice to find the net. Harvard tied the game early in the third period on a power-play goal by John Murphy, only to have Dave Tomlinson, a Boston University freshman from North Vancouver, British Columbia, tally the eventual game-winner. BU and Northeastern would thus reprise the overtime epic from the previous February.

For the fourth time in five years, the Beanpot would belong to the dogs. Would the Huskies or the Terriers seize the moment and bring home the coveted trophy? It was BU's twenty-eighth appearance in the finals to Northeastern's seventh. The 1980s Beanpot-play record between the two was deadlocked at 3–3. A youthful Terrier team was coming in on a positive note, having won seven of their last eight, the only loss a 2–1 decision at Northeastern. The contrast at the goaltending position seemed to be significant. Northeastern's Racine was a former tournament MVP, and Boston University's Peter Fish was an unheralded junior who had been a key factor in the Terriers' success against Harvard the previous week.

The distance from Brookline's Whiskey Point to Boston Garden isn't many miles, but the journey native David O'Brien took with the Beanpot held aloft last night was a trip that took many years to complete.

BU defenseman Tom Ryan (at left) and Northeastern's captain in 1988, forward David O'Brien (right)
(Courtesy of Northeastern University)

"I've been waiting for four years to hold it," said O'Brien. "My dream's come true."

He was sitting off in a corner of a crowded Northeastern locker room, the proud captain of the latest team from Huntington Avenue to win a Beanpot. The forlorn Huskies of the '50's, '60's and '70's are the Beanpot team of the '80's, and O'Brien talked of the way it was as he led his team around the Garden ice. "It's heavier than I thought it was," he said of the pot. "We came in with a Beanpot, and we're going out with a Beanpot."

In a spirited game set off by the splendid goaltending of tournament-MVP Bruce Racine and punctuated by O'Brien's two goals in the third period that erased any doubt of the outcome, the Huskies won their fourth Beanpot of this decade and third in five years with a 6–3 victory over defending-champion Boston University before a raucous sellout crowd of 14,451 in the steamy Garden.

The issue seemed settled after two periods, when the Huskies forged a 3–0 lead and Racine extended his scoreless string through five periods of the 36th Beanpot. The Terriers came out and scored a pair of quick goals in the first 3:01 of the third period, but this was not to be their night, as Harry Mews came back to score a goal at the 4:51 juncture and O'Brien pumped in two more to ensure his place in Beanpot lore as a freshman and a senior. . . .

"The first Beanpot was a big lift for the hockey program," said O'Brien, who grew up watching the tournament and dreaming of going to a Beanpot school. "Kids are waiting to come to Northeastern."

The Terriers had won the Beanpot the last two years, but a team with seven freshmen in its lineup wasn't up to beating a team with eight seniors. . . .

The die was cast early, when Joe MacInnis was credited with the goal as he swooped in on BU goaltender Peter Fish and helped him sweep the puck into his own net.

"I was trying to make the goalie make a bad pass," said MacInnis. I think I just hit his stick. I think he panicked. His defenseman wasn't helping him. He wanted to go in the corner. I was surprised. I was skating behind the net and it was in the net."

The Huskies (14-9-1), who had beaten the Terriers (10-13-3) twice in the regular Hockey East season, went on top, 2–0, when Peter Schure swept in to pick up Paul Russo's rebound after Tom Bivona fed it out from behind the net at 7:46 of the second period. After Fish made a sprawling stick save on Dave Buda's bid, Mews swatted in the rebound at 14:05 of the second period to stake the Huskies to a 3–0 lead.

The Terriers finally ended Racine's scoreless streak after 100 minutes and 39 seconds when Mike Sullivan scored just as a penalty to Russo expired 39 seconds into the third

period. When Mike Kelfer, the MVP of the 1987 Beanpot, deflected the puck off a
raised stick past Racine, it was suddenly a one-goal game and the BU partisans were
aroused. Their enthusiasm was quickly doused, as the Huskies took the game in hand.

Mews, who had predicted a 6–4 victory in print, fed the puck out from the corner after
BU defenseman Kris Werner fell in front of Fish and had his stick poked away from
him. Buda picked up the set-up and rifled it in to lift the Huskies to a 4–2 lead at the
4:51 mark. Buda and BU's Mike Lappin were dealt matching unsportsmanlike-con-
duct penalties out of the flurry, and when BU's Steve Shaunessy drew a double minor
for cross-checking at 5:51, the Huskies had a four-on-three advantage.

O'Brien finished off a textbook sequence that started when defenseman Claude Lodin
sent the puck to Kevin Heffernan in the slot, and he put it on O'Brien's stick. He simply tucked it in the open side of the net, for a 5–2 lead (6:36), and O'Brien went in on
a shorthanded rush (11:35) to make it 6–2.

—Joe Concannon, *Boston Globe*, February 9, 1988

The four chiseled faces on the Beanpot's Mount Rushmore of coaching had undergone a complete overhaul over the course of the tournament's colorful history. Two
Boston College coaches, Snooks Kelley and Len Ceglarski, would lead the Eagles into
battle for forty tournaments. Two Boston University coaches, Jack Kelley and Jack
Parker, would lead the Terriers into thirty-eight tournaments. Northeastern's Jim Bell
and Fern Flaman had been behind the bench for a combined twenty-four Beanpot
seasons. At Harvard, "Cooney" Weiland and his pupil Bill Cleary would guide the
Crimson through thirty-eight renewals of midwinter madness.

1989   As the turbulent fourth decade of Beanpot competition approached in 1989,
the same four coaches—Flaman, Cleary, Ceglarski, and Parker—had been clashing
against each other continuously for fifteen first-two-Mondays-in-February. Like
Boston, its home, the Beanpot did not yield to change.

The announcement that Jack Parker, Boston University's coaching icon and, at forty-
three, the youngest of the four, was stepping down as head coach effective at the end
of the 1988–89 season to become the school's athletic director stunned the world of
college hockey. Parker had already coached the Terriers to six Beanpot titles, four
ECAC titles, a Hockey East crown, and a National Championship. A head coach since
age twenty-eight, Parker showed signs of burnout. The frustration of the past couple
of seasons in particular had exacted a heavy price on the ever-demanding head coach.
Parker had been a part of thirteen Terrier Beanpot championships—as player, assistant coach to Jack Kelley and Leon Abbott, and head coach. Beanpot 1989 would be
his Causeway Street farewell.

BU entered the tournament as the only team not in the top-ten national rankings.
In the first round's early match, the Terriers (12-15-1) faced a Northeastern team
that had defeated them eight times straight since the 1987 Beanpot final. In a dramatic third-period comeback, BU got goals from Mike Kelfer, 1987 MVP, and Mike
Sullivan in the final 5:20, sending the game into overtime. Defenseman Chris Lappin's

overtime goal on a shot from the left point sent the Terriers back to their accustomed position in the late game on the second Monday in February.

The marquee game on the first Monday featured 17-1 Harvard, the nation's number-one ranked team, and Boston College (17-5-3), ranked fourth. Unbeaten in their previous seven games, earlier in the season the Eagles had lost a fast-paced game at Harvard in overtime. The Crimson team, despite its impressive run during the 1988–89 campaign, had a Beanpot monkey on its back and it had grown to King Kong proportions. Eight long years had passed since Harvard had advanced to play for the Beanpot. They had last won the Beanpot in the first month of the administration of President Ronald Reagan. Now, another Republican president, George H. W. Bush, had just been inaugurated. Could the Crimson ride a Yale man's coattails to another Beanpot crown?

Harvard bolted to a pair of three-goal leads at 4–1 and 5–2, then barely hung on for a 5–4 victory. The Eagles unleashed a furious barrage on Crimson freshman goalie Chuck Hughes in the third period. Despite a 21-2 shots-on-goal advantage, BC never got even. Eagle senior forward Rich Braccia, who had scored just seven goals in seventy-one career games, scored a pair in the final session to get BC within one. But it just wasn't enough to prevent Harvard from a long-awaited journey back to the championship game.

The baby-faced Hughes made thirty-eight saves total, several of them in the "spectacular" category. "I've never played in a period that was so lopsided," said Hughes. "But when you're called upon to do a job, you've got to do it. And I'm only as good as my team out there. This game is what hockey's all about. I've never had more fun in my life."

BU and Harvard would be seriously challenged to equal the excitement of the third-period rally and third-period goaltending that highlighted the opening round. The subplot provided by the departure of a Beanpot coaching legend would be the emotional backdrop to this decade's final Beanpot.

 The time on the scoreboard clock had finally expired, and when this tumultuous championship game of the 37th Beanpot was history last night in the steamy Garden, Harvard captain Lane MacDonald hoisted the trophy above his head and took that elusive victory skate around the rink.

"It was a real relief," he would say, when the tumult subsided, "after being so frustrated for so long."

This was a time to exult, a time to savor the Beanpot. The Crimson, beaten in the opening round for seven straight years, rose to the occasion and beat Boston University, 9–6, to win their first Beanpot since 1981 in the highest-scoring championship game in tournament history. In the process, they presented coach Bill Cleary with his 300th career victory.

"Just to see a smile on these kids' faces was worth it," said Cleary. "Just to see them experience a Beanpot win. We've had a lot of good teams and players who haven't

Harvard forward Lane MacDonald,
1989 Beanpot MVP

(Courtesy of Harvard University)

won a Beanpot. I've won one myself. I just wanted the kids to experience it. We played before family and friends. It's such a big event now. That's what it is. An event."

The game was a turbulent exhibition of offensive hockey that saw the Crimson take a 3–0 lead and then trail, 4–3. BU scored a pair of goals 16 seconds apart in the second period, and Harvard got one 30 seconds later. There were four goals scored within a 2:11 stretch. . . .

This was Parker's Beanpot farewell. He was a part of 13 of BU's 14 Beanpot championships as a player (three), assistant coach (four) and head coach (six), and he will move up to athletic director and assume the role of spectator next year.

"Before the game, I'm smiling because of all the guys who came down to the bench," said Parker. "There were a lot of former players who came down. Once the game started, I forgot about it all.". . .

There was a measure of vindication for the Crimson, who have been to the NCAA-title game twice in these years of their Beanpot drought.

"I'm not used to feeling this way," said senior defenseman Josh Capian. "I'm used to being out of here around 8:30. I knew it wasn't going to be easy, but after being here for four years I'm just relieved.

"I was tired of coming in here the best team in the tournament every year and not winning it. We showed it tonight."

The Crimson, beaten Saturday night at Colgate for just the second time this season, surged to a 3–0 lead in the first 10:49 of the game. C. J. Young converted a power-play set-up from Peter Ciavaglia (6:05), and Paul Howley, a senior left wing on the money line, made it 2–0 when he poked in a rebound (7:40). The Crimson made it 3–0 when Mike Vukonich fielded a pass from Ted Donato and rifled it into the far corner. . . .

The Terriers (13-16-1) started to click when Mike Lappin deflected a shot by Mark Krys from the left point past freshman goalie Allain Roy at 16:51 of the first period.

The shootout began in earnest in the second period. Phil von Stefenelli scored his second goal of the season at 2:48 to pull the Terriers within one, and two goals within 16 seconds put them in the lead.

Mike Kelfer sent a blistering shot past Roy at the 4:11 mark, and Dave Tomlinson intercepted Nick Carone's centering pass in front of Roy and scored to create a 4–3 lead at 4:27.

The Crimson returned the favor 14 seconds later when John Weisbrod finished off Ciavaglia's set-up to tie the game, 4–4. Vukonich lifted the Crimson to a 5–4 lead with a shot from the top of the circle that broke off Fish's glove at 6:22.

MacDonald, the tournament MVP, made it 6–4 when he scored a shorthanded goal as he sank to his knees.

So it went.

Roy juggled a shot by David Sacco to cut the deficit to a goal on a power play. Donato's shot on a break up the left wing made it 7–5, and then the game came down to a few desperate moments in the early stages of the third period.

The Crimson's Kevan Melrose had been given a 5-minute major and game disqualification for a butt end as time ran out in the second, and MacDonald was called for hooking by Hockey East–referee Joe Albert, 59 seconds into the third.

Joe Sacco took a pass from brother Dave and cut it to 7–6, and there was still 3:39 left on the power play because of the major.

The Crimson won this game in those minutes when they killed off the penalty. Tom Harig scored an insurance goal (16:19) and Weisbrod finished it off with 1:20 to go in this cauldron.

—Joe Concannon, *Boston Globe,* February 14, 1989

Crimson forward Ted Donato kisses the Beanpot.
(Courtesy of *Boston Herald*)

From Bruin to Husky

Northeastern University's head coach, Fern Flaman

(Courtesy of Northeastern University)

Ferny Flaman arrived in Boston from Dysart, Saskatchewan, at the tender age of fifteen and has remained part of the Boston hockey scene as a player, coach, scout, and all-around legend for better than a half-century. As a player, first with the semi-pro Boston Olympics and later during a sixteen-year NHL career that included two tours of duty with the Bruins (1946–50 and 1955–61, when he was captain), Flaman earned a reputation as a rock-solid defenseman.

A six-time NHL all-star and hall-of-famer, Ferny was the principal of the "old time hockey" school, with his defense-first, physical style of play. It was no surprise that Detroit Red Wings' great Gordie Howe referred to Flaman as the "toughest defenseman" he ever faced during his illustrious career. After several years as a coach and administrator at the minor league level, in 1970 Flaman seized the opportunity to return to Boston as head coach of the Northeastern Huskies. The former Bruin worked diligently to revive the Huskies' hockey fortunes. During Flaman's first years at the helm, the Huskies' Beanpot disappointments continued. But then came the 1980s. The Huntington Avenue Hounds became the Beanpot's team of the decade, capturing four 'Pots under Ferny's tutelage.

"The 1970s are tough to recall but the '80s I remember very well," Ferny quipped recently.

It all began to turn around in the 1980 tournament. "John Montgomery, a little guy, got the game-winning goal for us on a shot from just inside the blue line," Flaman remembered. "Everybody forgets about him but that was the overtime goal that got us past BU in the first round."

The heroics of the following week's title match with Boston College have become the stuff of local hockey legend—arguably the Beanpot's defining moment.

"Wayne Turner's [overtime] goal that won our first Beanpot was something I'll never forget," said the former Northeastern mentor. "When you watch the tape, the play Dale Ferdinandi made starting out of our end and getting the puck up the ice to Wayne was tremendous. Another guy who really got the job done for us that night was defenseman Dave Archambault."

The Huskies' resounding victory was instrumental in paving the way for future success. "We had two or three recruits at the game that night, one of which was Ken Manchurek [Northeastern's Number 8, their all-time leading scorer], who became one of the best players on our 1982 ECAC Championship and Final Four team," said Flaman. The 1982 season also saw Northeastern's all-time winningest coach garner recognition as National Coach of the Year.

Northeastern followed up its 1980 Garden success with back-to-back Beanpots in 1984 and 1985. The 1984 tournament provided perhaps the Beanpot's most emotional moment when Fernie's terminally ill son, Terry, a former Beanpot champion for Harvard (1969), was presented the coveted trophy by the Northeastern victors. "That year was very tough, with Terry and my wife [Jean] both in wheelchairs (she had injured her kneecap)," the coach recalled. "The players skated over and presented the Beanpot to my family."

The 1985 team was determined to "follow up their success," as Flaman offered, and led by freshman netminder Bruce Racine, they did just that. The rookie's thirty-two-save performance versus Boston University earned him MVP honors and his first of two Eberly trophies. As a senior, Racine would again prove instrumental in another victory over BU, a 6–3 win, with future Huskies hall-of-famer David O'Brien scoring twice.

The 1988 Beanpot crown proved to be Flaman's last as head coach. Currently retired, Ferny hasn't strayed very far from the game. He is still employed as a part-time special-assignment scout by the New Jersey Devils.

Flaman arrived for opening-round Beanpot action in 2000, fresh from the NHL all-star-weekend festivities in Toronto, where he was honored as a legend alongside former Bruin teammates Milt Schmidt and Woody Dumart, with whom Flaman initially played when he was barely eighteen years old.

"I guess I'm a legend," the affable Flaman said, tongue planted firmly in cheek.

No argument from those who hold the first two Mondays of February sacred.

THE TERRIERS
TAKE CHARGE
1990–1995

As the new decade commenced, a coach was missing from the Beanpot lineup. Boston University's Jack Parker had announced his "retirement" from behind the Terrier bench the previous season. The results of the 1989 championship game appeared to be a bitter last waltz at the Beanpot cotillion for the still youthful coach.

But, after only ten days as the school's athletic director, the position he had accepted after relinquishing his coaching duties, the six-time tournament champion head coach changed his mind. And so, Parker returned, with a renewed sense of purpose, to lead the Terriers into battle for the 1989–90 season. The disappointment of back-to-back sub-.500 seasons had stoked the competitive fires of the ever-intense Terrier mentor. Through the 1990s, life would be miserable for the other three Beanpot schools.

Instead, the coaching change for the 1990 tournament was at Northeastern University. The Huskies, the Beanpot team of the 1980s (with four titles), had announced the retirement of head coach Fern Flaman, which was effective at the end of the 1988–89 season. His successor was Don McKenney, Flaman's assistant coach for nineteen years and his former Boston Bruins teammate.

With all four teams rated in the nation's top fifteen late in January, the prospects seemed to point toward tournament parity among the foursome. "I usually like to pick out a favorite and give them the kiss of death," said Jack Parker, "but there is no outright favorite."

Boston College, the team with the longest Beanpot championship drought and best record coming in (17-8-1), was hungry to rebound. "We're hoping we can turn the tables," said coach Len Ceglarski. "I think we're playing pretty well." In fact, the Eagles were soaring on a 9-1-1 run through the eleven games prior to visiting Causeway Street for their first-round match with their traditional nemesis BU (13-10-2). The Terriers, on a 6-1-1 pre-Beanpot streak, had split two previous games with BC.

1990   In another Beanpot game of wildly shifting momentum, BU jumped to a 3–0 lead by the halfway mark. The Eagles then surged back to tie the game at 3–3 before the second intermission. The lone third-period goal, by Terrier senior right-wing Ed Ronan, came on his shot from behind the net, off the stick of Boston College forward Doug Brown, which proved to be the game-winner. The Eagles and their dejected coach suffered yet another February night of frustration. "We've had a lot of tough luck in this tournament," said Len Ceglarski, "and this was more of it. The thing that makes me feel the worst is the type of goal that won the game." For the twenty-fourth time in twenty-seven years, the Terriers were headed back to their more accustomed later face-off time on the second Monday in February.

The feature first-round game was highlighted by its own ebb and flow. Harvard, the defending Beanpot and national champions, allowed a 3–1 third-period lead to become a 4–3 deficit on a goal by Northeastern's Mike Roberts. The Crimson rallied, tying the game on Peter Ciavaglia's power-play marker, and won it, with 21 seconds remaining, on a nifty give-and-go finish by Duluth, Minnesota, native Mike Vukonich off a pass from John Murphy. Two dramatic one-goal matches for the sellout crowd of 14,448.

Both the Terriers and Crimson fashioned impressive stretches prior to their rematch at the Beanpot summit. BU avoided the pitfall of the between-the-Beanpot game by rallying from a 4–0 deficit to defeat Merrimack 5–4. Meanwhile, Harvard's five unanswered goals brought them back from a 2–0 deficit to clinch the Ivy League title, scoring a 5–2 victory over Cornell. Despite a loss to Colgate the next night, which ended an eight-game winning streak, coach Bill Cleary's club was hungry for a repeat as Boston hockey's ruling class.

 They didn't want to leave the ice; they wanted to savor the magic of the moment forever. They skated the old trophy over to a corner of the rink where their faithful had watched this championship game of the 38th Beanpot Hockey Tournament with understandable glee. Yes, in this magical moment of their athletic lives, they were in no hurry to go anywhere. The record will duly note that, on this night in steamy Boston Garden, a Boston University hockey team that was struggling as the calendar turned to a new decade dispatched defender Harvard, 8–2, in one of the most decisive and thorough beatings in the tournament's history. . . .

If there was a goal that broke the Crimson's back and left little doubt as to which team would win, it was the one scored by tournament MVP David Tomlinson to give the Terriers a 5–0 lead at 7:12 of the second period. The Crimson had a two-man advantage, but Tomlinson broke into the Harvard zone, intercepted goaltender Allain Roy's clearing pass and shot it into the open net as he zipped by. This game was about to become history. "I was trying to get the puck out primarily," said Tomlinson, who had two goals and a pair of assists. "Once I saw it was going down to their goalie and he wasn't handling the puck too well, I kept going. Their players were holding me

Dave Tomlinson, BU forward, accepts 1990 MVP award from Steve Nazro.

(Courtesy of Boston University)

up, but not concentrating on where the goalie was going; I anticipated which way he was going to go. He didn't get too much on it. It was anticipation on my part, but the goalie didn't make too much of a play."

There was a slew of BU heroes. Joe Sacco, who grew up in Medford and had dreamed of this all his life, had two goals and wore a smile as big as the Beanpot itself.

"We worked real hard the whole game," he said. "The goals were going in for us. We've been ready to explode for awhile. We're on a roll and we're not going to stop."

The Beanpot? "I've been dreaming of this ever since youth hockey," said Sacco. "I skated it over to show my parents."

BU goalie Scott Cashman, who made some big early saves and was credited with 29 for the game, saw the Beanpot as a recruit out of Kanata, Ontario, and decided on that night he wanted to play in it.

"This year has been a lot more than I could have hoped for, and this kind of made it even better," said Cashman. "I was there last year and I said, 'I want to play in that game.' I played it and we won. What more can you ask for?"

Mike Sullivan, the captain and one of just two BU seniors, played on a winning Beanpot team as a freshman and has seen this team mature.

"Everybody just stuck together," said Sullivan. "We went 1-6 in December. The guys didn't get down. Every individual on the team knew we had some talent. It was only a matter of time before we put some wins together and gained some confidence."

Sacco started the Terriers on their way to a 3−0 lead in the first period when he moved through the slot on a power play, took a feed from Alexandre Legault, and rifled a shot into the right corner past Roy at the 8:04 mark. Phil von Stefenelli picked up a pass from Ed Ronan and saw his shot from the left point go in at 11:53. Shawn McEachern, who has been a vital cog in the team's resurgence, made it 3−0 when he cut in and put a high backhander home at 16:56.

The Terriers, who had an 18−7 edge in shots in the first 20 minutes, forged a 4−0 lead when Sacco followed up his own rebound 2:28 into the second period. Tomlinson then converted to finish off his dazzling rush and the Terriers seemed as if they were on the power play even though they were still killing off two penalties.

The Crimson's dangerous Mike Vukonich finally broke through when Tod Hartje sprung him into the BU zone on a breakaway to cut the deficit to 5−1, but Tomlinson artfully deflected Peter Ahola's shot past Roy (11:35) and McEachern finished off a pass from Sacco (13:34) and BU was on top, 7−1.

—Joe Concannon, *Boston Globe*, February 13, 1990

Northeastern University goalie Tom Cole made fifty-one saves versus Boston College in the schools' 1991 opening-round match.

(Courtesy of Northeastern University)

1991   Six weeks after capturing the 1990 Beanpot, a youthful Terriers squad had made its first final-four appearance in twelve years. The expectations of being the pre-season number-one team in the nation weighed heavily on the team. Having suffered four defeats in the six games that preceded the 1991 Beanpot tournament, BU was uncharacteristically searching for answers. Farther along up the Green Line's B-trolley tracks, Boston College (22-7) had been on an 11-2 roll since the first of the year. The ancient rivals were rated as the often-cursed pre-tourney favorites to meet again for the Beanpot trophy.

The early opening-night contest between BC and Northeastern (4-21-2) featured one of the greatest goaltending exhibitions in tournament annals. Northeastern netminder Tom Cole turned back fifty-one of fifty-six Eagle shots—including an amazing twenty-seven saves in the second period—en route to a 5–3 BC victory. On a team populated by outstanding offensive performers, such as 1991 Hobey Baker Award–winner and all-American David Emma (who became the Eagles' all-time leading scorer on this night), it was the most unlikely of goal scorers who deposited the game-winner. Fresh-man center Jack Callahan, a true hometown hero from the Newton village of Chestnut Hill, scored on the power play from a goal-mouth scramble just beyond the halfway point of the third period. Callahan, a second-generation Eagle, had followed his father Jack (class of 1963) to the Boston College hockey program.

The first-round victory was BC coach Len Ceglarski's first in five years. These February Mondays at the Garden had become the gentlemanly Eagle mentor's private hell. "Nobody's any more disappointed than I am," reflected Ceglarski. "It's no fun to hear what we hear every year. But believe me, I'm more disappointed for the kids. I'd like these seniors to win one in their four years." In order to accomplish their goal they would have to defeat—guess who—BU.

The struggling Terriers needed nothing more than a dose of the time-tested winter elixir—a visit to Causeway Street—to turn around their fading fortunes. BU matched the score of the 1990 final with an 8–2 demolition of Harvard. Harvard's former assistant coach Ronn Tomassoni, who had replaced Bill Cleary (unlike his close friend Jack Parker, Cleary had retired permanently from coaching to become athletic director), fared no better than his predecessor. The Terriers built a 5–1 lead by the end of the first period and never looked back. BU's Ed Ronan, he of the first-round game-winning goal versus Boston College the previous year, led the Terriers' onslaught with two goals. For the eighth year in a row and the twenty-fifth time in twenty-eight years, BU headed to the final. "We seem to be pumped up for this," commented Coach Parker on his team's perennial first-round game effort. "They remember who wins the championship game."

The unprecedented level of talent on both sides for this Beanpot title bout was particularly memorable. In one corner, the defending Hockey East champion and NCAA final-four participant, Boston College. In the other corner, the defending Beanpot champion and NCAA final-four participant, Boston University. Sixteen of the thirty-six skaters in this Beanpot title match would go on to play in the National Hockey League. More than a decade later, eight are still active. The 1991 Beanpot final shaped up as a true heavyweight championship fight and the player who took control of the bout rose from the canvas after a KO.

 In a remarkable stretch of offensive hockey, Boston University turned the 39th Beanpot Hockey Tournament into another triumphant ride on the Green Line to the Back Bay campus, as a sellout crowd of 14,448 last night at Boston Garden watched the Terriers conquer a demoralized Boston College team that offered little resistance over the final 30 minutes.

So complete was this dismaying 8–4 rout that people started heading for the exits with 7:39 to go, and as time ran down with their 16th Beanpot securely in their grasp, captain Mark Krys ended it all by sweeping the puck up the ice and counting down the precious moments until he could joyously skate the trophy around the Garden ice.

The Eagles, whose Beanpot history has been painfully punctuated by games such as this, saw it blown apart when MVP Tony Amonte picked this evening to rise above the rest of his teammates. In a wondrous stretch, he set a Beanpot record with three goals in 5:24 of the second period, as the Terriers outscored the dazed Eagles, 5–1, over the final 7:42 of the period.

There wasn't a happier person in the rink than BU goaltender John Bradley. He'd waited four long and sometimes agonizing years for a game such as this. The scintillating stop he made in the early moments of the second period, when Bill Guerin took dead aim at the open side of the net, set the tone for the fireworks that followed. . . .

"The puck was bouncing in the net for us," said BU coach Jack Parker, who matched BC's legendary Snooks Kelley by winning his eighth Beanpot. "We played so hard. We played with a lot of intensity. I knew we were in good shape because Bradley played so well. The MVP was deservedly Amonte's, but the big plays all night were made by our goaltender."

The Eagles (24-8) owned the first three leads of the game. Emma opened the scoring just 54 seconds into the game, when he took a feed from Joe Cleary and swept a backhand past Bradley. Krys, a mainstay on the BU defensive corps, scored his first collegiate goal in 125 games, rifling a shot over Scott LaGrand's shoulders at the 1:57 mark.

Steve Heinze, who returned to the BC lineup for the first time since January 29, staked his team to a 2–1 lead, when he went up the right boards, cut back and around defenseman Kevin O'Sullivan, and tucked it behind Bradley at 6:08. The Terriers (20-9-2) answered when Petteri Koskimaki teamed up on the Finnish Connection and took a setup from Peter Ahola at 7:44.

The Eagles went on top, 3–2, when they owned a two-man advantage following penalties to Keith Tkachuk (8:41, interference) and Ed Ronan (9:01, holding). Cleary's shot from the top of the left circle went past Bradley at 9:25. After the Terriers held up for the duration of Ronan's penalty, the onslaught began.

Amonte started it when he picked up Phil von Stefenelli's rebound and flipped it home at 12:18. Amonte came back on a power play, swooping in to pick up Shawn McEachern's rebound and shooting it in at 13:03. The Eagles tied it at 4 when David Franzosa burst through traffic to score what would be his team's final goal at 13:21.

Amonte, who had just one multiple-goal game in two years, triggered a mild barrage of hats onto the Garden ice when he swept in to pick up a loose puck and shoot it between Cleary's legs and past LaGrand at 17:43 for a 5–4 lead. Doug Friedman made it 6–4 with a blistering shot from the right wing at 18:28. The Eagles looked like a beaten team, and with just one second left in the period, Mark Bavis spun around and put a weak shot on net that went in for a 7–4 lead. Chris McCann closed out the scoring at 14:43 of the third period with a cannon shot from the left wing.

—Joe Concannon, *Boston Globe*, February 12, 1991

1992   The Beanpot turned toward middle age in 1992, attaining the benchmark of forty. Most of the pretournament discussion focused on Boston College's head coach, Len Ceglarski. The Eagles' mentor had announced his retirement, effective at the end of the 1991–92 season. Although the Walpole native and former BC two-sport standout would culminate his illustrious coaching career as college hockey's all-time winningest coach, the Beanpot had long ago become his annual crucible. Ceglarski's role as Captain Ahab, the Beanpot his elusive Moby Dick, made his remarks at his final Beanpot luncheon appearance all the more poignant: "I know how much the Beanpot means, and I wish I could have won the Beanpot more, just for you," Ceglarski said apologetically to his athletic director, Bill Flynn.

In order for the sub-.500 Eagles (9-12-3) to give their esteemed coach one more Beanpot title opportunity, they would have to defeat a favored Crimson team (10-3-3). With a pair of victories on the weekend preceding the tournament, Harvard had become just the second school in college hockey history to win one thousand games. Unfortunately for Coach Ceglarski, one of the game's classiest representatives, his February horror movie would receive a renewed engagement.

The Crimson bolted to a 5–2 advantage. Boston College goals by John Joyce and Rob Canavan narrowed the Harvard lead to a single goal until Tim Burke found the vacant BC net with 47 seconds remaining. Harvard 6, Boston College 4. Another familiar player on the Causeway Street stage would exit disheartened yet again. "I have pride, our kids have pride," observed Ceglarski. "That's what made it so disappointing. If we had played the first forty minutes the same way we played the final ten, things might have been different." Second-year Crimson head coach Ronn Tomassoni got his first opportunity to capture the coveted trophy.

In the other opening-round match, an extremely youthful Boston University team (17-5-2), with nine freshmen in the lineup, was favored to extend their string of Beanpot championship appearances to nine in a row. Their opponents from Northeastern (12-11) were playing solid hockey and would need to be in peak form to upset the Terriers, who were on a 10-1-2 run since early December.

Jumping to an early 3–0 advantage, led by the offensive contribution of freshman John Lilley (two goals), BU appeared to be in control. But the Huskies stormed back and finally got even on a Sebastian LaPlante goal with 8:11 remaining in the third period. Then, with under three minutes left, a scarlet hue descended once again upon the Garden ice, as David Sacco's follow-up of a Rich Brennan shot from the point nestled in behind Northeastern netminder Tom Cole (thirty-four saves), giving the Terriers a 5–4 lead they refused to relinquish. Despite losing twelve players from their 1991 NCAA finalist and Beanpot championship squad, Jack Parker now tied Snooks Kelley for all-time Beanpot victories—twenty-six. A victory over Harvard the following Monday would give the Terrier mentor both his twenty-seventh victory and the overall championship record (nine). These were the compelling stories for championship Monday. The sentimental favorite had been relegated to playing in the early game.

 They are largely a young team, but perhaps young and yearning is a better way to put it. Put them in the uniforms of the Boston University hockey team, put them on the ice for a Beanpot Hockey Tournament in Boston Garden, and they seem to go from year to wonderful year in this parochial exercise of the college game played out in this tournament they rule with such aplomb. . . .

This time it was a 5–2 decision over Harvard before a sell-out crowd of 14,448 in the Garden to win the Beanpot for the third straight year and the 17th time in 40 tournaments. They've also been in the final nine straight years and 32 of 40. "It's a great feeling to see all the fans up there," said forward David Sacco. "They're loyal to us. We wanted to give something back to them."

The heroes on this team that is 13-1-2 in its last 16 games and 15-2-2 in its last 19 (20-5-2 overall) were freshman–right wing Mike Prendergast and goaltender Scott Cashman. It was Prendergast's dash up the ice to score the fourth goal just 16 seconds into the third period that ruined the Crimson, and it was Cashman who was credited with 33 saves as the Terriers wore down Harvard, which played its third game in four days and sixth in the last 11.

BU coach Jack Parker, who was a part of three championship teams as a player in the late 1960s, became the Beanpot's winningest coach with his 27th victory and ninth Beanpot, surpassing the legendary John (Snooks) Kelley of Boston College, whose teams owned the Beanpot in an earlier era. "He was something really different," said Parker of Kelley's legacy. "He was a legend."

BU freshman forward Mike Prendergast took home the MVP award in 1992.

(Courtesy of Boston University)

Boston University forward Mark Bavis with the 1992 Beanpot. Bavis, a passenger on United Airlines flight 93, died in the terrorist attacks on September 11, 2001.

(Courtesy of Boston University)

Prendergast—one of seven freshmen in the lineup—also had a pair of goals disallowed in the second period but still scored two, and with one in an opening 5–4 victory over Northeastern, was named the tournament's most valuable player. "That was probably the only four-goal game I've ever had in my life," said Prendergast.

The goal that Crimson (11-4-5) coach Ronn Tomassoni said did in his team was the fourth goal, and it was a solo effort once Prendergast poked the puck away from Crimson captain and defenseman Kevin Sneddon and flew in alone on goaltender Chuckie Hughes. "I just saw a lot of open ice," said Prendergast. "We were four on four. The defenseman just mishandled it, so I broke away. I came down on Chuckie. I was going to take a slap shot, but I got his legs to open up, and I just slid it through."

The Terriers seized a 1–0 lead on Prendergast's first goal at 6:27 of the first period. Sacco took a pass, Prendergast broke for the right post, and Sacco delivered it right to his stick to complete a two-day celebration for the Saccos of Medford. Brother Joe was on the winning US team in the opening game of the Olympics, [on] Sunday, in Albertville, France. "He called me last night," said younger brother David. "He was pretty happy."

The Crimson, who were tied at Yale (5–5) and Princeton (4–4) over the weekend, tied the game, 1–1, when Tim Burke moved in front and rerouted Steve Flomenhoft's set-up past Cashman at 12:37 of the period. The Terriers took a 2–1 lead when Tom Dion's shot from the top of the circle glanced off the leg of Crimson defenseman Rich DeFreitas at 14:35, but the Crimson evened it, 2–2, when freshman-center Brad Konik won a face-off and slid the puck out to Sneddon, who drilled it into the net at the 18:04 mark for just the second goal of his four-year career.

The second period was Prendergast's frustrating stretch. He put in his second rebound on a power play, but referee John Gallagher had whistled the play dead. The Terriers took a 3–2 lead when freshman-defenseman Rich Brennan's shot from the right point found its way home after Mark Bavis had won a face-off out to Kevin O'Sullivan. He slid the puck across to Brennan, who pulled the trigger at 7:06 of the period. Prendergast's next goal was disallowed when Doug Friedman was called for slashing Hughes.

The Terriers are 15-1 when they lead after the second period, and Prendergast sent them on their way to a celebration at the Dugout Cafe. Mike Bavis closed out the scoring at 5:07 of the period. The Terriers skated the Beanpot around the Garden ice as their faithful cheered, and the Crimson skaters filed off the ice in despair. They could only stand there for an eternity in the BU end as the fans rocked the building, and the cheers cascaded down.

—Joe Concannon, *Boston Globe*, February 11, 1992

1993   The 1992–93 Boston University hockey team approached the Beanpot well aware of the historic opportunity that the tournament presented. The Terrier squads that spanned from 1970 to 1973 were the only skaters in tournament history to claim four consecutive championships while representing one school. The 1993 scarlet-and-white senior class was in a position to put a more personal stamp on the perfect four-for-four parlay. Since freshmen were not varsity eligible by1970 NCAA rules, the youngest Terrier pups that contributed to that year's championship were sophomores. The BU classes of 1972 and 1973 matched their predecessors from 1968 and the BC seniors of 1965 as the only other Beanpot participants never to lose a tournament game. The 1993 BU group would be the first in the forty-one-year midwinter college hockey celebration actually to play and win four consecutive Beanpots.

The pretournament analysis targeted two prohibitive favorites. Harvard (13-1-1) was led by returning 1992 Olympian Ted Drury, who was happy to be back and to have a chance to skate on the Garden ice rather than being an ocean away making friendly Beanpot wagers, with fellow Team USA skaters from BC and BU, as he had been the previous year in Meribel, France. The captain celebrated his return to February Garden hockey by leading the Crimson to a 7–5 triumph over Northeastern (8-14-1) with a goal and three assists. Harvard made its task more difficult by drawing twelve penalties, but managed to survive four Northeastern power plays.

The late semifinal matched two programs that had been skating in opposite directions. Boston University (17-5-2) prepared to face a Boston College team (7-14-4) that they had already defeated three times earlier in the season. The fourth time proved no charm for the Eagles and their first-year coach, Steve Cedorchuk. The Terriers submitted a dominant effort, leading 4–0 early in the third period before BC briefly cut the deficit to three on a goal by John Joyce. The teams traded goals again quickly before BU iced the game with authority. A pair of markers by unsung Terrier Ken Rausch sandwiched around a goal by Jacques Joubert set the final score at 8–2. BU goalie Scott Cashman, one of the seven members of the Class of 1993, improved to a perfect 5-0 in the Garden.

A battle that hearkened back almost two decades to the epic championship games of 1974 and 1975 was set for the second Monday. Harvard, ranked second in the country, would have a chance not just to get mad, but to get even with the nation's number-four ranked team, Boston University. The Terriers had defeated them 4–3 in November, the Crimson's only pretournament loss. On a 16-1-1 roll since early December, the Crimson appeared to be a formidable challenger. Beaten by BU in two of the three finals since their Beanpot- and national-championship season of 1989, Harvard was motivated to exact a measure of revenge. Beanpot fandom was primed for a potential classic.

Harvard University forward and team captain Ted Drury was named Beanpot MVP in 1993.

(Courtesy of Harvard University)

 They'd been on the outside looking in for too long, this Harvard team that grudgingly must earn respect in this city. Even though they are the most recent Eastern team to win the NCAA championship and took a lofty 14-2-1 record into the title game of the 41st Beanpot before a roaring crowd of 14,448 last night against Boston University, the Crimson still had to go out and do it.

They did, with style, elan and a resolute application of their hockey skills in an enthralling game that is easily the best Beanpot final played since any of the participants had laced up a pair of skates for their colleges. This was a game that either side could have won, but thanks to a glittering performance by freshman-goaltender Tripp Tracy and the presence of U.S. Olympian Ted Drury and his band of brothers, the Crimson won it, 4–2, for their first Beanpot since the NCAA championship season of 1988–89.

It's interesting to note that the Crimson had two freshman goaltenders in that season of glory, and when Allain Roy and Chuckie Hughes reached the end of their careers, two freshmen named Tripp Tracy and Aaron Israel stepped in and have been the back-bone of a surprising, youthful team. Tracy was in the nets Friday night when the Crimson lost to RPI, 6–3—their first ECAC defeat of the season—but he was ready to go last night, making 30 saves and keeping the Terriers (19-6-2) at bay. Tracy, who grew up in the Detroit suburb of Grosse Pointe Farms, and saw his only previous Beanpot as a freshman at Milton Academy, said, "There's nothing like this in Michigan.

"I wasn't nervous. It was more pure excitement, because I saw it as an opportunity. I lost my first game on Friday and I saw this as a chance to come back and forget about it. I had always dreamed of going to Harvard and I'm glad I had the opportunity."

Terriers goalie Scott Cashman—the only three-time Eberly Award winner (Courtesy of Boston University)

There are just two seniors on this team, Steve Flomenhoft and Matt Mallgrave, and they helped end the dreams of the four BU seniors who were hoping to win four Beanpots.

"It's just an awesome feeling," said Mallgrave. "I can't really describe it. We've lost to BU all three years, so it ended some frustration. I hope we can use it as a stepping stone for the rest of the season. We could have used that RPI game two ways. We could have fallen asleep. We used it as a motivator for this game."

The Terriers, who were ranked No. 3 in the nation and were 16-1-1 since November 28, took a 1–0 lead out of a scramble in front that wound up with Doug Friedman sweeping the puck past Tracy at 10:14 of the first period. The Crimson tied it on the power play when Flomenhoft won the face-off, sending the puck into the corner, where Tom Holmes dug it out and fed it to Steve Martins, whose shot went over Scott Cashman's glove. A stretch of about five minutes in the second period was a hockey purist's delight, with the teams going up and down the ice without any stoppage of play. Cashman, who had 19 saves and lost his first game in six Beanpot decisions, made a glorious sprawling save on Flomenhoft at 9:08, but the Crimson came back at the end of this stretch to take a 2–1 lead. Brian Farrell stood at the goal mouth and rerouted a perfect set-up from Drury at 11:11.

The Crimson ended up two men down when Flomenhoft (12:22, boarding) and Peter McLaughlin (12:35, high stick) were sent to the penalty box. Even though the threesome of Drury, Chris Baird, and Lou Body did some yeoman penalty killing, the Terriers tied it when David Sacco took a pass from Stephen Foster and rifled it in at the 13:59 mark.

Harvard took a 3–2 lead 6:29 into the third period when Drury cut in front and moved the puck to his backhand to score.

Martins, who has been prone to injuries in his two seasons, made it 4–2 at 16:13, when he picked up a bouncing puck just outside the blue line, broke in alone and lifted it over Cashman's glove. It was his second goal of the night and numbers two and three in the five games he's played. "The puck just ended up on my stick," said Martins. "It hit a defenseman and took a bad bounce and it ended up on my stick. I was able to get a breakaway."

The Terriers were in their 10th straight championship game, 27th in the last 32 Beanpots, and 33rd of 41 overall.

"We might have been a little too jacked up," said BU coach Jack Parker, whose team beat the Crimson, 4–3, in Brown Arena on November 24. "We were all over them in the first ten minutes, but when we didn't score, we went from playing sky high to being a little deflated.

"I thought we played well in the second and third periods. They did a nice job of taking center ice away from us."

—Joe Concannon, *Boston Globe,* February 9, 1993

1994 After ending an eight-year 'Potless drought the previous season, Harvard (11-3-2) had to begin their defense against Boston University (18-5). Once again, the two schools were among the college hockey elite, with Harvard third and BU second in the national rankings. The Crimson exhibited a suffocating defensive effort led by captain Sean McCann, who also contributed offensively with a goal and an assist. The 4–2 final score did not fully reflect Harvard's mastery on this night. The Terriers could muster only seventeen shots on goalie Tripp Tracy, while the Crimson peppered BU netminder J. P. McKersie with thirty-six shots of their own. In fact, until Terrier junior center Steve Thornton scored, with just forty-eight seconds remaining in the game, BU was looking at its first single-goal offensive output in a Beanpot game since 1963. The Terriers' unprecedented run of ten straight championship appearances had come to a halt.

The "early" semifinal on opening night 1994 had become the late show. A Northeastern team (15-6-4), guided by Ben Smith, former Harvard player (1968) and BU assistant coach (1982–90), entered the tournament playing their best hockey, climbing to the eleventh position in the national rankings. Their first-round opponents from Boston College (10-12-3) were unquestionably the tourney underdogs, having won just one of their previous eight games. The Eagles' Beanpot drought now stretched to a full decade. Like Smith, beleaguered second-year coach Steve Cedorchuk (BC class of 1969) had known only disappointment as a Beanpot player. He had the considerable task of rallying his team from their recent doldrums.

"I wanted it as a kid from Charlestown; I've played in it, coached in it, and it's something you can't put into words. You just say the word Beanpot and all kinds of feelings go through your body and mind," said Cedorchuk. The feeling he sought for his team was one of improved confidence in their ability. "This is a showcase for college hockey and it brings out the best in the players," he continued. Could the best in his Eagles carry them past Northeastern? It would take a long time to find the answer.

Boston College senior right wing John Joyce's fifteen-foot wrist shot beat Northeastern goalie Mike Veisor at 6:52 of the second overtime period to deliver Boston College a dramatic 5–4 upset victory over Northeastern. The frenetic overtime periods featured a multitude of end-to-end rushes and game-sustaining saves until Joyce's definitive salvo "Jack Callahan took a shot as I was going around the cage," said Joyce. "The rebound came to me and when the goalie went down I just lifted it high and that was it."

The sensational goaltending by freshman Greg Taylor (forty saves), who hailed from Androssan, Alberta, keyed the Eagle victory. A two-goal third period was not enough for BC, as the Huskies stormed back to tie the game on a Jason Melong goal off a Dan Lupo rebound with less than five minutes remaining in regulation play. Although he had been battling the flu in the days preceding the tournament, Joyce became the Eagles' brand-new Beanpot hero. For just the second time in thirty-one years, the heavyweights of the tournament's infancy would face off to settle the midwinter Beantown bragging rights.

After so many years of frustration, a sophomore defenseman out of Western Massachusetts named Tom Ashe shot the puck into the net at 8:05 of overtime last night to lift underdog Boston College to a wondrous 2−1 victory over Harvard for the 42nd Beanpot championship in a haunted house called Boston Garden.

The dramatic goal enabled a generation of hockey followers at the Heights to see the demons of the past exorcised in a victory that may mark the dawn of a new era. The Eagles had won this parochial exercise just twice since 1965 [1976 and 1983], and there were so many teams and players that knew only heartache every February.

This one belongs in the lore of the Beanpot, a marvelous game set off by the goal-tending brilliance of MVP Greg Taylor and his Crimson counterpart, Aaron Israel. The victory was an emotional one for BC coach Steve Cedorchuk, who has struggled in his first two seasons but now has the first jewel to cherish as a reward for his years of dedication to the program and the hard-work ethic he instilled in his team. It was Cedorchuk's finest hour.

"It just makes you grateful," said Cedorchuk. "It shows if you work hard and you have persistence what can happen—I was an assistant for seventeen years.

"It shows if you have determination and you keep at it every day, the puck can bounce your way and life can bounce your way. It's as simple as that. We don't have any illusions, but we're going to enjoy this until Wednesday.

"I'm not going to kid anybody. I've been around a long time, so this is very special to me for a whole bunch of reasons. The first is that when I started watching the Beanpot a long time ago, BC won a lot of Beanpots. This is a young team that should be able to build on this. We have to preach that, but we're going to enjoy the heck out of this tonight and tomorrow."

The end came suddenly in a game that was tied by BC's Don Chase with 4:32 left in regulation and Israel staring at a shutout.

"I just skated in," said Ashe, who resides in Springfield and played at Avon Old Farms. "I pulled up looking for a trailer. There was no one there, so I just put it on net. It was really a lucky break. I think the goalie just moved a bit thinking there was a trailer and I just got a lucky break."

Legions of BC alumni will toast it as much more than a lucky break, as the Eagles (12-12-3) beat the nation's second-ranked Crimson (15-4-2) in a classic. Harvard had given up just four goals in four games until Ashe's shot went in.

—Joe Concannon, *Boston Globe*, February 15, 1994

1995   The 1995 tournament had the distinction of being the first of the Boston Garden lasts, as the venerable building prepared for its final curtain. After sixty-seven years and forty-one of the forty-two Beanpots, all agreed it was time for a change.

"This really is The End," said Garden vice president and Beanpot tournament director Steve Nazro. "I have seriously thought about the ramifications for some time now. It's not really, by the way, sad. None of this is sad. It's just time."

For the four coaches, especially Jack Parker (BU), Ben Smith (Northeastern), and Jerry York (BC), all three of whom had played in the Beanpot, the motivation to be the team to close the Garden era as champion enhanced the significance of this particular February's renewal of familiar acquaintances. "We know each other so well," said Parker at the final Beanpot luncheon at the Blades & Boards Club. "These are games you want to remember. We'd love to be the last team to win the last Beanpot in the old Boston Garden."

In order to advance halfway to achieving their coach's objective, the Terriers (18-5-3) would have to get past Northeastern (12-10-4) in the early match of round one. A balanced Terrier scoring attack comprising six goals from six different players along with solid goaltending from senior Derek Herlofsky (twenty-seven saves) carried BU back to the finals after its one-year hiatus. Senior center and captain Jacques Joubert and defenseman Rich Brennan led the Terriers' offense with three assists apiece, for a 6–2 victory over the Huskies.

Beanpot 1995 was Jerry York's first as head coach at his alma mater, Boston College.

(Courtesy of Boston College)

The defending champions from Boston College (9-15-2) came into Beanpot play riding the wave of a three-game winning streak. Harvard (11-7-2), meanwhile, had split a pair of games the previous weekend as the players came off their January-exam break. The Eagles surged to a 4–0 first-period lead, then barely withstood sustained Crimson pressure through the second and third periods, to emerge with a 7–6 win and a championship date with BU. Boston College goaltender Greg Taylor, the shutout hero of the Eagles' championship victory over Harvard the previous year, once again turned in a stellar demonstration of netminding.

Perhaps destiny had intervened to provide the aging edifice with its fiercest rivalry for an encore championship performance. For the twelfth time, the bitter adversaries of the Green Line would face off for the coveted trophy. After losing the first four championship meetings, BU had dramatically turned things around, winning six of the last seven to hold a slim 6-5 edge overall. The favored Terriers had also defeated the Eagles twice in January, including a 5–1 decision highlighted by a spectacular sixty-save performance by Taylor.

"Everybody says BU owns the Beanpot," observed BC's sophomore goalie, "but we skated [it] around last year, and the year before that I know Harvard skated it around. I haven't seen BU skate it around yet. I know BU's a great team and it's not going to be one of those things [where], if we play our best, we're going to be guaranteed a win. We just have to play as good a game as we can."

After lengthy coaching stints at Clarkson (1972–79) and Bowling Green (1979–94), the captain of the 1967 Eagles and a 1965 Beanpot champion during his sophomore year at BC had been reintroduced to the Beanpot's unique brand of winter madness. Now, as prodigal son and rookie head coach, Watertown native Jerry York mused: "It's all Beanpot, Beanpot, Beanpot. I always thought it was a great event, but I'd forgotten about the magnitude of it because I was so far away."

On the Terrier bench, BU's head coach, Jack Parker, long at the eye of the Beanpot hurricane, was forthright about his sense of Beanpot history on this occasion. "I don't know what it would mean to me if we won," he said, "but I'd be happy for the seniors and I certainly would like BU to win the last Beanpot in the Garden." The stage was set for the last twirl around the Garden ice.

Boston Garden—home of the Beanpot for forty-one years, from 1954 to 1995

(Courtesy of *Boston Globe*)

 They lowered the Beanpot curtain for the final time in 66-year-old Boston Garden last night, a suitably nostalgic occasion in the barn on Causeway Street that has staged 42 of the tournament's 43 renditions.

The Beanpot: Fifty Years of Thrills, Spills, and Chills

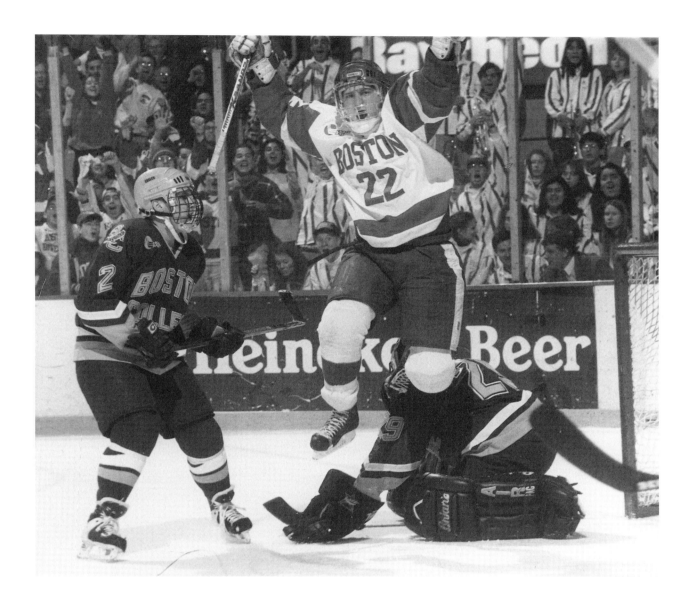

BU's Matt Wright scores the final goal of the last Beanpot played at Boston Garden.

(Courtesy of Boston University)

The Beanpot has been a town-and-gown occasion in the building through parts of five decades, and this was a night for the 14,448 who managed to secure a ticket to become part of Garden lore before it gives way to Shawmut Center [sic] later this year.

There was a good dose of deja vu for the Boston University faithful who have been a part of the school's tradition here. The Terriers have been the dominant team in the Beanpot since the mid-1960s. Coach Jack Parker, who won three titles as a player and had been an assistant coach before taking over the reins in the mid-1970s, kept saying how nice it would be to hoist the last Beanpot on Garden ice.

So they went out against Green Line rival Boston College and showed why they were the preseason pick to be the nation's No. 1 team, erupting for three goals within 3:34 of the second period en route to a 5–1 victory that clinched the first leg of Eastern college hockey's triple crown. . . .

"We felt if we played our game we were going to win," said BU captain Jacques Joubert, whose team has beaten the Eagles twelve straight times, including three this season, with one game to go. "We had success against them earlier in the year. It was nice to see all those great BU fans looking down on you. We don't want to get overly psyched about this. It's a nice thing, but we're going to have to put it in the back of our minds."

Tournament MVP Ken Rausch, a walk-on who didn't play very much as a freshman, scored the first and third goals. The first was on a shorthanded rush when he poked the puck between two defensemen at his blue line and went in alone on Greg Taylor.

"They almost hit themselves, the puck was free and I just poked it free," said Rausch. "I saw nothing but ice in front of me, and I just got my legs going and put it home."

The Terriers (21-5-3) then erupted in the second period, forcing the Eagles to play catch-up against a quicker and more explosive opponent. Bob Lachance created the second goal when he carried the puck around the net and slid it across to a breaking Mike Prendergast, whose low wrist-shot went past Taylor (34 saves) at 4:59 to make it 2–0.

They stormed right back again, just 18 seconds later. Chris Drury of Trumbull, Connecticut, who earned early fame as the winning pitcher of the Little League World Series, fed Rausch on the opposite wing, and Rausch put his own rebound between Taylor's pads for a 3–0 edge.

"He made a great pass," said Rausch. "Taylor made the first save. I just happened to stop in front of the net and the puck came right back to me."

Before the period was over, BU goalie Derek Herlofsky—winner of the Eberly Award for having the tourney's best save percentage (.917)—came up with one of his several big stops, getting his right pad to the open side of the net to blunt a golden chance by David Hymovitz.

Mike Grier lifted the Terriers to a 4–0 lead when he swooped in to tip Chris O'Sullivan's shot into the upper part of the net at 8:33 of the period.

The Eagles finally broke through when Timmy Lewis was in position to take Rob LaFerriere's pass at 17:18. The Terriers made it 5–1 at 8:31 of the third period when Matt Wright converted a pass from Joubert, who had circled the net.

—Joe Concannon, *Boston Globe*, February 15, 1995

Technically Knocked Out

Boston University forward Tony Amonte

(Courtesy of Boston University)

This piece was written for the 2001 Beanpot Program by Bill Doherty, who was assistant director of sports information at Northeastern for twenty years and is currently the color analyst for Northeastern hockey.

"When the game's on the line, it's coming down to the wire, and you can feel the electricity in the building, those are the moments you want to play in," said Tony Amonte, who was Beanpot chatter-ready, even after a long road trip with the Blackhawks. "You can tell when they are there, and I believe they provide what separates the great players from the good players."

Right here on Causeway Street, in a smoky joint that begat this FleetCenter, that distinction crystallized one decade ago on February 11, 1991, on a night when most might have wondered whether Amonte would rerack his skates, never mind win the Beanpot MVP. Somewhere before midnight in the 1991 title game against the Eagles, BU's Amonte took a brutal open-ice check that sent him crashing to the old Boston Garden ice. Momentum, already in the direction of Len Ceglarski and Steve Cedorchuk's Maroon-and-Gold, appeared to be in a tailwind toward Chestnut Hill.

"Most people might have thought, geez, this game is over now, he's definitely out for the night," remembers Cedorchuk, a Charlestown product and former BC mentor, who now runs clinics nationwide while not teaching students mathematics at West Roxbury High School. "That check would have put most people out of the game. But I remember thinking, 'O my God, we've woken him up.' " Amonte, ever the diplomat, concurred—sort of.

"Maybe it was a wake-up call," he remembered. "Well, it was kind of silly, too. It was one of my good friends who hit me. He knocked me out, and knocked himself out a little bit, too, he told me years later."

Either way, Cedorchuk's wake-up nightmare came true. Amonte not only regained his legs after the Joe Cleary hit, but he also returned for one of the memorable microcosms in Beanpot history. With the Eagles in control of the scoreboard and the play after one period, he came back to score a hat trick in the second period and engineer one of his school's greatest Beanpot victories ever.

In the span of five minutes and twenty-four seconds, Amonte not only induced the tossing of chapeaus from Garden rafters, he also painfully reminded all of his erstwhile college suitors just how great an impact he could have had in one of their jerseys. Though he played just two seasons for Parker's Terriers, Amonte was around long enough to have at least given them the pleasure of a union worth pursuing.

The toughness, explosiveness, and command of the moment accentuated by that ebony-wafer direct-deposit was conspicuous to every pro scout in the old building that night. All of college hockey, but, more immediately, the parochial fans of the Beanpot, might have fancied themselves spectators for the short term only. They would have been right.

Amonte, like the good hustler, wore panache underneath the threads, as the redoubtable Terrier Bernie Corbett sees it. Corbett, executive director of Giant Sports Associates and the sixteen-year radio voice of BU hockey, could almost be overheard recently during a quiet Tuesday evening at his satellite headquarters, the Dugout Cafe, on Commonwealth Avenue.

"Lightning in a bottle," Corbett burst out, when asked to describe Amonte. "As for pure offensive ability, electrifying a crowd, he's got to be absolutely at the top."

Amonte's combination of off-ice humility and on-ice braggadocio was never lost on Corbett, who has witnessed the best of the best on Babcock Street. "It was his ability to pounce," he explained. "He could change the complexion of a game in an instant.". . .

Far from through resurrecting, Amonte played Lazarus again in the Hockey East title, also usurped at Boston Garden. Then, on March 30, 1991, having just helped BU dispatch Clarkson with a hat trick–infused semifinal performance, Amonte (30-36-66), along with centerman [Shawn] McEachern (33-46-79), and freshman left wing Keith Tkachuk (17-22-39), primed the Terriers for what would be a four-hour, triple-overtime loss to Northern Michigan in one of the best NCAA finales ever.

Amonte had a goal and an assist in that memorable marathon, as Parker's seminal vision of an NCAA championship came within several rattled posts of reality.

Just two days after that epic NCAA battle, Amonte was flush with a three-year, one-million-dollar New York Rangers contract and back in the play-off fray, this time in the Patrick Division, with new linemates Adam Graves and a journeyman by the name of Mark Messier. Skating for Mike Keenan in his first full NHL season of 1991–92, Amonte punctuated a college-bestowed nickname of "Broadway" by finishing second in the NHL rookie-of-the-year voting to Pavel Bure.

Ten years and an NHL-jersey change later, Amonte owns a professional career line of 290-304-594 in three campaigns with the Rangers and seven with the Chicago Blackhawks. In 1999, his journeys through the collegiate, international, and pro ranks intersected when the NCAA named him to the golden anniversary squad that includes Kenny Dryden, Chris Chelios, Billy Cleary, and Red Berenson, to name a few.

Today, as one of hockey's brightest stars at hockey's most conspicuous level, he no longer needs to hustle.

SWEEPING INTO THE FLEET

1996–1999

C H A P T E R
T E N

The FleetCenter—new home of the Beanpot

(Courtesy of FleetCenter)

The sparkling new FleetCenter hosted its first Beanpot in 1996. Although removed physically a mere nine inches from the soon to be demolished Boston Garden, the tournament itself was making a quantum leap to a state-of-the-art facility. The four rivals were anxious to christen the new building with some Beanpot moments to call its own.

The defending Beanpot, Hockey East, and NCAA champions, Boston University's Terriers (19-3-3), entered the tournament motivated to embark on another quest for the "triple crown." BU was only the second team in history—along with the 1972 Terriers—to capture all three titles in one season. Coach Jerry York's Boston College skaters matched up with BU, riding a five-game winning streak that began after a 10–3 loss to BU, which followed a 4–4 tie with the Terriers—a game in which junior goalie Greg Taylor made an astounding sixty-one saves.

1996 Backstopped by the thirty-save effort of sophomore goalie Tom Noble, the Terriers ground to a 4–1 victory over BC. The former Catholic Memorial High School star

improved to a perfect 10-0 all-time on Causeway Street, as his 9-0 mark amassed in the Garden (8-0 state high school, 1-0 Hockey East semifinal) made a successful transition to the FleetCenter. "I was sorry to see the old building go," said Noble, "but so far this building's treated me pretty well. I don't think it was so much me. The defense played really well. They covered my rebounds, and our forwards came back all night."

Trailing 1–0 early, BU tied the game with a goal by winger Matt Wright. Forward Mike Grier stuffed in the eventual game-winner early in the second period. His empty-net goal in the final minutes secured the Terriers' twenty-ninth trip to the finals during the preceding thirty-three years.

In the early game on opening night, the Northeastern team (9-13-4), searching for an identity, fashioned an impressive defensive effort, defeating Harvard (10-9-1) by a 4–1 score. The Huskies, who had dropped six agonizing one-goal decisions during the campaign, utilized the defensive leadership of captain Dan McGillis and a fellow senior, goalie Todd Reynolds, to reverse an identical Crimson victory from a game played earlier in the year. Northeastern's coach, Ben Smith, would have an opportunity to face his former boss and close friend, Jack Parker, for the Beanpot championship. The Huskies' mentor would have the unique status of having taken part in the annual hockey ritual as a Harvard player, an assistant coach for Boston University, and now Northeastern's head coach. Unfortunately for the affable Smith, this new role would not provide a pleasant experience.

 The Beanpot has been Boston University's private preserve for stretches of the past four decades, and the Terriers hung onto it again last night with an avalanche of goals in the 44th rendition of this midwinter athletic rite, as if to say they can move this tournament across the alley from old Boston Garden, but it just doesn't matter.

Erupting for eight straight goals—six in that second period, which followed a zany opening twenty minutes—the Terriers recorded a rousing 11–4 triumph over Northeastern to win this championship for the nineteenth time overall and fifth time in the 1990s. To put it in perspective, the previous record for goals by one team in the championship game was nine; the Terriers scored their eleventh at 10:12 of the second period.

This was the first leg of what could be a countdown to BU's second straight "triple crown." The Terriers won the Beanpot, Hockey East, and NCAA tournaments a year ago. Considering the way they can explode, backed up by solid defense and goaltending, who'd bet against this 22-3-3 team, which is ranked second in the nation? Certainly not NU coach Ben Smith, who could only watch in dismay. . . .

This game was actually tied, 3–3, into the fifteenth minute of the first period before the Terriers exploded to an 11–3 lead after two. Five of the game's first six goals were on power plays, as the contest was marred by thirty-one penalties.

BU's Mike Grier, who had a 2-1-3 game, tipped in Chris Kelleher's shot for a 1–0 lead 3:17 into the game. The Terriers went on top, 2–0, when Bob Lachance (2-1-3) ripped home Jon Coleman's rebound at 6:40. Then Chris Drury—whose hat trick made him tour-

Boston University forward Chris Drury, the 1996 Beanpot MVP

(Courtesy of Boston University)

nament MVP, joining brother Ted, who was so honored for Harvard in 1993—was set up by Grier at 9:34. BU 3, NU 0, and the Terriers had a 9–2 edge in shots, to give the early impression that this might be a blowout.

But the Huskies (9-15-4) stormed back to create a 3–3 deadlock. Dan Lupo lifted a loose puck over Noble at 12:15. Arttu Kayhko sent a pass across to Dan McGillis, who rifled a shot past Noble less than a minute later, to cut it to 3–2 with the game's fifth power-play goal. And McGillis tied it on the game's first even-strength goal, rifling a shot through traffic at 14:38.

The Terriers wasted little time before regrouping. Lachance scored out of a scramble (15:07) and Drury finished off a two-on-one with Chris O'Sullivan at 18:30, making it 5–3 after one.

The Terriers were awesome in the second period. Drury started the onslaught with a pretty solo rush (2:21), Bill Pierce lifted the puck over two fallen players (6:02), Pandolfo registered his shorthanded goal after Lachance fed from the side of the net (6:34), Albie O'Connell tipped one past back-up goalie Todd Reynolds (9:53), and [Mike] Grier greeted the returning [Mike] Veisor (10:12).

The Terriers had six goals and this game was history.

—Joe Concannon, *Boston Globe*, February 13, 1996

1997 Only two-time defending champions Boston University (14-6-5) approached the FleetCenter's second Beanpot with a winning record. The nine-inch journey from old to new tournament venue caused no adverse effect on the Beanpot's winningest institution. The Terriers had not faced their first-round opponents from Harvard (7-11-2) in Beanpot play since the 1994 tourney opener. In fact, the Crimson could boast of a two-game Beanpot winning streak over BU that dated to their 1993 championship-match victory. The 5–1 early-season Terrier victory over the Crimson was another matter.

The early opening-round game between Boston College (10-13-3) and Northeastern (6-18-2) seemed to hold promise of an Eagle revival. Now in his third season as mentor at his alma mater, BC head coach Jerry York was beginning to win some important recruiting battles. Behind the other bench, Northeastern's first-year head coach Bruce Crowder was struggling. Following in the footsteps of legendary Huskies head coach Fernie Flaman, Crowder was also a former Boston Bruins player. Crowder had decided to make the trek south to Northeastern after enjoying great success elsewhere in Hockey East, at University of Massachusetts, Lowell.

A thorough defensive effort by York's young group of Eagles resulted in a 4–1 victory. Playing in his final Beanpot, senior goalie Greg Taylor (twenty-three saves), who won the MVP and the Eberly awards when he was a freshman, was almost flawless. The lone Northeastern tally, by Todd Barclay on a shot from the right face-off circle, with his team a man down, tied the game late in the first period. It would remain knotted until a bad-angle shot by BC's Chris Masters squeezed by Northeastern's netminder Marc Robitaille. The Eagles' line of Marty Reasoner, Jeff Farkas, and Blake Bellefeuille combined for a pair of goals to lead the resurgent Boston College offensive attack. The surprising Eagles appeared ready to return to their perennial position among college hockey's elite.

The other first-round match, between Boston University and Harvard, was no contest. With a six-goal third period eruption, the Terriers erased the memory of consecutive-tournament defeats versus the Crimson. Outshot 18–15, but leading 1–0 through two periods on a Chris Kelleher power-play goal, BU broke the game wide open halfway through the third period on a shorthanded tally by 1996 MVP Chris Drury. Harvard answered back, less than a minute later, before BU's Peter Donatelli and captain Billy Pierce closed out the scoring for a resounding 7–1 BU victory.

Terriers forward Bill Pierce was named Beanpot MVP in 1997.

(Courtesy of Boston University)

The BU-BC championship-game pairing once again captured the imagination of the local hockey populace. The two teams seeking the title were primed not only to decide who got bragging rights on Cape Cod beaches on the Fourth of July weekend, but also to make some history at the FleetCenter. The previous year, the new venue's first championship game had not been competitive. The 1997 edition of Beanpot championship hockey would be quite different.

 Billy Pierce traveled from his family home in Burlington to the old Boston Garden many times as he was growing up. He was a young hockey player with dreams of playing in the Beanpot Tournament, which had moved next door to the FleetCenter by the time he entered his junior year at Boston University.

The Beanpot? "It's part of being a Terrier," said Pierce a short time ago. He remembers watching the seniors skate around the Garden ice in a farewell to the arthritic building that had been the tournament's home for 42 glorious years, and last year he watched the seniors skate the trophy around the FleetCenter in [the Beanpot's] debut in the new building. So Pierce decided it was time to do it once more with feeling, in a personal adieu, and he did it in the grandest manner by scoring the goal that sent the Terriers to a 4–2 victory over Boston College last night.

Pierce worked his magic with 8:24 left, in one of the best Beanpot finals of this decade, as he gathered in a little poke pass from Chris Heron, busted in on goaltender

Greg Taylor, and went to the roof in a split-second reaction shot that lifted the Terriers (17-6-5) into a 3–2 lead in a game they had trailed, 2–0. Chris Drury's shot into the open net with thirteen seconds to go put the lid on the third straight Beanpot for the Terriers, their sixth this decade and twentieth overall as they continue to rule the city's college hockey scene with an iron hand.

This one didn't come easy, as a rousing game saw the full range of emotions return to the tournament in the cavernous FleetCenter.

The Eagles (11-15-3) came to play, riding the glittering 28-save performance of Taylor and the rousing play of forwards Marty Reasoner and young Jeff Farkas to the brink of something special. It wasn't to be, though, as Tom Noble was immense when he had to be in the BU nets and Pierce lived out his dream of dreams.

"It's the greatest goal I've ever scored," said the captain of a team that may have shifted gears and taken its play to the next level in a season of ups and downs. "I usually don't get too many breakaways. I really didn't have much time to think. I was trying to get the puck off edge. I just kept trying to settle the puck. I looked up and I was pretty close. I saw the upper corner and the puck went in."

From the first drop of the puck, it was apparent that this would be a bristling game between the old Green Line rivals. The Terriers had won the last five times they met BC at the Beanpot summit and held a 17-2 edge in the last 19 Beanpot encounters overall. . . .

As Taylor made thirteen saves in a brisk first period, the Eagles took a 1–0 lead on a brotherly connection. Chris Masters won a face-off in the BU zone, and the puck slid out to brother Peter at the left point. He rifled a shot that glanced off defenseman Tom Poti and past Noble just 5:38 into the game.

There it would remain until a jolly-good third period that was launched when Reasoner zoomed in on defenseman Jeff Kealty and put a rising shot into the far upper corner at 1:25. BC 2, BU 0.

The response came just 22 seconds later. Dan LaCouture put in a puck that slid through the crease after Shawn Bates shot it out in front. BC 2, BU 1.

Pierce set up the tying goal when he gathered in the puck just inside the blue line, spun around, and found Brendan Walsh heading to the net at 2:57.

After LaCouture's jarring elbow dropped Chris Masters and led to his exit with a mild concussion at 3:57, it was back and forth until Pierce's majestic goal.

"We had a player on him," said York, "and he let Pierce go to another player. It was a case of a flagrant miscommunication."

There was still one critical save to be made by Noble, who sprawled moments after Pierce's goal to stop Jamie O'Leary's bid.

"It was quite a show," said BU coach Jack Parker, "and no matter who won, it was going to be something good for our history and our rivalry and something good for college hockey in Boston."

—Joe Concannon, *Boston Globe*, February 11, 1997

1998   The Boston University class of 1998 had been "triple crown"—Beanpot, Hockey East, and NCAA—champions as freshmen. The next two years brought two more Beanpots to Walter Brown Arena, which bears the name of one of the tournament's founding fathers. The BU seniors also had a streak of three consecutive excursions to the NCAA final four on the line. Led by senior co-captains, center Chris Drury and defenseman Chris Kelleher, the Terriers (16-4-2) were looking to round into their familiar stretch-run mode of supremacy. Their first-round opponents from Northeastern (16-7-2) were also playing well. The Huskies' 10-3-1 record, through their last fourteen games, included a hard-fought split of a weekend series (a 2–1 loss and a 3–2 victory) with the Terriers in January.

Beanpot fans and the sports community at large offered good thoughts for BU coach Jack Parker, who had undergone surgery to relieve blockage in a coronary artery less than one week before the Beanpot's forty-sixth renewal. The feeling among the most perceptive Beanpot aficionados was that it would take more than a heart procedure to keep this Jack away from his Beanpot. It would indeed take more.

With Parker at his customary post, the Terriers defeated Northeastern by a score of 4–1. A collection of callow pups, including seven freshmen and four sophomores, smoothly accepted the torch from their forebears in scarlet and white, as freshman Carl Corazzini of Watertown and St. Sebastian's got the game-winner during a second period dominated by BU. Trailing 1–0 after one, the Terriers outshot the Huskies 18–3 and outscored them 3–0 in the middle twenty minutes. A Northeastern goal by Roger Holeczy halfway through the third period would have made it a one-goal game at 3–2, but was disallowed by video replay. The ruling that he had kicked the puck into the net baffled coach Bruce Crowder. "I thought it was a goal and knew nothing about goal reviews on the tape," Crowder said afterward. The Huskies could draw no closer, as Mike Sylvia and Chris Drury, two members of the Terriers' senior class, closed out the scoring. The duel between goaltenders Michel Larocque (twenty-six saves) and Marc Robitaille (thirty-three saves) turned out to be a memorable one.

The formidable-looking Eagles' rise (15-7-3) back toward the pinnacle was the biggest story of the college hockey season locally. A sub-.500 Harvard (6-9-2) team would attempt to slow down the swift skaters from Chestnut Hill. BC had a 4–3 overtime win and a 6–6 tie to their credit in two meetings with the Ivy Leaguers. With the team coming off a twenty-three-day exam break, without its number-one goalie, J. R. Prestifilippo, who had succumbed to mononucleosis, Harvard coach Ronn Tomassoni and all the Crimson nation turned their eyes toward seldom-used backup Oliver Jonas. On Causeway Street, with the painful memories of a winless Beanpot career (0-6) weighing heavily on them, the Crimson trailed 3–0 after one period. Goals by senior Henry Higdon and freshman Chris Bala narrowed the Eagles' lead to a single goal in the final period, but BC defenseman Bobby Allen's

Chris Bala scored the winning overtime goal in Harvard's 1998 upset of Boston College.

(Courtesy of Harvard University)

rocket from the point on a five-on-three power play restored the team's two-goal lead.

The night then seemed to take on an "only in the Beanpot" form as forward Trevor Allman and defenseman Ben Storey evened the game for the Crimson. Storey's goal came with the Harvard net vacant and just twenty-six seconds left in regulation time. As the hour passed to a new day, Chris Bala, a freshman from Phoenixville, Pennsylvania, became the newest addition to the pantheon of unlikely heroes. His game-winning goal at 2:41 into the overtime period gave Harvard an improbable 5–4 victory. Crimson captain Jeremiah McCarthy, who wryly described the warm-up before his first Beanpot game as his most memorable tournament experience, now had a moment to savor. "I think this might have made my career," commented McCarthy. "It was phenomenal."

The downcast Eagles would be denied a shot at the title and BU, but they would also return to the same ice twice, where they would win the Hockey East title and play for the national crown over the next two months.

The Crimson was the first team, since Boston College in 1994, to play for the coveted trophy despite a losing record. The six Terrier seniors seeking their fourth straight title would receive their historic opportunity.

 They finally could hoist the Beanpot, skate it around the FleetCenter ice, and show the world they had accomplished something very special. For the six senior members of Boston University's hockey team, this was a historic moment to seize and treasure.

Oliver Jonas, Crimson goalie

(Courtesy of Harvard University)

They'd just beaten a gritty Harvard team, 2–1, in overtime in last night's forty-sixth rendition of Boston's parochial midwinter sporting event, to win the Beanpot for the fourth-consecutive time. No class had ever done this before. It was their time to shine, and they did.

Given all they could handle by an unheralded Crimson team that wasn't given much of a chance before the tournament, the Terriers won it on a power-play goal by Nick Gillis at 5:51 of overtime. Gillis ended an emotionally draining game that saw the Crimson storm back to create a 1–1 tie on freshman Harry Schwefel's goal with 6:47 left in regulation.

On the night when the six seniors wrote a dramatic chapter, it was two freshmen who scored the biggest goals of the night.

And it was a night when BU-defenseman Tom Poti showed flashes of greatness.

Defenseman Tom Poti, 1998 Beanpot MVP, set up the game-winner for Boston University.

(Courtesy of Boston University)

It was Poti, a towering sophomore out of Worcester and Cushing Academy, who set up the first goal, by Chris Drury at 9:16 of the second, with a magnificent rush the length of the rink. In overtime, it was Poti who kept the puck in the zone on the fateful power play and fired it in to Gillis, who put it in the net.

"When they couldn't clear," said Gillis, "it went out to Poti. I saw him walk in the middle and I just tried to get in front of the net for a screen or a tip and I just tipped it in there." The Terriers poured onto the ice, and Gillis had become a part of Beanpot lore. . . .

J. R. Prestifilippo, the Crimson's rising sophomore goaltender, who came down with mononucleosis late in December and only returned to the ice last Friday night, came up big with thirty-four saves against the firepower of the Terriers.

The teams left the ice scoreless after the first period, but Drury soon forged a 1–0 lead. The play was started in motion by Chris Kelleher, and Poti did the work up the left wing.

"I had a lot of open room to skate it up," said Poti. "I just beat the defenseman wide, and I saw Drury cut to the net. I supplied it to him, and he put it in. No problem."

The Crimson kept coming, seemingly getting stronger as the game wore on, much as they did a week ago in a 5–4 overtime victory over Boston College. After Steve Moore failed on a couple of rebound opportunities, Schwefel tied it as Brice Conklin carried the puck into the zone, hesitated for position just inside the blue line, and then fed it to the freshman in the middle. Schwefel unloaded a bomb that went past senior goaltender Tom Noble, who is sitting on top of the world today with a 15-2 career record in championship games.

After Noble came up with his seventeenth and final save on Mark Moore's bid, [Brett] Chodorow was penalized and the Terriers went to work on the power play. Poti kept the puck in the zone, saw Gillis break to the net, and led him to the winning goal.

"The puck just came to me at the blue line," said Poti. "I made one fake to the guy who was coming out on me, and he kind of took it a little bit. I went to my backhand, and I saw him in front. I passed to him, and he put it home."

For Jack Parker, who underwent heart surgery two weeks ago, his Beanpot record is now 37-13 in 25 seasons.

"I'm so happy for the seniors," said Parker, who broke the goaltending rotation with Michel Larocque so Noble could join his classmates for this game. The seniors are Drury, Kelleher, Noble, Mike Sylvia, Jeff Kealty, and Peter Donatelli.

—Joe Concannon, *Boston Globe*, February 9, 1998

1999   The final Beanpot of the tournament's first century presented an intriguing configuration of the four schools. Boston College (15-8-2) was the only team to enter February with a winning record. The Eagles had been a preseason number one in the national rankings, but they plummeted to eighth just before their first FleetCenter appearance since the previous April, when they lost the national championship to Michigan in a volatile overtime decision.

Meanwhile, the defending champion team from Boston University (8-13-2) was deep in the throes of its most disappointing season in a decade. A heartbreaking loss to

The Beanpotters

The original Beanpotters, shown in 1966. Seated (from left to right): Northeastern's Jack Grinold, BU's Art Dunphy, the *Boston Globe*'s Fran Rosa, and Boston Garden's Tony Nota.
Standing (from left to right): The Garden's Herb Ralby, Boston Bruins Tom Johnson and Tom Carlton, Kevin Walsh of the *Globe*, the Bruins' Milt Schmidt, Eddie Powers from the Garden, *Boston Herald* writer Jack Sheehan, the *Globe*'s Bob Monahan, BC's Eddie Miller, Harvard's Ken Boyce, and photographer Dick Raphael.
(Courtesy of Beanpot Hall of Fame)

Fran Rosa, a retired *Boston Globe* sportswriter, who handled the Bruins beat during the 1970s and 1980s, remembers coining the term.

"We had a weekly college hockey luncheon," Rosa remembers. "I said the week before the Beanpot one year that there would be a meeting of the 'Beanpotters' for dinner and cocktails on Monday at 4 P.M., Durgin Park, Dutch treat. From there it began to grow. Once the word got out that Eddie Powers [Boston Garden treasurer and, later, president] was picking up the tab, we started getting flooded with people, picking up a lot of strangers. Some of the original group pleaded with Eddie not to pay. So we had pins made up. If you forgot your pin you had to buy a round of drinks for everyone. One year I grabbed Tom Johnson [then the Bruins coach] and asked him to come with me for a drink before the game. He didn't know about the 'no pin' rule. Upon our arrival, he got the house a round and turned and thanked me for the most expensive drink he ever had.

"We've had some great memories. One year Channel 2 wanted to do a television special. They set up the floodlights and suddenly a couple in the corner—probably not man and wife—were ducking under the table. We had the same waitress, Dottie, for so many years. John Hennings brought his son Greg for the first time. He was a young kid so we asked Dottie to tone down her salty language. You can't print her response.

"The manager at Durgin Park, Danny Roberts, was a college baseball umpire. He was the guy that Tony Nota got the original Beanpot trophy from. He also gave us one each year at dinner to present to one of our crowd, sort of a 'good guy' award."

Long live the Beanpotters and their fraternal spirit.

UMass (Lowell), dispatched a BU team to Causeway Street that had been winless for the month of January (0-5-1).

The irony of being the wearer of the unprecedented mantle of four-time defending champion *and* an underdog simultaneously was not lost on the Terriers' head coach, Jack Parker. "It's unusual for only one of the Beanpot teams to be ranked in the top ten in the nation, but I think it's fortunate for us we're playing them," commented the tournament's all-time winningest coach. "They've brought out the best in us over the years, and I think it's true vice versa." Although BU and BC had split a pair of November games, the Eagles were still given a decided edge. The present seemed to belong to Boston College.

The Terriers appeared much more comfortable pointing to the past: a perfect Beanpot record (10-0) versus their ancient rivals that began with the 1982 title game. Could a second straight group of seniors put their indelible stamp on this revered tournament with four straight titles? In order to have that opportunity, they would have to overcome a formidable opponent.

BU initiated the scoring at 5:09 of the first period on a goal by defenseman Juha Vuori, one of three regulars benched by Parker for the previous Terriers game. A Boston College power-play tally by Jeff Farkas, off a setup by defenseman Mike Mottau, evened the game six minutes later. Early in the second period, speedy BU forward Carl Corazzini wheeled around BC defenseman Bobby Allen and scored, allowing the Terriers to regain the lead. It then took the ever-dangerous Farkas just four minutes to pounce on a Chris Masters rebound to tie the game at two goals apiece. With the play often approaching a frenetic pace, and the skillful Eagles in control for numerous stretches, the game turned on an official's call—for the second year in a row.

Referee Tim Benedetto went to replay-official Jim Villandry for a ruling on an apparent goal by BC's Chris Masters. The ruling that Masters had directed the puck in deliberately off his skate denied BC a 3–2 lead. The ruling proved pivotal as the game remained tied through the third period and on into overtime.

At 5:10 of the extra session, BU sophomore center Russ Bartlett and junior Chris Heron busted in on a two-on-one break created by a brilliant two-zone pass by fellow junior forward Tommi Degerman. Bartlett fielded Heron's feed, streaked in, and beat Eagle goalie Scott Clemmensen. And yes, Bartlett and Heron were the other two BU players benched by Jack Parker during the previous game.

"I thought our team played very well," said dejected BC coach Jerry York. "We played very hard. We competed very hard. We had good chances, but the bottom line is you have to convert good chances into goals."

On the winning side, Parker's immense pride in his underdog team's clutch performance came through in his postgame commentary. "I was so pleased we played with some poise tonight and we played with some intensity," said Parker. "We had a number of guys who played extremely well." None better than the three who skated smoothly from the veteran mentor's doghouse to send the Terriers back to the championship game for the fifteenth time in sixteen years.

The BU-BC late show played out until 12:15 A.M. before a resolution was reached. But, on this compelling night of hockey, it was not the only game that needed overtime play to render a decision. For just the third time in tournament history—the first since 1965—both opening-round games were extended beyond sixty minutes.

The early/late game between Harvard and Northeastern was as compelling as the match between BU and BC. The Huskies fought back from a 2–1 deficit early in the second period, killing off a pair of Harvard power plays, before they reclaimed the lead on goals by junior co-captain Billy Newson and freshman Willie Levesque. Northeastern goalie Jason Braun (twenty-six saves) successfully protected the one-goal advantage until Crimson defenseman Matt Scorsune's screened shot from the point found the net with just five seconds remaining in the third period. At the 4:35 mark of overtime sophomore right wing Brian Cummings of West Roxbury deposited a rebound of a Ryan Zoller shot up high past Harvard goalie J. R. Prestifilippo. Cummings was yet another in the long line of unlikely Beanpot heroes. "One of the reasons I picked Northeastern was to play in the Beanpot," Cummings said after the game.

He did more than play. He stepped to the forefront, leading a Northeastern team with seven freshmen and seven sophomores, to its second Beanpot final in eleven years.

As the decade winds down and the new millennium approaches, perhaps it was appropriate that Boston University's struggling hockey team would suddenly shift into high gear for the forty-seventh Beanpot Tournament. The Terriers have ruled this event with an iron fist in the 1990s, so it was fitting that they stamp their imprint on the final game of the decade.

BU goalie Michel Larocque, 1999

Eberly Award winner and MVP

(Courtesy of Boston University)

With Michel Larocque leaving his personal mark on Boston's parochial hockey festival—becoming the first Terrier to win the tournament's Eberly Award as best goaltender *and* to be named MVP—the Terriers rose to the occasion last night and upended a Northeastern team that played more than well enough to win for the first time in thirteen seasons.

The final was BU 4, NU 2, before a FleetCenter crowd of 17,565, who saw an exhibition of the college game at its best. Larocque came up with 36 saves, Carl Corazzini put in a rebound at 18:35 of the second period to break a 2–2 tie, and Tommi Degerman sealed it when he took a pass from Chris Heron in the left slot and fired the puck past NU goaltender Jason Braun with 3:21 left. . . .

"I thought we played very well technically the first two periods," said BU coach Jack Parker. "It was a real cautious game. I don't think we played with anywhere the emotion we played in our last two games. I told them we had to go out and win the third period, and we went out and sat around and watched as they took it to us."

The Huskies, whose only four Beanpot titles came in the 1980s, swarmed the Terriers for good stretches in that final period. They allowed the Terriers only two shots on goal in the entire period. They're good, they're young and yearning, and they had nothing to be ashamed of on this night.

"We decided we were going to go out in the third period and not leave anything in the tank," said NU coach Bruce Crowder. "I'm proud of my players. We're a very young team."

Seniors on the Boston University hockey team—(left to right) Albie O'Connell, Michel Larocque, and Dan Ronan—celebrate BU's win with Travis Roy as tournament director Steve Nazro and coach Jack Parker look on.
(Courtesy of Boston University)

As hard as they played, the Huskies could never seize the lead. The Terriers had a 4–1 shot edge in the first eight minutes of the game, then were outshot, 5–1, over the next 4 minutes 15 seconds. That was when Larocque seemed to say, "Test me."

The Huskies did, and Laroque was up to the task.

The Terriers headed to the locker room with the lead, after freshman Jack Baker finished off a pass from captain Albie O'Connell at 13:54 of the first period.

The Huskies created a 1–1 tie when freshman Ryan Zoller snapped the puck into the net at 4:30 of the second, after Kevin Welch started the play with a pass out of his zone to Jim Fahey. The Terriers responded, as Bartlett followed up his own rebound, for a 2–1 lead just 59 seconds later. Zoller registered his second of the game at 8:35 on a power play.

Corazzini, who had the winning goal a year ago in the opening round against the Huskies, scored the key one of this championship, when he picked up Scott Perry's rebound and lifted it into the net for his fifth goal, at 18:25 of the second period.

"The coach has been telling me all year if I drive the net I'll be rewarded," said Corazzini. "That's all I was trying to do, and Scott had a great shot."

"I'm real happy to see these guys perform," said Parker, who won his fourteenth Beanpot in his twenty-fifth season as a head coach.

This was his second straight group of seniors—Larocque, O'Connell, and Dan Ronan—to win four straight Beanpots.

"The only difference," said Parker, "is these seniors won four Beanpots to give BU five in a row. I'm real happy with this one."

—Joe Concannon, *Boston Globe*, February 9, 1999

The Boston University seniors on the ice amidst the tumult of the postgame celebration numbered four. Team captain forward Albie O'Connell, defenseman Dan Ronan, goaltender Michel Larocque, and Travis Roy.

In October 1995, Travis Roy's hockey career had ended tragically when he crashed into the boards, suffering a paralyzing injury. With goaltender Larocque holding the trophy, a tearful Roy, seated in his wheelchair on the FleetCenter ice, kissed the coveted mug. The moment clearly transcended athletic competition. It was a scene akin to that of Northeastern coach Fernie Flaman's dying son, Terry, in the midst of the Huskies' 1984 postgame locker room.

"I'm glad for the seniors that were playing, that Travis felt a part of the team and felt a part of [the Beanpot championship]," observed Captain O'Connell. "He gave a speech before the third period and before the BC game. It was inspirational. He asked the guys before we played BC to put a piece of red tape around the top of their stick as a little remembrance of him, and I don't think the guys have stopped doing it since."

Inspired by Travis Roy's testament to the indomitable strength of the human spirit, the Terriers again found a way to keep the Beanpot at Walter Brown Arena. The tournament passed toward the new millennium on a poignant note.

Edward J. Powers, 1907–1973

Eddie Powers began his career at Boston Garden as a junior accountant in early 1929. From that humble beginning, the native of Haverhill rose to the position of treasurer of the Garden Arena Corporation.

As the alter ego to legendary Garden president Walter Brown, Powers developed a well-deserved reputation for integrity, imagination, and fierce loyalty. When Brown helped found the Beanpot, it was Powers who nurtured the fledgling tournament into a Boston tradition. Upon Brown's death in 1964, Powers was elevated to become the Garden's president. During a tumultuous period in America, he kept the Garden running smoothly while gaining national recognition for standards of excellence in arena management.

Overseeing a facility with two million customers annually and a wide range of events, Powers personally made it his business to become familiar with every aspect of the Garden's day-to-day operation. From ushers and concession workers to members of the board of directors, Powers treated everyone the same. "He was the most Christian man I ever knew. Everybody was exactly the same with him," recalled Steve Nazro, FleetCenter vice president and director of events, in an interview with Russ Conway of the *Lawrence Eagle Tribune*. "He made it a point every day of saying hello to people: the barber, the shoeshine man, the cab driver, and the peanut vendor."

Of all the events Powers was involved in promoting during his forty-four-year association with the Boston Garden—ice shows, circuses, concerts, boxing and wrestling matches—the Beanpot stood out as extra special. Something about the college kids on the ice the first two Mondays in February captured Eddie Powers's imagination, just as it has for the thousands of hockey fans who have made the Beanpot the unique event it is.

After Powers's death, in 1973, the Beanpot trophy was formally renamed the Eddie Powers Memorial Trophy—a fitting tribute to the man who played so prominent a role at the Boston Garden, a building he called the "House of Magic."

AT THE HALF-CENTURY

2000–2002

CHAPTER ELEVEN

As the tournament passed into the twenty-first century, the same old question was being asked: can anyone beat BU? The 1999 Terriers, who won a record-extending fifth consecutive title, had relied heavily on the MVP- and Eberly Award–winning performance of goaltender Michel Larocque. But, after nine straight appearances in the NCAA tournament, the Terriers had slumped uncharacteristically to a 3-6-1 post-Beanpot record, which included an early elimination from the Hockey East Tournament.

Meanwhile, Boston College had sustained a dramatic turnaround in their hockey program. Under head coach Jerry York, the Eagles had shaken their mid-1990s malaise to become, once again, a major player, both regionally (1998 and 1999 Hockey East champions) and nationally ("Frozen Four" appearances in 1998 and 1999). Locally, however, the Beanpot still belonged to BU.

2000   Both Commonwealth Avenue rivals entered the Beanpot tournament playing well. An experienced and all-around highly skilled Boston College team was on a 12-2-1 run, after a four-game losing streak in November. By completely dominating Northeastern, 6–0, the Eagles demonstrated why they were installed as pretournament favorites. Freshman center Krys Kolanos from Calgary, Alberta—not a recruiting locale with which Snooks Kelley would have been familiar—took control of the game with two second-period goals in less than two minutes, en route to a three-goal, one-assist evening. Eagles junior netminder Scott Clemmensen registered a rare tournament shutout, the thirteenth in Beanpot history.

In late first-round action, Boston University, on a 6-0-4 unbeaten streak of their own—including one win and a tie versus Boston College since the dawning of the new year—pitched a shutout of their own. In goal, Rick DiPietro, a freshman sensation from Winthrop, stopped twenty-one Harvard shots, completing the first ever double first-round shutout in tournament annals. Terriers sophomore forward Jack Baker matched Kolanos's earlier goal-scoring performance with a three-goal hat trick of his own, in a 4–0 victory over Harvard. The favorites had advanced, setting up another installment of the Beanpot's most frequently played serial drama.

Only one head coach—Jack Parker or Jerry York—would have a happy Valentine's Day.

The offensively prolific Eagles came out flying in the first period, outshooting BU 11–5, but they couldn't get a puck by goalie Rick DiPietro, the latest February Eaglekiller. After a scoreless first period, Boston College's co-captain Blake Bellefeuille scored his first career Beanpot goal. It took just twenty-four seconds for Boston University senior Chris Heron to deposit his own rebound past BC freshman goalie Tim Kelleher, whose brother, Chris, had been BU co-captain in 1997. Boston University captain Tommi Degerman—who, while growing up in Helsinki, Finland, had not heard of the Beanpot—got the eventual game-winner, at 7:11 of the second period, by completing a nifty passing play with Heron and defenseman Chris Dyment. The 1998 Beanpot-overtime hero Nick Gillis added a late goal for the Terriers in the final seconds of the second period, putting them on their way to an unprecedented sixth straight tournament triumph. The Terriers, class of 2000, led by Captain Degerman and Assistant Captain Heron, had become the third perfect four-for-four group of Beanpot skaters. Outdueling Kelleher, his former St. Sebastian's teammate,

Rick DiPietro, goalie for Boston University, was named 2000 MVP and Eberly Award winner.
(Courtesy of Boston University)

The Terriers' Tommi Degerman, of Finland, was the first European-born team captain to win a Beanpot.
(Courtesy of Boston University)

and setting records for goals-against-average and save percentage, Rick DiPietro garnered both MVP and Eberly honors.

"I've experienced for the first time what the BU experience is all about," he said in the middle of the Terriers' jubilant postgame celebration. It would also be his last time.

2001   Both the Terriers and the Eagles finished strong in 2000. BU returned to the NCAA tournament, after its one-year absence, and was defeated by St. Lawrence in the longest game in NCAA history (four overtimes), canceling an NCAA semifinal match with Boston College. The Eagles advanced to the NCAA championship game for the second time in three years, only to be denied a title by the winning North Dakota team.

Goaltender Rick DiPietro's sudden departure for the professional ranks was a devastating blow to Terrier fortunes. A sputtering BU team regrouped and put together a modest four-game winning streak prior to the tournament's 2001 renewal. Facing a Northeastern team that had handled them by a score of 4–1 in an early-season meeting, BU rode a thirty-four-save performance by junior goalie Jason Tapp and the hat-trick heroics of sophomore Brian Collins to a 6–4 victory. The Terriers witnessed a 4–1 lead become a precarious 5–4 advantage through the final minutes, as Northeastern's Mike Jozefowicz blasted home a power-play slap shot from the point with 9:13 remaining.

Although outshot 38–22, BU survived, with captain Carl Corrazini icing the game with an empty-net goal.

The numbers continued to be staggering: a seventeenth championship game appearance in eighteen years—BU's thirty-fourth since 1964. The Terriers were in position to roll a lucky seven.

Boston College had won seven of their last eight matches since an early-January loss at BU's Walter Brown Arena. Though small of stature, the line made up of senior captain Brian Gionta (5' 8") and freshmen Ben Eaves (5' 8") and Tony Voce (5' 8") proved to be huge of influence. The sniping Gionta got the Eagles started versus Harvard with an early first-period goal on a drive from the right face-off circle. A tip-in goal by another offensively proficient freshman, Chuck Kobasew, on the power play late in the period, extended the Eagles' lead to 2–0, but Gionta and Eaves set up senior Marty Hughes in the final minute of the period, giving the Eagles control, at 3–0. A third-period goal by BC's Voce and a tally by the Crimson's Kenny Turano cost goalie Scott Clemmensen his bid for a second career opening-round shutout and set Boston College's final count at 4–1. The six senior-class Eagles—Gionta, Bobby Allen, Mike Lephart, Rob Scuderi, Hughes, and Clemmensen—would have one more chance for Beanpot glory. To achieve February vindication, however, they would have to vanquish the six-time defending champion.

 Boston College finally accomplished last night what no Eagles team had done in a quarter-century: beat archrival Boston University in a Beanpot final. BC exorcised its BU demons, turning back a valiant effort by the Terriers to take a 5–3 victory before a Beanpot-record crowd of 17,953 at the FleetCenter.

It was the Eagles' twelfth all-time Beanpot title and the first in its last eight finals against BU, which was stymied in its quest to extend its record of six straight tournament crowns. . . .

"The champion goes down hard," said BC coach Jerry York, who played on the Eagles' 1965 'Pot winner as a sophomore forward. "It was a difficult task for us. BU really hung in there. They don't give you that trophy, we had to earn it.". . .

BU coach Jack Parker hailed the new owners. "We had won fourteen straight Beanpot games and six straight titles. All good things must come to an end," said Parker, who won three titles as a player. . . .

After a shaky start, in which BU nearly connected twice on close-in bids by captain Carl Corazzini, BC got untracked. The Eagles opened a 3–0 lead and appeared to have control before BU rallied to make it 3–2 heading into the final period.

Freshman defenseman J. D. Forrest opened the scoring at 9:33 of the first with a 30-foot shot that eluded the catching glove of BU-junior Jason Tapp (26 saves).

It was 2–0 at 13:12, after a point drive by defenseman Brett Peterson got behind Tapp, where Beanpot-MVP Krys Kolanos scooped up the puck, swung the net, and

fired home his twentieth goal of the season. . . . It became 3–0 at 4:47 of the second when freshman Chuck Kobasew beat Tapp after taking a blind, backhand pass from Kolanos. BU answered with an open-side goal from the right circle by freshman right winger Frantisek Skladany at 9:22 of the second. Tapp then made a long clearing feed to sophomore center Brian Collins, the hat-trick hero of BU's 6–4 opening-round win over Northeastern. Collins steered the puck to a streaking Kenny Magowan, who held off BC blue-liner Bill Cass and fired high over Scott Clemmensen to make it a seat-squirming 3–2 show.

BC-senior, defenseman Rob Scuderi, arguably the Eagles' best player in the tournament, gave the Eagles a two-goal cushion when his 30-foot blast broke off Tapp's catching glove at 2:19 of the third.

Mike Pandolfo kept [the] Terriers' hopes alive when he flicked home his eighth goal of the season in front at 3:38 of the third.

Brian Gionta, Eagles captain in 2001

(Courtesy of Boston College)

But freshman-center Ben Eaves cemented the win with a backhander at 12:31.

—John Connolly, *Boston Herald*, February 13, 2001

2002 Fifty. A half-century. The Beanpot was now easing its way into middle age, having become firmly entrenched as a staple of the Boston sports calendar. The first two Mondays in February have long been established as high holy days for college hockey aficionados and young hockey players across North America—and even across the ocean, in Europe.

The 2002 Beanpot luncheon, now held in the Legends Club at the FleetCenter, featured a keynote address by William J. Cleary, Jr. (Harvard Class of 1956). The choice was easy for anyone who truly knew the tournament. Only Billy Cleary could reflect on the experience of playing and coaching in, and officiating at, the fabled tournament. Factoring in Cleary's years as an assistant coach and athletic director, there is no question that he holds clear title to the greatest number of years of official involvement—forty-one of the first forty-nine.

After the traditional speaking program of coaches and captains, the gathering moved upstairs, to the Sports Museum of New England. The Beanpot Hall of Fame, which began inducting members in 1995 to commemorate the final year of the Boston Garden, has an honor roll that has grown to include thirty-one names. The museum was pleased to announce that the Beanpot Hall of Fame now makes its permanent home at the FleetCenter, where its opening exhibition was presented in January 2002 by B&M Baked Beans, of course. The gala reception was a fitting and proper tribute to honor a half-century of hockey excellence, but now it was time for the games to begin.

As in the previous forty-nine, a multitude of questions and subplots surrounded the fiftieth tournament. After suffering the ending to which their record six consecutive Beanpot-championship winning streak had come, could the Terriers bounce back to regain the title? Could Harvard bring third-year head coach Mark Mazzoleni to the finals for the first time? Could Northeastern end the longest Beanpot-title drought that had afflicted any of the four schools?

At 5:08 p.m., on February 3, 2002, the puck was dropped and Beanpot number fifty was under way. The opening game between a 9-9-3 Harvard team, whose players were forced to jump directly from final exams into a grueling weekend-long road trip to Colgate and Cornell, then back for an opening-night Beanpot game, was no match for a better-rested 15-10-3 Northeastern team that, for the past month, had been one of the nation's best.

The offensive hero for the Huskies fit a familiar Beanpot profile. Mike Ryan, a local skater from Milton and Boston College High School, had attended the tournament from the time he was twelve and played at the FleetCenter as a schoolboy. Now a Northeastern junior forward, Ryan initiated the scoring at 9:24 of the first period with a power-play goal set up by center Jason Guerriero. Harvard evened the score at 1–1 on a goal by Brendan Bernakevitch early in the second period. The Huskies responded with tallies by Ryan Dudgeon and Eric Ortlip to take a two-goal lead into the second intermission. Ryan got back on the offensive in the final period, scoring an even-strength backhander, then on a Huskies power play, with his linemate Guerriero assisting on both goals. "I did hope to come in here and maybe pop one or two goals, but to get a hat trick is something I thought about when I was a kid," said Ryan.

The Crimson would add a late goal, but the final score of 5–2 did not truly indicate the Huskies' overall mastery. Northeastern freshman goalie Keni Gibson (twenty-two saves) was not severely tested. "The team played great defense. I didn't have to make too many big saves. I thought our team played exceptionally well and made my night really easy," said Gibson. The Huskies were now in position to end their Beanpot-title drought.

The late first-round game was a rematch of the 2000 and 2001 title games. The defending Beanpot champions from Boston College (13-13-2) were reeling from injuries. A school record six-game losing streak had been snapped with a win at UMass (Amherst) the previous Friday. Boston University (17-7-2), meanwhile, exhibited strong indications that they were capable of returning to the finals. The 14-20-3 season record from 2000–2001 was already a distant memory.

Although able to dress only fifteen skaters, three below the minimum, BC exited the first period with a 1–0 lead on a goal by Tony Voce. The Terriers' Jack Baker, who hailed from the same South Boston neighborhood as former Terriers Dennis O'Connell (1966 captain) and Mike Prendergast (1992 MVP), dashed down the right wing and converted an unassisted goal to level the game in the opening minute of the second period. The two teams then traded shorthanded goals. First, Eagles freshman defenseman Andy Alberts rerouted a pass from J. D. Forrest; then Terriers junior forward John Sabo deposited a rebound of a slap shot by co-captain Mike Pandolfo, tying the game at two after two periods. A flurry of two goals, 1:50 apart, six minutes into the third period, swung the game to the Terriers. A torrid rush by Ryan Whitney jump-started BU. The freshman defenseman's wrist shot was stopped by BC goalie Matti Kaltiainen, but the carom glanced into the net off BC defenseman Brett Peterson, whose attempt to clear the puck went awry. A textbook give-and-go passing play, completed by Sabo on a perfect feed from center Brian McConnell, accounted for the eventual game-winning goal.

Eagles defenseman Forrest connected on a power-play slap shot from the point with under five minutes remaining, then walked in nearly to tie the game in the final minute. Instead, the Terriers scored the final goal. Mike Pandolfo found the empty net after junior forward Brian Collins separated an Eagles defenseman from the puck. BU 5, BC 3. A twenty-third BU victory in thirty-two Beanpot meetings with BC. A forty-first trip to the finals overall, and the eighteenth in nineteen years.

When asked if making the Beanpot final by beating Boston College provided a "bigger incentive," the ever-glib Coach Parker had an answer that explains a rivalry dating back to 1917: "It's a bigger incentive to beat BC," he said. "Even if you were playing at the Skating Club of Boston at 3 A.M.!"

The following Monday, at the FleetCenter at 8 P.M., would have to suffice. Terriers and Huskies—a dogfight for the golden Beanpot.

"There's no question it's become a very hot ticket," Parker said. "It's amazing this year, with Northeastern and BU in the final, it's as hot a ticket as I've seen in a long, long time." After a late-January sweep by New Hampshire, Parker's Terriers seemed to be back on track, winning four straight leading into the championship match.

Northeastern had constructed an 8-1-1 record through their last ten games. The streak began in early January, with a first-ever 3–0 shutout versus BU at Walter Brown Arena. The Huskies' captain, Jim Fahey, was particularly hungry for Beanpot success. "We'll be ready to go," said the former Catholic Memorial standout. "BU has pretty much dominated this tournament, but we'll see what happens. We've had a pretty good stretch going. Obviously, going out a winner and bringing the trophy to Huntington Avenue would be great. I can't lie to you and say this is going to be just another game."

Fahey, the Huskies' leading scorer from his defense position, could only dream of the Beanpot-winning feeling that BU's co-captain, Mike Pandolfo, had already experienced twice—and was anxious to savor once again. "It's a pretty even matchup and it should be a great game," said Pandolfo, a Burlington native. "Both teams are coming into the game with a lot of confidence."

When the puck that commenced the Beanpot's 2002 championship game was dropped, it was Pandolfo and his fellow Terriers who played with remarkable confidence. Freshman right wing Justin Maiser initiated the game's scoring on a goal-line extended wrist shot to the near side, after taking a pass from David Klema at 7:52 of the opening period. The Terriers dominated the opening period, outshooting Northeastern by a 14–7 margin. Huskies rookie goalie Keni Gibson kept the deficit 1–0 by making several spectacular saves. "I thought we should have had a bunch of goals early, but we didn't," observed Coach Parker.

A scintillating stick-handling play by freshman defenseman Ryan Whitney allowed the Terriers to extend their lead to 2–0 less than five minutes into the middle period. Then, just beyond the game's halfway mark, with BU in abundant control, a pair of penalties led to two Northeastern power-play goals by forward Chris Lynch. With only ten seconds left in the period, Fahey took the game into his own capable hands. Racing over the Terrier blue line, the former Milton peewee player blasted a slap shot that broke through BU goalie Sean Fields to give Northeastern a 3–2 lead. An ill-advised Pandolfo penalty at the second-period buzzer dug a deeper hole for BU.

A successful Terrier penalty kill opened the third period. Then, on a power play of their own, Pandolfo took advantage of a fortuitous bounce on a clear-in by defenseman Bryan Miller. The puck suddenly on his stick, the Terrier senior left wing deposited his shot behind Gibson to tie the game at the 3:54 mark. For the next fifteen

The Beanpot's fiftieth MVP (2002)—Justin Maiser, BU forward (Courtesy of Boston University Photo Services)

The Beanpot: Fifty Years of Thrills, Spills, and Chills

Terriers Chris Dyment and Mike Pandolfo skate the trophy in 2002.

(Courtesy of Boston University Photo Services)

minutes, the sold-out FleetCenter was treated to Beanpot hockey at its best, with both netminders making big stops. As had happened in countless Beanpot finals before this one, the clock wound down toward the moment a new February hero would be anointed. On this night, it was a nineteen-year-old freshman from Edina, Minnesota—Justin Maiser.

Terrier center David Klema won the face-off to the right of Gibson and directed it to left wing Kenny Magowan, who was able to nudge the puck back to Klema. A nifty play by Klema (also a Minnesotan) to kick the puck back to his stick and then thread a pass to Maiser, who was parked in front of the Northeastern net, set up the game-winning goal. A quick backhand-to-forehand shift and the shot beat Gibson high to the stick side. It was 4–3 BU, with 1:12 on the clock. The Terriers stemmed the tide of the Huskies' final offensive, with Gibson pulled for an extra attacker. BU senior forward Jack Baker took a feed from Whitney and placed the exclamation point on the Terrier victory with an empty-net goal in the waning seconds.

The scarlet-and-white captured their twenty-fourth Beanpot, matching the number of Stanley Cups won by the bleu-blanc-et-rouge of the Montréal Canadiens. The victory was also the Terriers' one-hundredth all-time win on Causeway Street.

Although now a three-time champion player, Pandolfo had a confession to make. "Me and Chris Dyment [his co-captain] have talked about how we've won two of them but we never actually touched the Beanpot," said Pandolfo. "When they brought the Beanpot down to show the crowd, for some reason the two of us got passed over both years. We didn't want to say we've won the Beanpot without ever actually touching it. That was so important to both of us and to have gotten it and touched it is the greatest feeling in the world."

At the postgame press conference, Maiser spoke for the hundreds of young men who had competed for the unique prize. "Growing up in Minnesota, I had always heard about [the Beanpot] and I wondered what it was," he said. "It's been an amazing experience. And then to win it—there's nothing better." Maiser was only the second Minnesotan ever to be named tournament MVP—Harvard goalie Wade Lau was the first, in 1981.

From the senior co-captains who finally touched the coveted trophy, to the freshman who etched his name forever in the tournament's illustrious annals, to the more than one million fans who, for a half-century, have been enthralled by its spirit of competition, there is indeed nothing better than this unique annual on-ice passion play.

Billy Cleary——Renaissance Man

He is the Beanpot's Renaissance man. Nobody has seen Boston's parochial midwinter rite of passage from as many different angles as William J. Cleary, Jr.

As a player, he was the Beanpot's first legend in 1955. As an assistant coach to his former mentor, Cooney Weiland, he learned his coaching craft and was part of the 1969 championship team. As a coach he climbed to the very pinnacle of his profession, winning the Beanpot in 1974, 1977, 1981, and 1989, and a national championship in 1989. As a highly respected on-ice official, he had the unique opportunity to experience the tournament from yet another, completely different perspective. And as Harvard athletic director from 1990 to 2001, Cleary unquestionably became, as tournament director Steve Nazro recently commented, "the Beanpot's conscience."

There was no doubt in the mind of any true Beanpot tournament aficionado that Billy Cleary would be the keynote speaker at the fiftieth tournament luncheon. All of the speakers to follow the *Boston Globe*'s John Powers, in 1987, in occupying the luncheon's special place of honor have followed in the spirit of Boston College coaching legend Snooks Kelley. It was particularly fitting and proper, therefore, for Cleary to speak at this golden-anniversary milestone. For some thirty years, in his annual state-of-the-Beanpot address—also known as the "Beanpot Charge"—Kelley never failed to mention Cleary's game-winning, shorthanded, overtime goal for the Crimson versus Snooks's Boston College team, in 1955.

It is truly a testament to the man that Cleary chose to speak of two moments from his own Beanpot experience that, as Harvard's Joe Bertagna, Cleary's former netminder, wrote, "have nothing to do with his own performances." At the luncheon, Cleary recounted two stories that embody the unique Beanpot spirit.

"In 1974, I called up a kid named Lyman Bullard. He was a varsity soccer and tennis player. A terrific all-around athlete who played on the JV hockey team. His roommate was our goalie, Brian Petrovek. When I called their room, Lyman answered the phone. He told me how he'd be at the Beanpot rooting the next night and wished me luck. Then I asked him, 'How would you like to play tomorrow night?' He thought I was kidding. He couldn't believe it. The next night he scores a goal and we win the Beanpot. He never played another varsity game.

"The other moment that comes to mind happened a few years earlier. We had a player on our team, Steve Janasak, from Ontario. He had a little brother who had come down for the Beanpot and was the same age as my son Billy. The two of them were stick boys on the bench that night against BU. We were getting hammered after the first period and had to walk across the ice from our bench to the locker room with the two boys leading us.

"As we got to the big, spoked Bruins B at center ice, the kid drops down into position to take a face-off. There's fourteen thousand people watching, we're behind in the game, and he has no idea what's going on around him. His total focus was on that center-ice B he had seen so many times on 'Hockey Night in Canada' broadcasting from Boston Garden. Now he was actually there and it was his turn to take a face-off."

We would be remiss to let the hero escape without describing, himself, the definitive goal of the tournament's first quarter-century—Cleary's overtime game-winner versus Boston College in 1955. Snooks Kelley's version is well known; now the Renaissance man receives equal time:

"BC had tied the game with two late goals by Dick Dempsey. We got a penalty, with seconds left in the third period. Before the overtime I was feeling sick and I went over to the bench and took off my shoulder pads. As we were killing the penalty in our zone, one of our guys deflected a pass intended for Dick Gagliardi [later head coach at Yale], just a little flick of his stick that sent the puck out toward the blue line. Snooks Kelley always needled me by saying I was out of position reading *Playboy* when the puck came to me. Hey, we were shorthanded. I saw the puck and raced after it and beat their defensemen. I had a breakaway from my own blue line. I was going in alone on their goalie, Chick D'Entremont. Now, when I had a chance like that, I used to come down the right wing and cut across the goal to my backhand, so I faked as if I was going to cut across and Chickie started to lean that way. That's when I went back to my forehand and scored. As the years have gone by, [the myth surrounding] the goal grew and grew. Somebody even swore that I was skating backwards when I scored."

Not Snooks Kelley. He had his *Playboy* story—and he stuck to it for thirty years.

Hall of Fame

Tony Amonte
Boston University Forward 1990–91
The 1991 Beanpot Most Valuable Player; in the title game, after taking a bone-jarring check and being down on the ice for several minutes, got back up to score an amazing second-period hat trick within a span of 5:24 to lead the Terriers past Boston College for the championship; finished collegiate career with 56-70-126 in only 79 games with the Terriers; left after two years to play in the NHL.

Dave Archambault
Northeastern Defenseman 1977–80
The Most Valuable Player of the 1980 Beanpot, the first ever won by Northeastern; played over forty minutes in each of NU's upset overtime wins over BU, 6–5 in round one, and BC, 5–4 in the championship; was elected co-captain as a junior and senior; voted team MVP as a junior and senior; one of only eight two-year captains for the Huskies and also one of only eight two-time team MVPs for NU.

Joe Cavanagh
Harvard Forward 1969–71
The tournament's all-time scoring leader with 7-12-19; led all scorers with 3-5-8 as the Crimson won the 1969 title; a two-time Harvard team Most Valuable Player; ranks fifth in career scoring (60-127-187) and set the school record for single-season assists with 50 as a senior; a three-time first team All-Ivy and All-ECAC pick, earning ECAC Rookie of the Year honors in 1969; a three-time all-American (1969–71).

Art Chisholm
Northeastern Forward 1959–61
Tied for third on all-time Beanpot scoring list with 15 points on six goals and nine assists; led all scorers in 1960 tournament with 2-5-7 line; member of Northeastern's Hall of Fame; set Husky records for most goals (100) and most points (182) when he graduated; remains NU's all-time leader in goals and fourth in points; voted all-America in 1960 and 1961; winner of 1961 Walter Brown Award (Most Outstanding American Player in New England).

Bill Cleary
Harvard Forward 1955; Coach 1971–90; Athletics Director 1990–2001
As a coach for 19 seasons, collected 324 wins, a National Championship in 1989, two ECAC Tournament titles, four Beanpots, and eleven Ivy League crowns; as a player, established single-tournament Beanpot scoring record (7-4-11) that still stands today, and led the Crimson to the 1955 Beanpot title; his shorthanded overtime game-winning goal against Boston College in the '55 final is arguably the most legendary in tournament annals; member of the 1960 U.S. Olympic gold-medal team.

John Cullen
Boston University Forward 1984–87
The Terriers' all-time leading scorer with 241 points in 160 games; starred on the team's 1986 and 1987 Beanpot-winning teams; in the 1986 tournament, had two goals and three assists, highlighted by a pair of assists in the 4–1 title-game victory over BC; the following year, in the title game against Northeastern, assisted on the game-tying goal, helping the Terriers to go on for a 4–3 overtime win.

John Cunniff
Boston College Forward 1964–66
A member of the 1964 and 1965 Beanpot championship teams and Most Valuable Player in both tournaments; scored 153 career points in 75 games at the Heights; was 1965 All-East Most Valuable Player and 1966 Walter Brown Award winner; a two-time all-American and three-time All-New England selection; member (1968) and an assistant coach (1998) of U.S. Olympic teams.

Ferny Flaman
Northeastern Coach 1970–89
Won Beanpot titles in 1980, '84, '85, and '88; provided the tournament's most dramatic moment—Northeastern's initial win in 1980—and, in 1985, its most emotional when, upon winning, the Huskies presented the Beanpot to Flaman's terminally ill son Terry; member of the College Hockey and the NHL hall of fame; was named coach of the year in 1982 after winning the ECAC tournament and advancing to the Frozen Four; the winningest coach in Northeastern's history, with 255 career victories.

Mark Fusco
Harvard Defenseman 1980–83
Led the Crimson to the 1981 Beanpot title; tournament scoring co-leader as a freshman in '80; holds three school records for scoring by a defenseman; a four-time first team All-Ivy pick, three-time all-American and 1983 Hobey Baker Award winner; three-time winner of Harvard's John Tudor Memorial Cup as the team's MVP; was a member of the 1984 U.S. Olympic hockey team and played two years for the NHL's Hartford Whalers.

Herb Gallagher
Northeastern Coach 1952–55; Athletics Director 1956–76
One of the Beanpot's founders; originated the concept of a "Boston Hockey Invitational" along with Boston Garden President Walter Brown; a 1935 graduate of Northeastern, where he earned nine varsity letters in soccer, hockey, and baseball; coached baseball and hockey at NU for 15 seasons; coached NU in first three Beanpots; served NU for 45 years as player, coach, and athletics director; served as NU Athletics Director from 1955 through 1976; member of College Hockey and Northeastern halls of fame.

Walt Greeley
Harvard Forward 1952
Named Most Valuable Player of the first Beanpot in 1952; scored overtime game-winner versus Boston College in 1952 semifinals, propelling Crimson into finals against BU, where he netted a hat trick to lead Harvard to a 7–4 win; finished inaugural tournament with four goals and two assists; captained the team as a senior in 1952–53, helping the Crimson to an 11-5-1 overall record.

Billy Hogan
Boston College Forward 1961–63
A member of the Eagles' 1961 and 1963 Beanpot championship teams; had an 8-4-12 Beanpot career line; scored four goals and two assists en route to the 1961 title; 1963 Beanpot Most Valuable Player with one goal and two assists in the tournament; scored 130 points in 84 career games at Boston College; a 1962 all-American; the winner of the Walter Brown Award in 1963; a two-time All-East and All-New England selection.

Jack Kelley
Boston University Coach 1963–72
Graduated in 1952, about six months before the first Beanpot was played; instead, he established his own Beanpot lore as one of the tournament's most successful coaches; from 1963–72, his teams advanced to title games nine times and won the Beanpot six times; his overall Beanpot winning percentage (.750) ranks third, while his overall record as a Terriers coach was 204-78-8 (.721).

John "Snooks" Kelley
Boston College Coach 1952–72
Led Boston College to eight of the first thirteen Beanpot titles; won three straight titles (1963–65), marking the first time a school would win three in a row; coached the Eagles to the 1949 national championship and eight NCAA tournaments; the first collegiate coach to win 500 games; Spencer Penrose Award winner in 1959; inducted into the U.S. Hockey Hall of Fame and received the NHL's Lester Patrick Trophy in 1972.

Gene Kinasewich
Harvard Forward 1962–64
Played in 1962 and 1963 Beanpot finals; helped the Crimson defeat Boston College (6–1) and Boston University (5–0) to capture the 1962 Beanpot title; named Most Valuable Player as he shared the scoring title (2-4-6); as a sophomore and senior, led the Crimson in scoring; is among top-10 all-time for Harvard in career goals (61); All-ECAC pick when a senior.

Bob Marquis
Boston University Forward 1958–60
One of the most prolific scorers in Beanpot and Boston University hockey history; in the 1958 tournament's title game, helped lead the Terriers to a 9–3 win over Northeastern; the following year, he

was the Beanpot's leading scorer, with 3-4-7; in six Beanpot games covering three years, finished with 8-8-16 and is tied for second on the tournament's career scoring list; had a career 98-66-164 line in 73 games with the Terriers.

Tom "Red" Martin
Boston College Defenseman 1959–61
Won the Beanpot with Boston College in 1959 and 1961; first defenseman to be honored as Most Valuable Player (1961); netted three goals and three assists in the 1961 tournament; an all-American in both 1960 and 1961; was an All-New England and All-East selection each of his three seasons; third among BC defensemen in career scoring (23-111-134) and second in career assists; member of the 1964 U.S. Olympic team.

Rick Meagher
Boston University Forward 1974–77
Only Terrier to named first-team all-American three times; played on teams that won four consecutive ECAC titles; appeared in four straight NCAA tournaments; played in four Beanpot finals, including on the 1975 winning team; best Beanpot game was the '76 tournament opener against Harvard, in which he had one goal and two assists; 5-8-13 line in eight Beanpot games; 90 goals and 120 assists for 210 points in 124 games while at Boston University.

Joe Mullen
Boston College Forward 1976–79
A member of the 1976 Beanpot championship team; scored four goals during the 1979 tournament; a two-time all-American; when he graduated, held the Eagles' record for career scoring, goals, and assists (110-102-212); Walter Brown Award recipient in 1978; an 18-year NHL veteran, he was inducted into the National Hockey League Hall of Fame in 2000; member of three Stanley Cup winning teams; all-time leading American-born point scorer (1,063) in the NHL.

Jack O'Callahan
Boston University Defenseman 1976–79
A member of the Terriers' 1978 and 1979 Beanpot title teams; was the Most Valuable Player of the 1978 "Blizzard Beanpot" after scoring 1-5-6 in the two games; that year (1977–78), the Terriers finished with a 30-2 record and won the NCAA title; during his collegiate career, finished with 18-102-120 in 121 games; went on to play on the 1980 U.S. Olympic Hockey Team, which won the gold medal in Lake Placid, N.Y.

Jack Parker
Boston University Forward 1966–68
Coach 1974–Present
As a player and coach, has won the Beanpot 19 times; won three straight Beanpots (1966 to 1968) as a player for Boston University; that success has carried through during his illustrious career as a coach—his teams have won the title a record 16 times, including a record six consecutive times from

1995 to 2000; has a .750 winning percentage in the Beanpot; has won over 600 games and coached over 1,000 for BU; has won two NCAA titles and five Hockey East titles.

Eddie Powers
Beanpot Tournament Founder 1952
As Boston Garden President Walter Brown's top associate, then as president of the Garden himself (1964–73), Powers was the heart of the Beanpot, which he warmly referred to as "our little college tournament"; under his guidance, the Beanpot rewarded him by becoming one of the Garden's top yearly attractions; Powers worked at the Garden from its opening in 1928 until his death in 1973.

Bruce Racine
Northeastern Goalie 1985–88
Led Northeastern to titles when he was a freshman (1985) and again in 1988; both won the Eberly Trophy and was named Most Valuable Player each year—the only goalie to win two Beanpot MVPs; the tournament's all-time save leader (237); was named all-American and All-New England in 1987 and 1988; led NU to the Hockey East Championship in 1988, where he was again named MVP; holds five different Northeastern goaltending records and is a member of the university's hall of fame.

Randy Roth
Harvard Forward 1973–75
Played in two Beanpot finals; led the Crimson to the 1974 title with a 2-1-3 MVP performance in the championship game; posted 4-5-9 overall for his Beanpot career; named the 1974 ECAC Player of the Year, and was an All-ECAC and all-American pick as both a junior and a senior; helped the Crimson to two NCAA semifinals appearances; twelfth in all-time career scoring (54-88-142) in Harvard's annals.

Tim Sheehy
Boston College Forward 1967–70
Played in the 1970 Beanpot championship game; recorded 15 career points (nine goals, six assists) in the Beanpot; graduated as Boston College's career scoring leader (74-111-185 in 80 games) and still ranks in the top 10; two-time all-American, two-time Walter Brown Award winner, two-time All-East, and three-time All-New England selection; All-East Most Valuable Player (1970); captained the 1972 U.S. Olympics team.

Paul Skidmore
Boston College Goalie 1976–79
As a freshman, led Boston College to the 1976 Beanpot title with a 36-save effort against Boston University; awarded both the Most Valuable Player and Eberly Awards that year (1979); as a senior (1979), won a second Eberly Award when the Eagles fell in the final to Boston University; fourth in Boston College career saves (2,761) and third in career wins (55); a two-time All-New England and All-East selection (1976, 1977).

Ritchie Smith
Boston College Forward 1973–76
Led the Eagles to the 1976 Beanpot title; scored four goals and twelve assists in eight career Beanpot games; in his freshman-year Beanpot game (1974)—Boston College's 9–8 overtime victory over Northeastern—netted four assists; added one goal and two assists in 1976 championship game; is BC's fifth-leading career scorer, with 94 goals and 104 assists for 198 points; led the Eagles in scoring in each of his four years at the Heights.

Vic Stanfield
Boston University Defenseman 1973–75
The top-scoring defenseman in Beanpot history with 4-11-15 from 1972 to 1975; during his sophomore year, had 1-5-6 as he became the first defenseman in Beanpot history to lead the tournament in scoring; in 1975, he had 2-4-6, again leading in tournament scoring; each of those years, the Terriers won the tournament, and he was named the Most Valuable Player; finished his Terrier career with a 31-129-160 line in 92 games.

Wayne Turner
Northeastern Forward 1977–80
Known as "Beanpot" Turner for his overtime goal to defeat Boston College 4–3 in 1980 to give Northeastern its first ever Beanpot championship; in the opening round of the '80 Beanpot, scored two goals in a 6–5 overtime upset win over Boston University; member of Northeastern's Hall of Fame; graduated with 108 points to place eighteenth in NU records; had 51 goals and 57 assists in 102 career games; was co-captain of 1979–80 team.

Herb Wakabayashi
Boston University Forward 1967–69
A two-time all-American; helped the Terriers to win the 1967 and 1968 Beanpot titles; in the 1967 tournament, had six assists—a record he still shares with Boston College's Billy Daley and the Terriers' David Silk; 1967 Beanpot MVP; the following year, had two goals and three assists in Boston University's 7–4 opening-night win over Northeastern; finished his collegiate career with 55-90-145 in 92 games; played for his native Japanese hockey team at the 1992 Olympics in Sapporo.

Ralph "Cooney" Weiland
Harvard Coach 1952–71
Coached the Crimson to the first Beanpot title in 1952; captured five tournament crowns; played on the Bruins' first Stanley Cup championship squad in 1929 and coached the Bruins when they won the 1941 Cup; as the Harvard coach, won two ECAC tournament crowns and five Beanpot titles, compiling 315 wins in his 21-year tenure; in both the 1954–55 and 1970–71 seasons, won the Spencer Penrose trophy for National Coach of the Year.

Eberly Award Winners

The Eberly Award, first presented in 1974, is given annually to the Beanpot goalie with the best save percentage. The winning goalie must participate in two games to qualify. The award is named after Glen and Dan Eberly, former Beanpot goaltenders for Boston University and Northeastern University, respectively.

Year	Player (School)	Saves	Goals	Save %	GAA
1974	Ed Walsh (BU)	50	6	.893	3.00
1975	Brian Durocher (BU)	54	5	.915	2.50
1976	Paul Skidmore (BC)	70	6	.921	3.00
1977	Brian Petrovek (HU)	46	5	.902	2.50
1978	Ed Arrington (NU)	51	7	.879	3.50
1979	Paul Skidmore (BC)	57	6	.905	3.00
1980	George Demetroulakas (NU)	40	9	.816	4.50
1981	Wade Lau (HU)	36	2	.947	1.00
1982	Bob O'Connor (BC)	67	5	.930	2.50
1983	Bill Switaj (BC)	58	6	.906	3.00
1984	Tim Marshall (NU)	54	5	.915	2.50
1985	Bruce Racine (NU)	63	4	.940	2.00
1986	Scott Gordon (BC)	51	6	.895	3.00
1987	Terry Taillefer (BU)	70	6	.921	3.00
1988	Bruce Racine (NU)	50	3	.943	1.50
1989	Rich Burchill (NU)	67	9	.882	4.50
1990	Scott Cashman (BU)	52	5	.912	2.50
1991	Tom Cole (NU)	86	5	.945	2.50
1992	Scott Cashman (BU)	59	6	.908	3.00
1993	Scott Cashman (BU)	41	6	.872	3.00
1994	Greg Taylor (BC)	66	5	.930	2.11
1995	Derek Herlofsky (BU)	51	3	.944	1.50
1996	Tom Noble (BU)	52	5	.912	2.64
1997	Marc Robitaille (NU)	68	4	.944	2.00
1998	Marc Robitaille (NU)	75	7	.915	3.51
1999	Michel Larocque (BU)	65	4	.942	1.92
2000	Rick DiPietro (BU)	52	1	.981	0.50
2001	Scott Clemmensen (BC)	36	4	.900	2.00
2002	Matti Kaltiainen (BC)	42	4	.913	2.02

Most Valuable Players

Year	MVP	School	Position
1952	Walt Greeley	Harvard	F
1954	Bob Babine	Boston College	F
1955	Billy Cleary	Harvard	F
1956	James Tiernan	Boston College	F
1957	Joe Celeta	Boston College	F
1958	Bill Sullivan	Boston University	F
1959	Jim Logue	Boston College	G
1960	Bob Bland	Harvard	G
1961	Tom Martin	Boston College	D
1962	Gene Kinasewich	Harvard	F
1963	Billy Hogan	Boston College	F
1964	John Cunniff	Boston College	F
1965	John Cunniff	Boston College	F
1966	Tom Ross	Boston University	D
1967	Herb Wakabayashi	Boston University	F
1968	Jim McCann	Boston University	G
1969	Joe Cavanagh	Harvard	F
1970	Mike Hyndman	Boston University	D
1971	Steve Stirling	Boston University	F
1972	Dan Brady	Boston University	G
	John Danby	Boston University	F
1973	Vic Stanfield	Boston University	D
1974	Randy Roth	Harvard	F
1975	Vic Stanfield	Boston University	D
1976	Paul Skidmore	Boston College	G
1977	Brian Petrovek	Harvard	G
1978	Jack O'Callahan	Boston University	D
1979	Daryl MacLeod	Boston University	F
1980	Dave Archambault	Northeastern	D
1981	Wade Lau	Harvard	G
1982	Tom O'Regan	Boston University	F
1983	Bob Sweeney	Boston College	F
1984	Tim Marshall	Northeastern	G
1985	Bruce Racine	Northeastern	G
1986	Terry Taillefer	Boston University	G
1987	Mike Kelfer	Boston University	F
1988	Bruce Racine	Northeastern	G
1989	Lane MacDonald	Harvard	F
1990	David Tomlinson	Boston University	F
1991	Tony Amonte	Boston University	F
1992	Mike Prendergast	Boston University	F
1993	Ted Drury	Harvard	F
1994	Greg Taylor	Boston College	G
1995	Ken Rausch	Boston University	F
1996	Chris Drury	Boston University	F
1997	Bill Pierce	Boston University	F
1998	Tom Poti	Boston University	D
1999	Michel Larocque	Boston University	G
2000	Rick DiPietro	Boston University	G
2001	Krys Kolanos	Boston College	F
2002	Justin Maiser	Boston University	F

Beanpot Records

All-Time Beanpot Coaching Records

Coach	Team	Tournaments	Years	W-L	Pct.	Finishes
Leon Abbott	BU	1	1973	2-0	1.000	1-0-0-0
James Bell	NU	15	1956-70	6-24	0.200	0-2-4-9
Steve Cedorchuk	BC	2	1993-94	2-2	0.500	1-0-0-1
Len Ceglarski	BC	20	1973-92	19-21	0.475	2-7-8-3
Bill Cleary	HU	19	1972-90	17-21	0.447	4-4-5-6
Harry Cleverly	BU	10	1952-62	10-10	0.500	1-5-3-1
Bruce Crowder	NU	6	1997-Pres.	4-8	0.333	0-2-2-2
Fern Flaman	NU	19	1971-89	14-24	0.368	4-2-4-9
Herb Gallagher	NU	3	1952-55	0-6	0.000	0-0-0-3
Jack Kelley	BU	10	1963-72	15-5	0.750	6-3-0-1
John Kelley	BC	20	1952-72	26-14	0.650	8-2-8-2
Mark Mazzoleni	HU	3	2000-Pres.	1-5	0.167	0-0-1-1
Don McKenney	NU	2	1990-91	1-3	0.250	0-0-1-1
Jack Parker	BU	29	1974-Pres.	44-14	0.760	16-9-3-1
Ben Smith	NU	5	1992-96	3-7	0.300	0-1-2-2
Ronn Tomassoni	HU	9	1991-99	5-13	0.277	1-3-0-5
Ralph Weiland	HU	19	1952-71	22-16	0.579	5-7-5-2
Jerry York	BC	8	1995-Pres.	9-7	0.563	1-3-4-0

Career Scoring Leaders

Player (School)	Years	GP	G	A	Pts
Joe Cavanagh (HU)	1969-71	6	7	12	19
Tim Sheehy (BC)	1968-70	6	9	7	16
Bob Marquis (BU)	1958-60	6	8	8	16
Richie Smith (BC)	1973-76	8	4	12	16
Lane MacDonald (HU)	1985-89	8	6	9	15
Art Chisholm (NU)	1959-61	6	6	9	15
Vic Stanfield (BU)	1972-74	6	4	11	15
Bill Daley (BC)	1959-61	6	4	11	15
Bob Cleary (HU)	1956-58	6	6	8	14
Mike Sullivan (BU)	1987-90	8	4	10	14
Shawn McEachern (BU)	1989-91	6	4	10	14
Billy Hogan (BC)	1961-63	6	9	4	13
Steve Owen (HU)	1969-71	6	7	6	13
Todd Johnson (BU)	1978-81	8	6	7	13
Dave Poile (NU)	1968-70	6	6	7	13
Rick Meagher (BU)	1974-77	8	5	8	13
David Tomlinson (BU)	1988-91	8	4	9	13
Bob Sweeney (BC)	1983-86	8	4	9	13
Scott Harlow (BC)	1983-86	8	6	6	12
Scott Fusco (HU)	1982-86	8	6	6	12
Dan DeMichele (HU)	1969-71	6	6	6	12
David O'Brien (NU)	1985-88	8	5	7	12
Dave Silk (BU)	1977-80	6	3	9	12
Herb Wakabayashi (BU)	1967-69	6	2	10	12

Scoring Records

Goals

Period	4 Billy Cleary (HU) vs. Northeastern, 1955 (HU, 12-3)
Game	5 Billy Cleary (HU) vs. Northeastern, 1955 (HU, 12-3)
	5 Ed Sullivan (BC) vs. Northeastern, 1961 (BC, 15-1)
	5 Mike Powers (BC) vs. Northeastern, 1973 (BC, 9-8)
Tournament	7 Billy Cleary (HU), 1955
Career	10 Joe Mullen (BC), 1976-79

Assists

Game	6 Billy Daley (BC) vs. Northeastern, 1961 (BC, 15-1)
Tournament	6 Billy Daley (BC), 1961
	6 David Silk (BU), 1977
	6 Herb Wakabayashi (BU), 1967
Career	12 Joe Cavanagh (HU), 1969-71
	12 Richie Smith (BC), 1973-76

Points

Period	5 Billy Cleary (HU) vs. Northeastern, 1955 (HU, 12-3), 4-1-5
Game	7 Billy Cleary (HU) vs. Northeastern, 1955 (HU, 12-3), 5-2-7
Tournament	11 Billy Cleary (HU), 1955, 7-4-11
Career	19 Joe Cavanagh (HU), 1969-71 6 gp; 7-12-19

Goaltending

Career Leaders (Two-tournament minimum)

Player (School)	GP	Periods	Saves	GA	Sv %	Years
Michel Larocque (BU)	4	13	115	6	.950	1997-99
Dan Brady (BU)	4	6	98	6	.942	1971-72
Jim McCann (BU)	3	9	79	5	.940	1967-68
Marc Robitaille (NU)	4	12	143	11	.929	1997-98
Tom Noble (BU)	4	12	96	8	.923	1995-98
Ed Walsh (BU)	4	12	109	10	.916	1973-74
Bob O'Connor (BC)	5	15	150	14	.915	1980-82
Sandy Galuppo (BC)	4	12	108	10	.915	1989-91
Tom Cole (NU)	3	12	107	10	.915	1990-91
Terry Taillefer (BU)	4	12	128	12	.914	1983-87
Bob Bland (HU)	5	15	117	12	.907	1960-62
Cleon Daskalakis (BU)	4	12	127	13	.907	1981-84
Godfrey Wood (HU)	3	9	58	6	.906	1962-63
Scott Cashman (BU)	6	18	156	17	.902	1990-93
Bob Barich (BU)	4	12	120	13	.902	1980-83
Greg Taylor (BC)	8	27	226	25	.900	1994-97
Paul Skidmore (BC)	8	24	235	28	.894	1976-79
Jim Craig (BU)	5	15	121	15	.890	1976-79
Scott Clemmensen (BC)	7	23	136	17	.889	1998-01
Bruce Racine (NU)	8	26	237	30	.888	1985-88
Charlie Flynn (HU)	6	18	130	18	.878	1954-56
Wade Lau (HU)	4	12	77	11	.875	1980-82

Shutouts

Year	Player (School)	Game
1952	Joe Carroll (BC) vs. Northeastern, 2-0	Consolation
1957	Al Pitts (BC) vs. Northeastern, 6-0	Semifinal
1959	Harry Pratt (HU) vs. Northeastern, 4-0	Consolation
1962	Godfrey Wood (HU) vs. Boston University, 5-0	Championship
1962	Charlie Driscoll (BC) vs. Northeastern, 4-0	Consolation
1967	Jim McCann (BU) vs. Northeastern, 4-0	Championship
1970	Jim Barton (BC) vs. Northeastern, 5-0	Semifinal
1975	Brian Petrovek (HU) vs. Northeastern, 9-0	Semifinal
1981	Wade Lau (HU) vs. Boston University, 2-0	Championship
1988	Bruce Racine (NU) vs. Boston College, 4-0	Semifinal
1991	Tom Cole (NU) vs. Harvard, 5-0	Consolation
1997	Marc Robitaille (NU) vs. Harvard, 2-0	Consolation
2000	Scott Clemmensen (BC) vs. Northeastern, 6-0	Semifinal
2000	Rick DiPietro (BU) vs. Harvard, 4-0	Semifinal
2002	Matti Kaltiainen (BC) vs. Harvard, 4-0	Consolation

Saves

Game	52 Jim Barton (BC) vs. Boston University, 1970
Tournament	91 Bill Fitzsimmons (HU) (8 goals allowed), 1965
Career	237 Bruce Racine (NU) (30 goals allowed), 1985-88

Penalty Shots

Beanpot Penalty Shots

Shooter (Team)	Opponent	Date	Time	Period	Result
T. Sheehy (BC)	NU	2/12/68	6:26	2nd	scored
B. Goodenow (HU)	BC	2/4/74	10:59	2nd	scored
R. Smith (BC)	BU	2/3/75	11:39	2nd	scored
W. Turner (NU)	HU	2/12/79	7:09	2nd	stopped
D. Burke (HU)	NU	2/12/79	18:15	2nd	scored

APPENDIX D

Results and Scoring 1952–2002

1st December 26, 1952 (5,105)
Boston University 4, Northeastern 1
1st Period
   (BU) Rodenheiser (Lee)
2nd Period
   (BU) Whalen (Lee)
3rd Period
   (BU) Burns (Cleary)
   (BU) Denning (Rodenheiser)
   (NU) Smith (Campion)
Goalies: (BU) Kelley, (NU) Picard
Harvard 3, Boston College 2 (OT)
1st Period
   (HU) Clasby (Greeley, Hubbard)
   (BC) O'Grady (unassisted)
2nd Period
   (BC) Maguire (Saltmarsh)
3rd Period
   (HU) Clasby (unassisted)
Overtime
   (HU) Greeley (Hubbard)
Goalies: (HU) Richardson, (BC) Carroll

December 27, 1952 (3,382)
Boston College 2, Northeastern 0
1st Period
   (BC) Burtnett (Babine, Canniff)
2nd Period
   No Scoring
3rd Period
   (BC) O'Grady (Babine, Burtnett)
Goalies: (NU) Picard, (BC) Carroll, Tarkey
Harvard 7, Boston University 4
1st Period
   (HU) Chase (unassisted)
2nd Period
   (HU) Greeley (Chase)
   (BU) Ccoria (unassisted)
   (HU) Greeley (unassisted)
   (HU) Manchester (unassisted)
3rd Period
   (BU) Zanetti (Whalen)
   (HU) Bliss (Bray)
   (HU) Greeley (Hubbard)
   (BU) Whalen (Kelley)
   (BU) Rodenheiser (unassisted)
   (HU) Hubbard (Greeley)
Goalies: (HU) Richardson, (BU) Kelley

2nd January 11, 1954 (711)
Harvard 3, Boston University 2
1st Period
   (BU) Murphy (Burns)
   (HU) Clasby (Mahoney)
2nd Period
   (HU) Bliss (unassisted)
   (HU) Cooledge (unassisted)
3rd Period
   (BU) Murphy (unassisted)
Goalies: (HU) Flynn, (BU) Bradley

Boston College 8, Northeastern 5
1st Period
   (BC) Duffy (Gallagher)
   (NU) Gilbody (Booker, Kelley)
2nd Period
   (BC) Canniff (Kiley)
   (NU) Vorderer (unassitsted)
   (NU) Gilbody (Kelley)
   (NU) Lally (Vorderer)
   (BC) Duffy (Gallagher, Cisternelli)
3rd Period
   (BC) Canniff (Babine, Gagliardi)
   (BC) Babine (Canniff, Gagliardi)
   (NU) Doherty (Watson)
   (BC) Forgues (unassisted)
Goalies: (BC) D'Entremont, (NU) Whynot

January 12, 1954 (2,399)
Boston University 5, Northeastern 3
1st Period
   (BU) Gurberg (unassisted)
   (BU) Dwyer (Driscoll)
   (BU) Murphy (unassisted)
   (NU) Dronsieko (Kelley)
2nd Period
   No Scoring
3rd Period
   (NU) Lally (Grayton, Vorderer)
   (BU) Driscoll (Dwyer)
   (BU) Driscoll (unassisted)
   (NU) Gilbody (unassisted)
Goalies: (BU) Bradley, (NU)
Boston College 4, Harvard 1
1st Period
   No Scoring
2nd Period
   (HU) Wood (Bray)
   (BC) Duffy (unassisted)
   (BC) Gallagher (Duffy)
3rd Period
   (BC) Babine (unassisted)
   (BC) Duffy (Canniff)
Goalies: (HU) Flynn, (BC) D'Entremont

3rd February 7, 1955 (2,560)
Harvard 12, Northeastern 3
1st Period
   (HU) Mahoney (Cooledge, Noyes)
   (HU) Crehore (Cleary, O'Malley)
   (HU) Manchester (unassisted)
2nd Period
   (HU) Cooledge (unassisted)
   (HU) O'Malley (Crehore)
   (HU) Cleary (Crehore)
3rd Period
   (HU) Cleary (unassisted)
   (NU) Lally (Williamson)
   (HU) Manchester (Cleary)
   (NU) Johanson (Vorderer)
   (HU) Cleary (unassisted)
   (HU) Little (Worthen)
   (HU) Cleary (Manchester)
   (NU) Lally (Bryant)
   (HU) Cleary (Manchester)
Goalies: (HU) Flynn, (NU) Lawn

Boston College 9, Boston University 5
1st Period
   (BC) Quinn (Moylan, Carroll)
   (BC) Tiernan (unassisted)
   (BC) Coakley (Tiernan)
   (BU) Dwyer (Quinn)
   (BC) Marino (Fox, Coakley)
2nd Period
   (BU) Murphy (Buell, Burns)
   (BU) Dwyer (Quinn)
   (BU) Murphy (Burns, Quinn)
3rd Period
   (BU) Murphy (Maddison)
   (BC) Moylan (unassisted)
   (BC) Coakley (Fox)
   (BC) Marino (Moylan)
   (BC) Donlan (Marino)
   (BC) Carroll (Tiernan, Gagliardi)
Goalies: (BC) D'Entremont, (BU) Aiken

February 8, 1955 (5,654)
Boston University 4, Northeastern 3
1st Period
   (BU) Murphy (McAdoo)
   (NU) Cavanaugh (Vorderer)
2nd Period
   (NU) Vorderer (Bryant)
3rd Period
   (NU) Buckley (Cavanaugh)
   (BU) Murphy (Manning)
   (BU) McComb (Quinn)
   (BU) Dwyer (McComb, Quinn)
Goalies: (BU) Aiken, (NU) Lawn
Harvard 5, Boston College 4 (OT)
1st Period
   (BC) Moylan (Marino)
   (HU) Little (unassisted)
   (HU) Cleary (Manchester)
2nd Period
   (BC) Quinn (Emery)
   (HU) Manchester (Cleary)
   (HU) O'Malley (Cleary)
3rd Period
   (BC) Dempsey (Tiernan)
   (BC) Dempsey (Carroll)
Overtime
   (HU) Cleary (Almy)
Goalies: (HU) Flynn, (BC) D'Entremont

4th February 6, 1956 (2,500)
Boston College 7, Northeastern 1
1st Period
   No Scoring
2nd Period
   (BC) Tiernan (Fox)
   (BC) Quinn (Michaud)
3rd Period
   (BC) Sheehy (Moylan, Fox)
   (BC) Quinn (Kane)
   (BC) Tiernan (Carroll)
   (BC) Fox (unassisted)
   (NU) Vorderer (Cavanaugh)
   (BC) Marino (Moylan, Smith)
Goalies: (BC) D'Entremont, (NU) Lawn

Harvard 6, Boston University 1
1st Period
    (HU) Ullyott (Owen, Crehore)
    (BU) Carriere (R. MacLeod)
    (HU) Summers (Cleary)
2nd Period
    (HU) Guttu (Summers, Cleary)
    (HU) Owen (unassisted)
    (HU) Crehore (Ullyott)
3rd Period
    (HU) Holmes (Copeland, Noyes)
Goalies: (HU) Flynn, (BU) Levin

February 8, 1956 (4,000)

Boston University 9, Northeastern 3
1st Period
    (NU) Vorderer (unassisted)
    (BU) Manning (Carruthers)
2nd Period
    (BU) Cicoria (Murphy)
    (BU) Sweeney (Sullivan, D. MacLeod)
    (BU) Sullivan (unassisted)
    (BU) Carriere (Dupuis)
    (BU) Cicoria (Murphy)
3rd Period
    (BU) Kinlin (unassisted)
    (BU) Manning (unassisted)
    (NU) Bryant (unassisted)
    (NU) Vorderer (unassisted)
    (BU) Kinlin (Cicoria)
Goalies: (BU) Levin, (NU) Lawn

Boston College 4, Harvard 2
1st Period
    (HU) Celi (unassisted)
    (BC) Carroll (Gagliardi)
2nd Period
    (BC) Quinn (Smith, Michaud)
    (BC) Carroll (Leary)
    (HU) Cleary (unassisted)
3rd Period
    (BC) Tiernan (Carroll)
Goalies: (HU) Flynn, (BC) D'Entremont

5th February 1, 1957 (4,038)

Boston College 6, Northeastern 0
1st Period
    (BC) Celata (unassisted)
2nd Period
    (BC) Celata (Tiernan)
    (BC) Celata (Coakley, Tiernan)
3rd Period
    (BC) Leary (Kane)
    (BC) Celata (Coakley, Tiernan)
    (BC) Marino (Sheehy, Fox)
Goalies: (BC) Pitts, (NU) Kerr

Boston University 5, Harvard 3
1st Period
    (HU) Guttu (Cleary)
    (HU) Vietze (Fischer)
2nd Period
    (HU) Kelley (Guttu, Owen)
    (BU) Carriere (Sweeney, Sullivan)
    (BU) Carruthers (Dupuis)

3rd Period
    (BU) Quinn (unassisted)
    (BU) McLeod (unassisted)
    (BU) Sullivan (unassisted)
Goalies: (HU) Bailey, (BU) Levin

February 5, 1957 (4,038)

Harvard 5, Northeastern 3
1st Period
    (NU) Cavanaugh (Salvucci)
2nd Period
    (HU) McVey (Owen)
    (NU) Salvucci (Cavanaugh)
    (HU) Cleary (unassisted)
    (HU) Guttu (Kelley, Cleary)
3rd Period
    (HU) Kelley (Guttu, Cleary)
    (HU) Reilly (McLaughlin)
    (NU) Bell (Spofford, O'Connor)
Goalies: (HU) Bailey, (NU) Kerr

Boston College 5, Boston University 4 (OT)
1st Period
    (BU) Kinlin (Manning)
2nd Period
    (BU) Kinlin (Manning, Cicoria)
    (BC) Bunyon (Kane)
    (BU) Creighton (Quinn)
3rd Period
    (BC) Kane (unassisted)
    (BC) Fox (Kane)
    (BU) Kinlin (Dupuis)
    (BC) Bunyon (Fox, Kane)
Overtime
    Celeta (unassisted)
Goalies: (BC) Pitts, (BU) Levin

6th February 3, 1958 (6,117)

Northeastern 5, Harvard 4
1st Period
    (HU) Cleary (McVey)
    (NU) Cronin (Lambert)
2nd Period
    (HU) Vietze (McVey)
    (HU) Kelley (Graney, Owen)
    (NU) Lambert (Cronin)
3rd Period
    (HU) Gillie (Vietze)
    (NU) Pareski (Lambert)
    (NU) Cronin (Lambert)
    (NU) Cronin (Lambert)
Goalies: (HU) Cleary, (NU) Kerr

Boston University 5, Boston College 4
1st Period
    (BC) Bunyon (Kane, Cassidy)
    (BU) Marquis (Kinlin, Sweeney)
    (BU) Sullivan (Creighton, Carruthers)
2nd Period
    (BC) Cusack (Pergola)
    (BU) Dupuis (Carruthers)
    (BU) Keith (D. MacLeod, McCormack)
3rd Period
    (BC) Mahoney (Cassidy)
    (BC) O'Neill (Mahoney, Walsh)
    (BU) Marquis (Kinlin, Sweeney)
Goalies: (BC) Pitts, (BU) Tansey

February 10, 1958 (4,784)

Harvard 7, Boston College 1
1st Period
    (HU) Fischer (McVey, Owen)
2nd Period
    (HU) Guttu (Cleary)
    (BC) Walsh (Madden, Mahoney)
    (BC) Kane (Bunyon)
    (BC) Bunyon (Kane)
3rd Period
    (HU) McLaughlin (Cleary, Guttu)
    (HU) Cleary (Guttu)
    (HU) Cleary (unassisted)
    (HU) Guttu (Cleary)
    (HU) Cleary (Duncan)
Goalies: (HU) Pratt, (BC) Pitts

Boston University 9, Northeastern 3
1st Period
    (BU) Sullivan (Creighton)
    (BU) Sullivan (Carruthers, Creighton)
    (NU) Walsh (Wenham, Bell)
    (BU) Don MacLeod (unassisted)
2nd Period
    (BU) Sweeney (Dupuis)
    (BU) Sullivan (Carruthers)
    (BU) Don MacLeod (Carruthers, Creighton)
3rd Period
    (BU) Dave MacLeod (McCormack, Keith)
    (BU) Dave MacLeod (Dupuis)
    (NU) Paresky (Cronin)
    (NU) Paresky (Lambert, Cronin)
    (BU) Marquis (Dupuis)
Goalies: (BU) Tansey, Levin, (NU) Kerr, Carroll

7th February 2, 1959 (5,920)

Boston College 6, Harvard 4
1st Period
    (HU) Forbes (Snow)
2nd Period
    (BC) O'Neil (Madden)
    (BC) Cusack (Leonard, Pergola)
    (BC) Walsh (Jangro)
3rd Period
    (HU) Higginbottom (Vietze, Graney)
    (BC) Pergola (Leonard, Cusack)
    (BC) Pergola (Leonard, Jangro)
    (HU) Fischer (Higginbottom, Anderson)
    (BC) Hughes (Daley)
    (HU) Kelley (Balboni)
Goalies: (HU) Pratt, (BC) Logue

Boston University 7, Northeastern 4
1st Period
    (BU) Keith (Marquis)
    (NU) Chisholm (Palmer, Spofford)
    (NU) D. Cronin (Paresky, Chisholm)
    (BU) McCormack (DiVencenzio)
    (BU) Quinn (Marquis)
    (BU) Keith (McCann, Quinn)
    (BU) McCurdy (McCann, Keith)
    (NU) G. Cronin (Chisholm, Weisbach)
2nd Period
    (BU) Marquis (Keith, Enright)
    (NU) Chisholm (unassisted)
3rd Period
    (BU) Marquis (Keith)
Goalies: (BU) Tanner, (NU) Carroll

February 9, 1959 (8,180)
Harvard 4, Northeastern 0
1st Period
    No Scoring
2nd Period
    (HU) Higginbottom (Fischer)
3rd Period
    (HU) Vietze (unassisted)
    (HU) Duncan (Collins)
    (HU) Forbes (Crosby)
Goalies: (HU) Pratt, (NU) Carroll
Boston College 7, Boston University 4
1st Period
    (BC) Daley (Martin)
    (BC) Martin (Pergda, Leonard)
    (BC) Boyle (Smith)
    (BC) Cusack (Riley)
2nd Period
    (BC) Martin (Smith)
    (BU) Keith (Marquis)
    (BC) Smith (Daley, Famigletti)
    (BU) Marquis (Creighton)
    (BU) McCormack (Marquis, Creighton)
3rd Period
    (BU) Creighton (unassisted)
    (BC) Smith (unassisted)
Goalies: (BC) Logue, (BU) Tanner

8th February 8, 1960 (10,909)
Harvard 5, Northeastern 3
1st Period
    (HU) Crosby (Forbes, Anderson)
    (HU) Ingalls (Heintzman)
    (HU) Morse (Grannis, Downes)
2nd Period
    (HU) Forbes (Crosby)
    (NU) Chisolm (unassisted)
3rd Period
    (NU) Cronin (Palmer)
    (HU) Morse (Eaton, Beckett)
    (NU) Vient (Waterman)
Goalies: (HU) Bland, (NU) LeBoeuf
Boston University 5, Boston College 2
1st Period
    (BC) Walsh (Hughes, Daley)
    (BU) McCormack (Marquis, Quinn)
    (BU) Goguen (Marquis)
2nd Period
    (BU) MacLeod (Enright, Jarasitis)
3rd Period
    (BU) Marquis (Quinn, McCann)
    (BC) Daley (McCarthy)
    (BU) Marquis (Quinn, McCormack)
Goalies: (BU) Urbanski, (BC) Logue

February 15, 1960 (5,713)
Northeastern 6, Boston College 5
1st Period
    (BC) Leonard (Smith)
2nd Period
    (BC) Daley (unassisted)
    (NU) Cronin (Chisholm)
    (BC) Walsh (Daley, Hughes)
3rd Period
    (NU) Cronin (Weissbach, Chisholm)
    (BC) Cusack (Mullowney)

    (NU) Dutczak (McGrath, McElholm)
    (NU) Weissbach (Chisholm, Cronin)
    (BC) Walsh (Daley, Martin)
    (NU) Cronin (Chisholm, Weissbach)
    (NU) Chisholm (Cronin, Weissbach)
Goalies: (NU) LeBoeuf, (BC) Logue
Harvard 3, Boston University 2
1st Period
    (HU) Morse (unassisted)
2nd Period
    (BU) McCann (Quinn)
3rd Period
    (BU) McCormack (Quinn)
    (HU) Grannis (Graney)
    (HU) Forbes (unassisted)
Goalies: (HU) Bland, (BU) Urbanski

9th February 6, 1961 (5,800)
Boston College 15, Northeastern 1
1st Period
    (BC) Sullivan (Hughes, Daley)
    (BC) Aiken (Lynch)
    (BC) Grant (Giles)
    (BC) Martin (Famigletti, Grant)
    (BC) Sullivan (Hughes, Martin)
    (NU) Connelly (Cronin)
    (BC) Hughes (Daley)
    (BC) Martin (Daley)
2nd Period
    (BC) Sullivan (Daley)
    (BC) Hogan (Leetch, Aiken)
    (BC) Hogan (Aiken)
    (BC) Hogan (Martin, Aiken)
    (BC) Sullivan (Daley, Martin)
3rd Period
    (BC) Hughes (Daley)
    (BC) Hogan (Leetch, Aiken)
    (BC) Sullivan (Larkin)
Goalies: (BC) Logue, (NU) Bishop
Harvard 3, Boston University 2 (OT)
1st Period
    (BU) Quinn (unassisted)
2nd Period
    No Scoring
3rd Period
    (BU) Smith (Denihan, Quinn)
    (HU) Ingalls (Heintzman)
    (HU) Ingalls (Alpine, Anderson)
Overtime
    (HU) Dwinnell (Morse)
Goalies: (HU) Bland, (BU) Urbanski

February 13, 1961 (13,909)
Northeastern 6, Boston University 2
1st Period
    (NU) Delaney (Connelly, Dutczak)
    (NU) Weissbach (Casey, Chisholm)
2nd Period
    (NU) Chisholm (unassisted)
    (BU) Rowan (Spinney, Connors)
    (NU) Chisholm (Casey)
3rd Period
    (BU) Spinney (Connors)
    (NU) Cronin (Chisholm)
Goalies: (BU) Urbanski, (NU) Brannelly

Boston College 4, Harvard 2
1st Period
    (BC) Hogan (unassisted)
2nd Period
    (HU) Ingalls (Alpine, Heintzman)
    (BC) Leetch (Hogan)
3rd Period
    (BC) Martin (Hogan)
    (HU) Alpine (Heintzman, Ingalls)
    (BC) Daley (Sullivan)
Goalies: (HU) Bland, (BC) Logue

10th February 5, 1962 (13,909)
Boston University 5, Northeastern 4
1st Period
    (BU) Welch (Spinney)
    (NU) Boden (Dupere)
2nd Period
    (NU) Frier (Dupere)
    (NU) Delaney (Johnston, Dutczak)
    (NU) Boden (Dupere)
    (BU) Ross (Denihan)
3rd Period
    (BU) Sampson (Denihan)
    (BU) Smith (Sampson, Denihan)
    (BU) Ross (Sampson, Denihan)
Goalies: (BU) Eberly, (NU) Tierney
Harvard 6, Boston College 1
1st Period
    (HU) Kinasewich (Taylor)
    (HU) Grannis (Ikauniks, Patterson)
2nd Period
    (BC) O'Connor (McCarthy, Duffy)
    (HU) Morse (unassisted)
    (HU) Taylor (unassisted)
3rd Period
    (HU) Taylor (Kinasewich, Patterson)
    (HU) Beckett (Kinasewich, Taylor)
Goalies: (HU) Bland, (BC) Apprille

February 12, 1962 (4,500)
Boston College 4, Northeastern 0
1st Period
    (BC) Lufkin (unassisted)
2nd Period
    (BC) Hogan (Aiken)
3rd Period
    (BC) Hogan (Callahan)
    (BC) Hogan (Callahan)
Goalies: (BC) Driscoll, (NU) Tierney
Harvard 5, Boston University 0
1st Period
    (HU) Ikauniks (Grannis)
    (HU) Taylor (Kinasewich)
2nd Period
    (HU) Ikauniks (Jorgenson, Heintzman)
3rd Period
    (HU) Kinasewich (Howell, Dwinnell)
    (HU) Taylor (Grannis)
Goalies: (HU) Wood, (BU) Eberly

11th February 4, 1963 (6,961)
Boston College 2, Boston University 1 (OT)
1st Period
    No Scoring

2nd Period
    (BC) Flaherty (Breen, Sullivan)
3rd Period
    (BU) McCabe (unassisted)
Overtime
    (BC) Hogan (Leetch, Aiken)
Goalies: (BC) Apprille, (BU) Eberly
Harvard 4, Northeastern 3 (OT)
1st Period
    (NU) Rossi (Dupere, McPhee)
2nd Period
    (HU) Taylor (Johnston)
    (NU) McPhee (Rossi, Dupere)
    (HU) Treadwell (Johnston)
    (NU) Lenormand (Powers)
3rd Period
    (HU) Ikauniks (Kinasewich, Taylor)
Overtime
    (HU) Thomas (Treadwell)
Goalies: (HU) Wood, (NU) Capizzo

February 11, 1963 (13,909)
Northeastern 4, Boston University 2
1st Period
    (NU) Dupere (unassisted)
    (NU) Boden (Fitzgerald)
    (BU) Denihan (Smith, Green)
2nd Period
    (NU) Boden (Dupere)
    (NU) Dupere (Boden)
3rd Period
    (BU) Martell (McCabe, Sylvia)
Goalies: (BU) Eberly, (NU) Capizzo
Boston College 3, Harvard 1
1st Period
    (HU) Kinasewich (Thomson, Taylor)
2nd Period
    (BC) Flaherty (unassisted)
3rd Period
    (BC) Aiken (Hogan, Leetch)
    (BC) Leetch (Hogan)
Goalies: (HU) Wood, (BC) Apprille

12th February 3, 1964 (8,396)
Boston College 7, Northeastern 4
1st Period
    (NU) Fitzgerald (Dupere)
    (BC) Flaherty (Kearns, Breen)
    (BC) Dyer (Latshaw)
    (BC) Dyer (Marsh)
2nd Period
    (NU) Rossi (Fitzgerald, Dupere)
    (BC) Flaherty (Toran, Breen)
    (NU) MacGillivray (Seabury, Campbell)
    (NU) MacGillivray (Seabury, Fitzgerald)
3rd Period
    (BC) Breen (Kearns)
    (BC) Downes (Duffy, McMullen)
    (BC) Downes (Cunniff)
Goalies: (BC) Apprille, (NU) Capizzo
Boston University 3, Harvard 2 (2 OT)
1st Period
    (BU) Fennie (Green, Comeau)
    (BU) McCabe (Green, Martell)
2nd Period
    (HU) Smith (Lamarche, Treadwell)

3rd Period
    (HU) Lamarche (Smith, Fryer)
1st Overtime
    No Scoring
2nd Overtime
    (BU) Carter (Conte, Fennie)
Goalies: (HU) Sweitzer, (BU) Ferreira

February 10, 1964 (13,909)
Harvard 7, Northeastern 5
1st Period
    (HU) Kinasewich (unassisted)
    (NU) Dupere (unassisted)
    (HU) Treadwell (Smith)
    (NU) Seabury (unassisted)
    (HU) Kinasewich (Ikauniks)
2nd Period
    (HU) Smith (Lamarche, Treadwell)
    (NU) Seabury (MacGillivray, Campbell)
3rd Period
    (HU) Kinasewich (Patterson)
    (HU) Smith (Clark)
    (NU) Bloh (MacGillivray, Seabury)
    (HU) Kinasewich (Fryer)
    (NU) Seabury (deBlois)
Goalies: (HU) Sweitzer, (NU) Capizzo
Boston College 6, Boston University 5
1st Period
    (BU) McCabe (Martell, Sylvia)
    (BU) Sylvia (McCabe, Green)
    (BC) Dyer (Duffy, Cunniff)
2nd Period
    (BC) Marsh (unassisted)
    (BU) Sylvia (Martell, McCabe)
    (BU) Fennie (unassisted)
3rd Period
    (BC) Cunniff (Toran)
    (BC) Flaherty (unassisted)
    (BC) Lufkin (Movian)
    (BC) Cunniff (Marsh)
    (BU) Martell (unassisted)
Goalies: (BC) Apprille, (BU) Ferreira

13th February 8, 1965 (13,058)
Boston University 5, Northeastern 4 (3 OT)
1st Period
    (BU) Conte (K. Ross)
    (BU) Bassi (D. O'Donnell, Fennie)
2nd Period
    (NU) MacGillivray (Seabury, Campbell)
    (NU) Turcotte (Leger, Bloh)
    (BU) Sobeski (unassisted)
    (NU) Bloh (Leu)
    (BU) Carter (K. Ross, Conte)
    (NU) Turcotte (DeBlois, Leu)
3rd Period
    No Scoring
1st Overtime
    No Scoring
2nd Overtime
    No Scoring
3rd Overtime
    (BU) Bassi (T. Ross)
Goalies: (BU) Ferreira, (NU) Thornton

Boston College 5, Harvard 4 (OT)
1st Period
    No Scoring
2nd Period
    (BC) Mullen (Cunniff)
    (HU) Mackey (Price, Zellner)
    (BC) Flaherty (Moylan)
    (HU) Gonzalez (Burnes, Sahlin)
    (HU) Smith (Clark, McCullough)
3rd Period
    (BC) Dyer (Cunniff)
    (BC) Moylan (Kearns)
    (HU) Gonzalez (Sahlin)
Overtime
    (BC) York (Kinsman, Kupka)
Goalies: (HU) Fitzsimmons, (BC) Murphy

February 15, 1965 (13,909)
Northeastern 3, Harvard 1
1st Period
    No Scoring
2nd Period
    (NU) Bloh (Bone)
    (NU) Leu (Bone, deBlois)
3rd Period
    (NU) O'Connell (Seabury)
    (HU) McCullough (Smith, Harrington)
Goalies: (HU) Fitzsimmons, (NU) Thornton
Boston College 5, Boston University 4
1st Period
    (BU) Sobeski (Quinn, T. Ross)
2nd Period
    (BU) O'Connell (Bassi)
    (BC) Kupka (Kearns)
    (BC) Mullen (Cunniff, Johnson)
    (BC) Cunniff (Kearns)
    (BU) Martell (Sylvia, T. Ross)
3rd Period
    (BC) Cunniff (Mullen, Dyer)
    (BC) Moylan (unassisted)
    (BU) O'Connell (Bassi, Fennie)
Goalies: (BC) Murphy, (BU) Ferreira

14th February 7, 1966 (13,909)
Harvard 5, Northeastern 1
1st Period
    No Scoring
2nd Period
    (NU) Bloh (McCarty, Seabury)
    (HU) Garrity (Carr)
    (HU) Burke (Clark, Miller)
    (HU) Price (Burke)
3rd Period
    (HU) Carr (unassisted)
    (HU) Parrot (McCullough)
Goalies: (HU) Fitzsimmons, (NU) Thornton, Heller
Boston University 6, Boston College 4
1st Period
    (BC) Cunniff (Hurley, Dyer)
    (BC) Fuller (Moylan)
2nd Period
    (BC) York (Kierstad, Clarke)
    (BU) Bassi (Fennie, Gilmour)
    (BU) Fennie (unassisted)
    (BU) Sobeski (Wood, Quinn)

3rd Period
  (BU) Sobeski (Gilmour, McLachlan)
  (BU) Bassi (Fennie)
  (BC) Moylan (Hurley, Fuller)
  (BU) Fennie (Bassi)
  Goalies: (BC) Murphy, (BU) Ferreira

February 14, 1966 (13,909)
Boston College 5, Northeastern 3
1st Period
  (BC) Mullen (Cunniff)
  (BC) Dyer (Cunniff, Hurley)
2nd Period
  (BC) Fuller (Moylan, Kupka)
  (NU) Leu (Turcotte)
  (NU) Leu (Jeanneault)
  (NU) Leger (Seabury)
3rd Period
  (BC) Clarke (York)
  (BC) Moylan (Fuller)
  Goalies: (NU) Thornton, (BC) Murphy
Boston University 9, Harvard 2
1st Period
  (HU) McCullough (Parrot)
  (BU) Sobeski (Wood)
2nd Period
  (BU) Wood (Conte, Quinn)
  (BU) Cooke (Parker, Riley)
  (BU) O'Connell (Bassi, Fennie)
  (BU) McLachlan (Parker)
  (BU) McLachlan (Gilmour)
3rd Period
  (BU) Cooke (Parker)
  (BU) Lumley (Quinn)
  (HU) Fredo (Price)
  (BU) Fennie (Gilmour)
  Goalies: (HU) Fitzsimmons, (BU) Ferreira

15th   February 9, 1967 (12,261)
Northeastern 6, Boston College 5 (OT)
1st Period
  (BC) York (Clarke)
  (BC) Clarke (York, Johnson)
  (NU) Leu (Porter)
2nd Period
  (NU) Coombes (Taylor)
  (BC) Kinsman (Prevett)
  (NU) Leu (Leger)
  (BC) York (unassisted)
3rd Period
  (NU) MacCausland (Leu, Porter)
  (NU) McCarty (McGranahan, O'Connell)
  (BC) Clarke (York, McCarthy)
Overtime
  (NU) Porter (Leu)
  Goalies: (NU) Thornton, (BC) McPhee
Boston University 8, Harvard 3
1st Period
  (BU) Boily (Wakabayashi, Hinch)
  (HU) Fredo (Garrity)
  (BU) Boily (Wakabayashi)
  (HU) Parrot (Smith, Scammon)
  (HU) Garrity (unassisted)
  (BU) Quinn (unassisted)
2nd Period
  (BU) McLachlan (unassisted)

3rd Period
  (BU) Boily (Wakabayashi)
  (BU) Sobeski (unassisted)
  (BU) McLachlan (Wakabayashi, Gilmour)
  (BU) Gray (Wakabayashi, Gilmour)
  Goalies: (HU) Fitzsimmons, (BU) Ryan, McCann

February 13, 1967 (12,910)
Boston College 6, Harvard 5 (OT)
1st Period
  (BC) Kupka (unassisted)
  (BC) Fuller (Hurley, Allen)
  (BC) York (Dowling)
  (HU) Mueller (Carr)
2nd Period
  (HU) Carr (unassisted)
  (HU) Carr (Johnson)
  (HU) Bauer (Ware, Carr)
3rd Period
  (BC) Allen (Hurley, Fuller)
  (HU) Ware (Smith, Bauer)
  (BC) Clarke (York)
Overtime
  (BC) Allen (Prevett)
  Goalies: (HU) Diercks, (BC) McPhee
Boston University 4, Northeastern 0
1st Period
  No Scoring
2nd Period
  (BU) McLachlan (unassisted)
  (BU) Boily (Wakabayashi, Gilmour)
3rd Period
  (BU) Gilmour (Quinn)
  (BU) Hinch (Riley, Cooke)
  Goalies: (BU) McCann, (NU) Thornton

16th   February 5, 1968 (11,818)
Boston University 7, Northeastern 4
1st Period
  (NU) McCarty (Hampe)
  (BU) Hyndman (Wakabayashi, Gray)
2nd Period
  (NU) MacCausland (Porter)
  (NU) Poile (Porter)
  (BU) Wakabayashi (Boily, Gray)
  (BU) Wakabayashi (Boily, Gray)
3rd Period
  (NU) Sarno (McCarthy, Hampe)
  (BU) Gray (Becker, Wakabayashi)
  (BU) Wright (Parker)
  (BU) Hyndman (Davenport)
  (BU) Boily (Gray, Dakin)
  Goalies: (BU) Jim McCann, (NU) Leu
Harvard 6, Boston College 4
1st Period
  (HU) Garrity (Smith, Fredo)
  (HU) Ware (Turco, McManama)
2nd Period
  (HU) Fredo (Garrity, Bauer)
  (BC) Prevett (Sheehy, Flynn)
  (BC) Snyder (Sheehy)
  (HU) Garrity (Bauer)
3rd Period
  (HU) Mark (unassisted)
  (HU) Flaman (Parrot, Mark)
  (BC) Cedorchuk (Ahearn)
  Goalies: (HU) Diercks, (BC) Cohen

February 12, 1968 (12,674)
Boston College 6, Northeastern 4
1st Period
  (BC) Snyder (Schilling, Sheehy)
  (BC) Schilling (Sheehy)
  (NU) Poile (unassisted)
2nd Period
  (BC) McCarthy (Snyder)
  (NU) Porter (Poile)
  (BC) Sheehy (Cedorchuck)
3rd Period
  (NU) McCarthy (DesJardins)
  (NU) Porter (Poile)
  Goalies: (BC) Cohen, (NU) Leu
Boston University 4, Harvard 1
1st Period
  (BU) Boily (Gray, Decker)
2nd Period
  (BU) Davenport (Hyndman, Toomey)
3rd Period
  (BU) Parker (Gamma, Wright)
  (HU) McManama (unassisted)
  (BU) Toomey (Hyndman)
  Goalies: (HU) Diercks, (BU) McCann

17th   February 3, 1969 (14,659)
Harvard 8, Northeastern 4
1st Period
  (NU) Eramo (Poile, Daniels)
2nd Period
  (HU) Owen (Cavanagh)
  (HU) Driscoll (Jones, Cavanagh)
  (HU) Otness (Jones, Turco)
  (HU) Owen (DeMichele, Cavanagh)
3rd Period
  (NU) Poile (Eramo)
  (HU) Cavanagh (Owen, Jones)
  (HU) Turco (Ware, Otness)
  (HU) Murphy (Mark, Bauer)
  (NU) Cain (MacCausland, Sarno)
  (NU) Tingley (Bell, Poile)
  (HU) DeMichele (Cavanagh, Owen)
  Goalies: (HU) Durno, (NU) Leu
Boston University 4, Boston College 2
1st Period
  (BU) Hyndman (Wright, Abbott)
  (BU) Davenport (Gray, Toomey)
2nd Period
  (BC) Sheehy (Snyder, Cedorchuk)
3rd Period
  (BU) Hyndman (Toomey, Delker)
  (BC) Schilling (Sullivan)
  (BU) Hyndman (Toomey, Davenport)
  Goalies: (BU) McCann, (BC) McPhee

February 10, 1969 (9,236)
Boston College 6, Northeastern 3
1st Period
  (BC) Sheehy (Schilling, Snyder)
  (NU) Poile (Daniels, Boyce)
  (BC) Cedorchuk (Hurley, Ahearn)
  (NU) Eramo (Abbott, Boyce)
2nd Period
  (NU) Poile (Eramo, Daniels)
  (BC) Flynn (Sheehy, Cedorchuk)
  (BC) Putnam (Cedorchuk, Flynn)

3rd Period
(BC) Smythe (Flynn, Putnam)
(BC) Toczylowski (Ahearn)
Goalies: (NU) Leu, (BC) McPhee
Harvard 5, Boston University 3
1st Period
(HU) Cavanagh (DeMichele)
2nd Period
(BU) Hinch (Gray, Stirling)
(HU) DeMichele (Cavanagh)
3rd Period
(BU) Hatton (Decker, Stirling)
(BU) Wakabayashi (unassisted)
(HU) Mark (Flaman)
(HU) McManama (Bauer, Ware)
(HU) Cavanagh (unassisted)
Goalies: (HU) Durno, (BU) McCann

18th   February 2, 1970 (14,835)
Boston College 5, Northeastern 0
1st Period
No Scoring
2nd Period
(BC) Mellor (Sheehy)
(BC) Sheehy (Sullivan)
(BC) Sheehy (Mellor, Schilling)
3rd Period
(BC) Callow (unassisted)
(BC) Sheehy (Mellor, Shanley)
Goalies: (BC) Barton, (NU) Eberly
Boston University 5, Harvard 3
1st Period
(BU) Gryp (Hyndman, Burrows)
(BU) Stirling (Toomey)
(BU) Davenport (Danby, Gowing)
2nd Period
(HU) J. Cavanagh (unassisted)
3rd Period
(HU) J. Cavanagh (Gurry, Owen)
(HU) Owen (Gurry, J. Cavanagh)
(BU) Toomey (Murray, Stirling)
(BU) Davenport (unassisted)
Goalies: (HU) Durno, (BU) Regan

February 9, 1970 (14,702)
Harvard 5, Northeastern 4 (OT)
1st Period
(HU) DeMichele (unassisted)
(NU) Poile (Daniels)
2nd Period
(HU) DeMichele (J. Cavanagh)
(NU) Archambault (Cain)
(NU) Bell (Anderson, Morrison)
(NU) Poile (unassisted)
(HU) Owen (J. Cavanagh)
3rd Period
(HU) Gurry (McManama)
Overtime
(HU) Owen (DeMichele, Gurry, Cavanagh)
Goalies: (HU) Durno, (NU) Eberly
Boston University 5, Boston College 4
1st Period
(BC) Sullivan (Ahearn)
(BC) Sheehy (Godfrey)

2nd Period
(BU) Thornton (Fenwick, Toomey)
(BC) Godfrey (Mellor, Sullivan)
3rd Period
(BU) Gowing (Danby, Davenport)
(BU) Davenport (Danby, Hyndman)
(BU) Gowing (Davenport, Hyndman)
(BC) Godfrey (Sheehy)
(BU) Gowing (Hyndman, Davenport)
Goalies: (BC) Barton, (BU) Regan

19th   February 8, 1971 (11,449)
Boston University 12, Northeastern 2
1st Period
(BU) Anderson (Dolloff, Burrowes)
(BU) Gowing (Gryp, LaGarde)
(BU) Cahoon (Stirling, Giandomenico)
2nd Period
(BU) Gowing (Gryp, Danby)
(BU) Jordan (Gowing, Stirling)
(BU) Dolloff (Burrowes, Anderson)
(BU) Stirling (Cahoon, Giandomenico)
(NU) Delaney (Shepard)
(BU) Abbott (Brown, Flynn)
(NU) Bell (Chaisson, Archambault)
3rd Period
(BU) Dolloff (Anderson, Yetten)
(BU) Giandomenico (Cahoon, Stirling)
(BU) Danby (Abbott, Yetten)
(BU) Dolloff (Anderson, Jordan)
Goalies: (NU) Eberly, (BU) Brady
Harvard 10, Boston College 4
1st Period
(BC) Callow (Ahearn, Kenty)
(BC) Keaveney (Kenty)
(HU) Owen (Hynes)
2nd Period
(HU) Riley (Burnes)
(BC) Lawrence (Bennett, Ahearn)
(HU) J. Cavanagh (Owen, Hynes)
(HU) DeMichele (Owen, J. Cavanagh)
3rd Period
(HU) Hynes (Owen)
(HU) Paul (J. Cavanagh, DeMichele)
(HU) Rosenberger (Riley, Paul)
(HU) J. Cavanagh (DeMichele, Hynes)
(BC) Keaveney (Reardon)
(HU) Owen (J. Cavanagh, DeMichele)
(HU) DeMichele (J. Cavanagh)
Goalies: (HU) Durno, (BC) Higgins

February 22, 1971 (14,994)
Boston College 8, Northeastern 2
1st Period
(NU) Costa (Chaisson, Bell)
(BC) Kenty (Shanley)
2nd Period
(BC) Mellor (Keny, Keaveney)
(BC) Callow (Shanley)
(BC) Keaveney (Haley)
(BC) Shanley (Kenty)
(NU) Scherer (Archambault, Cotter)
(BC) Keaveney (Reardon)

3rd Period
(BC) Haley (Kenty, Keaveney)
(BC) Shanley (Sico)
Goalies: (BC) Higgins, (NU) Eberly
Boston University 4, Harvard 1
1st Period
(BU) Giandomenico (Stirling, Cahoon)
2nd Period
(HU) Hynes (Corkery)
(BU) Stirling (Brown, Danby)
3rd Period
(BU) Dolloff (LaGarde, Murray)
(BU) Cahoon (Giandomenico, Stirling)
Goalies: (HU) Durno, (BU) Brady

20th   February 7, 1972 (8,159)
Harvard 8, Northeastern 3
1st Period
(HU) Hampe (Hands)
(HU) Corkery (McManama, Burnes)
(NU) Lovell (M. Archambault, Quinn)
(HU) Rosenberger (Havern)
2nd Period
(NU) Blanchard (Dunkle)
(HU) Hynes (Corkery, McManama)
(NU) Toal (Blanchard, Dunkle)
(HU) Paul (Goodenow, Desmond)
(HU) Hynes (Corkery, McManama)
3rd Period
(HU) McManama (Corkery, Hynes)
(HU) Reynolds (Rosenberger)
Goalies: (HU) Bertagna, (NU) Eberly
Boston University 4, Boston College 2
1st Period
No Scoring
2nd Period
(BU) LaGarde (Thornton)
(BU) Danby (Jordan, Brown)
(BC) Fidler (Reardon, Shanley)
3rd Period
(BU) Danby (Giandomenico, Thornton)
(BU) Giandomenico (Dolloff)
(BC) Fidler (Reardon)
Goalies: (BU) Brady, (BC) Higgins

February 14, 1972 (14,995)
Boston College 5, Northeastern 4
1st Period
(BC) Kimball (Taylor, Monahan)
(BC) Reardon (Lambert, Shanley)
2nd Period
(NU) Quinn (Condon)
(BC) King (Monahan, Kimball)
(BC) Taylor (Haley, Ahern)
(NU) Dunkle (Toal, Bryant)
3rd Period
(NU) Dunkle (Chaisson, Clegg)
(NU) Blanchard (Clegg, Chaisson)
(BC) Shanley (Reardon, Haley)
Goalies: (BC) Higgins, (NU) Eberly
Boston University 4, Harvard 1
1st Period
(BU) Danby (Anderson)
2nd Period
(BU) Jordan (Brown, Danby)

3rd Period
    (BU) Thornton (Anderson)
    (BU) Danby (Jordan, Cahoon)
    (HU) Burnes (McManama, Hynes)
  Goalies: (HU) Bertagna, (BU) Brady

21st February 5, 1973 (13,643)
Boston College 9, Northeastern 8 (OT)
1st Period
    (BC) Powers (Reardon, Smith)
    (BC) Powers (Reardon, Smith)
    (BC) Riley (Monahan, D'Arcy)
    (NU) DeJardins (McPhedran)
    (BC) Doyle (Fidler)
    (BC) Powers (Kenty, Doyle)
2nd Period
    (NU) Scherer (Dunkle, Toal)
    (NU) Martel (Lovell, Huck)
    (BC) Powers (Smith, Reardon)
    (NU) Condon (Toal)
3rd Period
    (NU) Toal (Dunkle)
    (BC) Doyle (Kenty, Fidler)
    (BC) Lambert (Kenty)
    (NU) Huck (Martel, Lovell)
    (NU) Toal (Dunkle, Reise)
    (NU) Huck (Martel, Condon)
Overtime
    (BC) Powers (Smith, Reardon)
  Goalies: (BC) Yetten, (NU) Blanchard
Boston University 8, Harvard 3
1st Period
    (BU) O'Neil (unassisted)
    (BU) Powers (Lowell, Stanfield)
2nd Period
    (BU) Wisener (Stanfield, Powers)
    (BU) O'Neil (Stanfield)
    (BU) Wisener (Dolloff, Stanfield)
    (HU) Goodenow (unassisted)
    (HU) Corkery (Goodenow, Roth)
3rd Period
    (BU) Cournoyea (Dolloff)
    (BU) Cournoyea (Dolloff)
    (HU) Hogan (Hampe, Gauthier)
    (BU) Wisener (unassisted)
  Goalies: (HU) Bertagna, (BU) Walsh

February 12, 1973 (15,003)
Harvard 8, Northeastern 5
1st Period
    (HU) McManama (Corkery, Desmond)
    (HU) Desmond (McManama, Noonan)
    (NU) Condon (Scherer)
2nd Period
    (HU) McMahon (Thorndike, Gauthier)
    (HU) Gauthier (Thorndike)
    (HU) McManama (Goodenow)
    (HU) Thorndike (Hampe)
    (NU) Condon (Sherlock)
    (HU) Corkery (Roth, Thomas)
3rd Period
    (NU) DeJardins (Condon, Sherlock)
    (NU) Dunkle (Finch)
    (NU) Scherer (Dunkle, DeJardins)
    (HU) Thorndike (McMahon, Gauthier)
  Goalies: (HU) Bertagna, (NU) Blanchard, McKenna

Boston University 4, Boston College 1
1st Period
    (BU) Stanfield (Robbins)
2nd Period
    (BU) Dolloff (Stanfield, Brown)
    (BU) Kuzyk (Lagarde)
    (BC) Powers (Reardon, Smith)
3rd Period
    (BU) Dolloff (Wisener)
  Goalies: (BU) Walsh, (BC) Yetten

22nd February 4, 1974 (8,033)
Boston University 6, Northeastern 1
1st Period
    (BU) Buckton (R. Meagher, Brown)
    (BU) Buckton (R. Meagher, Eruzione)
    (BU) Eruzione (unassisted)
2nd Period
    (BU) Robbins (T. Meagher, Marzo)
3rd Period
    (BU) Burlington (Stanfield)
    (NU) Condon (Lovell, Toal)
    (BU) Lowell (Burlington, Bishop)
  Goalies: (BU) Walsh, (NU) Blanchard
Harvard 11, Boston College 6
1st Period
    (HU) Thomas (Thorndike)
    (BC) Martin (Ferriter, Lambert)
    (HU) Thorndike (Hogan, Byrd)
2nd Period
    (BC) Albrecht (Powers, Smith)
    (HU) Thorndike (Hogan)
    (BC) Doyle (Martin, Powers)
    (HU) Goodenow (penalty shot)
    (HU) Carr (McMahon)
3rd Period
    (BC) Smith (Powers, Lambert)
    (HU) Bolduc (unassisted)
    (HU) Burke (Haley)
    (HU) Byrd (Burke)
    (HU) Haley (Burke, Byrd)
    (BC) Powers (Albrecht, Smith)
    (BC) Lambert (D'Arcy)
    (HU) Hogan (Thomas, Thorndike)
    (HU) Dagdigian (McMahon, Roth)
  Goalies: (HU) Murray, (BC) Yetten

February 11, 1974 (12,202)
Northeastern 4, Boston College 3
1st Period
    (BC) Lambert (Doyle, Riley)
    (NU) Condon (unassisted)
    (NU) Bryant (Huck, Sherlock)
    (NU) Toal (Lovell, Murphy)
2nd Period
    No Scoring
3rd Period
    (BC) Martin (Fernald, Lambert)
    (NU) Martel (unassisted)
    (BC) Smith (unassisted)
  Goalies: (NU) Blanchard, (BC) Yetten
Harvard 5, Boston University 4
1st Period
    (BU) T. Meagher (Marzo)
    (BU) Bishop (Burlington, Bannerman)
    (HU) Carr (Dagdigian, Hands)

2nd Period
    (BU) T. Meagher (Stanfield)
    (HU) Hogan (Thomas, Byrd)
    (HU) McMahon (Thomas, Roth)
    (HU) Roth (Goodenow)
3rd Period
    (BU) Stanfield (Burlington, McClellan)
    (HU) Roth (Byrd)
  Goalies: (HU) Murray, (BU) Walsh

23rd February 3, 1975 (8,694)
Harvard 9, Northeastern 0
1st Period
    (HU) Thomas (Burke, Piatelli)
    (HU) Roth (unassisted)
2nd Period
    (HU) Rossi (Haley, Carr)
    (HU) Thomas (unassisted)
3rd Period
    (HU) Roth (Thomas, Dagdigian)
    (HU) McMahon (Bell, Dagdigian)
    (HU) McMahon (Bell, Schuster)
    (HU) McMahon (Bell, Dagdigian)
    (HU) Haley (Bolduc, Carr)
  Goalies: (HU) Petrovek, (NU) McKenna
Boston University 5, Boston College 3
1st Period
    (BU) Robbins (Meagher, Stanfield)
2nd Period
    (BC) Hart (Barrett)
    (BC) Barrett (unassisted)
    (BC) Smith (unassisted)
    (BU) Stanfield (Fay, Marzo)
    (BU) Marzo (Fay, Stanfield)
3rd Period
    (BU) Stanfield (Burlington)
    (BU) Robbins (Meagher, Marzo)
  Goalies: (BU) Durocher, (BC) Redmond

February 10, 1975 (15,003)
Northeastern 5, Boston College 3
1st Period
    (BC) Martin (Barrett, Smith)
2nd Period
    (BC) M. Riley (B. Riley, Fernald)
    (NU) Holmes (Fidler)
    (NU) McPhedran (Biron)
3rd Period
    (NU) Haldane (Deck, Taylor)
    (NU) Fidler (McPhedran)
    (BC) Martin (Fernald, M. Riley)
    (NU) Sherlock (Martel, Huck)
  Goalies: (BC) Redmond, (NU) McElroy
Boston University 7, Harvard 2
1st Period
    (BU) T. Meagher (Marzo, Robbins)
2nd Period
    (HU) Thomas (Roth)
    (BU) Buckton (R. Meagher, Stanfield)
    (BU) Buckton (R. Meagher)
    (BU) Dudley (Powers)
3rd Period
    (BU) Fidler (Burlington, Kuzyk)
    (BU) Burlington (Fidler, Stanfield)
    (BU) R. Meagher (Eruzione, Brown)
    (HU) McMahon (Rossi, Thomas)
  Goalies: (HU) Petrovek, (BU) Durocher

24th   February 2, 1976 (11,118)
Boston College 5, Northeastern 3
1st Period
   (BC) Mullen (Smith)
   (BC) Barrett (Ferriter, Young)
   (NU) Huck (Martel, Holmes)
2nd Period
   (BC) Augustine (Albrecht, Smith)
   (NU) Sherlock (France, Martel)
3rd Period
   (BC) Barrett (Ferriter, Young)
   (NU) Huck (Martel, Holmes)
   (BC) Augustine (unassisted)
Goalies: (BC) Skidmore, (NU) Bowman
Boston University 6, Harvard 5
1st Period
   (BU) T. Meagher (Marzo, Robbins)
   (BU) Buckton (McLellan, O'Callahan)
   (HU) Neiland (Haley, Hughes)
2nd Period
   (BU) Kuzyk (Dudley, Sunderland)
3rd Period
   (HU) Burke (Purdy)
   (HU) Haley (Bell)
   (BU) Fidler (Dudley, Eryp)
   (BU) R. Meagher (Robbins, Eruzione)
   (HU) Hozack (Swift, Haley)
   (BU) Eruzione (R. Meagher, Brown)
   (HU) Beck (Trainor, Haley)
Goalies: (HU) Petrovek, (BU) Durocher

February 9, 1976 (12,250)
Harvard 4, Northeastern 2
1st Period
   (NU) Martel (Huck, Holmes)
   (NU) Martel (Huck, Holmes)
2nd Period
   (HU) Bell (Hughes, Haley)
   (HU) Purdy (Carr, Leckie)
   (HU) Purdy (Carr, Liston)
3rd Period
   (HU) Horton (unassisted)
Goalies: (HU) Petrovek, (NU) McElroy
Boston College 6, Boston University 3
1st Period
   (BC) Bartholomew (Smith, Barrett)
2nd Period
   (BC) Smith (McGuire)
   (BC) Ferriter (Young)
   (BU) T. Meagher (Brown, Fay)
3rd Period
   (BU) Fay (Brown, Dudley)
   (BC) Ferriter (Barrett, Bartholomew)
   (BU) T. Meagher (Eruzione, Fidler)
   (BC) Mullen (Albrecht, Augustine)
   (BC) Mullen (Smith, Albrecht)
Goalies: (BC) Skidmore, (BU) Durocher

25th   February 7, 1977 (13,674)
Boston University 10, Northeastern 5
1st Period
   (BU) Meagher (Silk, O'Callahan)
   (NU) Wilkins (unassisted)
   (BU) Silk (Lamby, Meagher)
   (BU) Lamby (Fay, Marden)
   (BU) Meagher (Silk)
   (NU) Simmons (Wilkins, Ferdinandi)

2nd Period
   (NU) Ferdinandi (Wilkins, Simmons)
3rd Period
   (BU) Meagher (O'Callahan)
   (NU) Derby (McMillen, Devlin)
   (BU) Boileau (Pidgeon)
   (BU) Marden (Silk)
   (BU) Lamby (Fay, Eruzione)
   (BU) Pidgeon (O'Callahan)
   (NU) Deck (unassisted)
   (BU) Bethel (Dudley)
Goalies: (BU) Craig, (NU) McElroy, Metz
Harvard 4, Boston College 2
1st Period
   (BC) Mullen (Burns)
2nd Period
   (HU) Purdy (G. Hughes, Bullard)
3rd Period
   (BC) Martin (Fernald, Songin)
   (HU) Cook (Nolen, Peterson)
   (HU) G. Hughes (Purdy, Bullard)
   (HU) Dea (Schuster, G. Hughes)
Goalies: (HU) Petrovek, (BC) Skidmore

February 14, 1977 (14,597)
Boston College 6, Northeastern 4
1st Period
   (NU) Wilkins (Ferdinandi)
   (BC) Young (Ferriter, Barrett)
   (NU) Walsh (Wilkins)
   (BC) Antotomaso (Fernald)
2nd Period
   (NU) Simmons (Walsh, Holmes)
   (BC) Ferriter (Barrett, McGuire)
   (NU) Simmons (Wilkins, Ferdinandi)
3rd Period
   (BC) Barrett (Augustine, Ferriter)
   (BC) Fernald (Riley, Augustine)
   (BC) Burns (Kyle, Reardon)
Goalies: (BC) Skidmore, (NU) Bowman
Harvard 4, Boston University 3
1st Period
   No Scoring
2nd Period
   (BU) Silk (McLellan)
   (HU) Purdy (Cook, G. Hughes)
   (BU) Eruzione (Silk, Lamby)
   (HU) J. Hughes (G. Hughes, Purdy)
   (HU) Horton (G. Hughes)
3rd Period
   (BU) Bethel (Dudley, Meagher)
   (HU) Garrity (Horton, Hozack)
Goalies: (HU) Petrovek, (BU) Craig

26th   February 6, 1978 (11,666)
Harvard 4, Northeastern 3 (OT)
1st Period
   (NU) Harvey (Coates, Simmons)
   (HU) Cook (Garrity, Scalamandre)
2nd Period
   (NU) Parks (Gruhl)
   (HU) Benson (Cochrane, Dea)
   (HU) Cook (G. Hughes, Cochrane)
3rd Period
   (NU) Turner (Holmes, Derby)

Overtime
   (HU) Purdy (Trainor, G. Hughes)
Goalies: (HU) Hynes, (NU) Arrington
Boston University 12, Boston College 5
1st Period
   (BU) O'Neill (Meagher, Bethel)
   (BC) Augustine (unassisted)
   (BU) Mullen (unassisted)
   (BU) Johnson (Lamby)
   (BU) Meagher (Lamby, O'Callahan)
   (BC) Hehir (Amidon)
   (BC) Switaj (Burns)
2nd Period
   (BU) Bethel (Fidler, O'Callahan)
   (BU) Meagher (Boileau, O'Neill)
   (BC) Barrett (Mullen, McClellan)
   (BU) Boileau (Nieland, O'Callahan)
   (BU) Lamby (Mullen, MacLeod)
3rd Period
   (BU) Boileau (Johnson)
   (BU) Fidler (Meagher, Bethel)
   (BU) Melanson (Cotter, Lamby)
   (BC) Riley (McClellan)
   (BU) Miller (Kimball, Cotter)
Goalies: (BU) Durocher, (BC) Skidmore, Cronin

March 1, 1978 (14,335)
Boston College 3, Northeastern 2 (OT)
1st Period
   (NU) Parks (Gruhl, Wilkins)
   (NU) Gruhl (Wilkins, Archambault)
   (BC) Kyle (Burns, Ewanouski)
2nd Period
   (BC) Mullen (Hehir, Augustine)
3rd Period
   No Scoring
Overtime
   (BC) Mullen (Barrett)
Goalies: (NU) Arrington, (BC) Skidmore
Boston University 7, Harvard 1
1st Period
   (BU) O'Callahan (Lamby, Silk)
   (BU) Mullen (McCloud, Miller)
2nd Period
   (BU) Mullen (LeBlond)
   (HU) Benson (unassisted)
   (BU) Mullen (LeBlond, Miller)
3rd Period
   (BU) Lamby (Hetnik, O'Callahan)
   (BU) Lamby (O'Callahan, Silk)
   (BU) LeBlond (O'Neill)
Goalies: (HU) Hynes, (BU) Craig

27th   February 5, 1979 (14,679)
Boston College 7, Northeastern 2
1st Period
   (BC) Ewanouski (Army, Hammer)
   (BC) Mullen (O'Dwyer, Smith)
   (BC) Enright (Sampson)
   (BC) Mullen (unassisted)
2nd Period
   (BC) Sampson (Barge, Burns)
3rd Period
   (BC) Hehir (Cowles)
   (NU) Ferdinandi (Harvey)

(NU) Turner (Harvey Ferdinandi)
(BC) Hehir (Antetomaso)
Goalies: (BC) Skidmore, (NU) Arrington, Ricciardi
Boston University 4, Harvard 2
1st Period
(HU) D. Burke (Olson)
2nd Period
(BU) MacLeod (Johnson, LeBlond)
(HU) Watson (G. Hughes, Purdy)
3rd Period
(BU) Whelton (O'Callahan, MacLeod)
(BU) Silk (Fidler)
(BU) Cotter (MacLeod, Johnson)
Goalies: (HU) Hynes, (BU) Craig

February 12, 1979 (14,456)

Northeastern 5, Harvard 4
1st Period
(HU) Millen (Andrews, Garrity)
(NU) Harrison (Hayes, Archambault)
(NU) Harrison (Hayes, Burke)
(NU) Harvey (Cowie, McDougall)
(NU) Cowie (McDougall, Harvey)
2nd Period
(HU) MacDonald (G. Hughes, Cochrane)
(HU) Murray
(HU) D. Burke
3rd Period
(NU) Cowie (Filipe, McDougall)
Goalies: (HU) Hynes, (NU) Arrington
Boston University 4, Boston College 3
1st Period
(BU) Cotter (Johnson)
2nd Period
(BU) Bethel (Silk, Fidler)
(BC) Mullen (Switaj)
3rd Period
(BU) Meagher (Miller, Hetnik)
(BC) Mullen (Amidon, Wright)
(BC) Ewanouski (Army)
(BU) MacLeod (Cotter)
Goalies: (BC) Skidmore, (BU) Craig

28th   February 4, 1980 (14,456)

Northeastern 6, Boston University 5 (OT)
1st Period
(BU) Cotter (unassisted)
(NU) Derby (Yaworski, Montgomery)
(NU) Beadle (Archambault, Iskyan)
(NU) Turner (Ferdinandi, Filipe)
2nd Period
(BU) Goegan (Meagher, MacLeod)
3rd Period
(BU) Goegan (Meagher)
(NU) Cowie (McDougall)
(BU) Goegan (Meagher, Whelton)
(BU) Fenton (unassisted)
(NU) Turner (Ferdinandi)
Overtime
(NU) Montgomery (Filipe, Yaworski)
Goalies: (BU) Barich, (NU) Demetroulakas
Boston College 4, Harvard 3
1st Period
(HU) Burns (Garrity, Britz)
(HU) Malmquist (Olson, Benson)
(HU) Britz (Burns)
(BC) Ewanouski (O'Dwyer, Murphy)

2nd Period
(BC) Blossom (Army, Murphy)
3rd Period
(BC) Switaj (Cowles)
(BC) Sampson (Hammer)
Goalies: (HU) Lau, (BC) Ellis

February 11, 1980 (14,456)

Harvard 7, Boston University 4
1st Period
(HU) T. Murray (Fusco, D. Burke)
2nd Period
(BU) MacLeod (Johnson, Miller)
(HU) Turner (G. Olson, Fusco)
(BU) Meagher (Marshall, Klapes)
3rd Period
(HU) G. Olson (Turner, Carter)
(BU) Fidler (Fenton, Nieland)
(HU) Fusco (T. Murray, McDonald)
(HU) Britz (Burns, Fusco)
(BU) Fidler (unassisted)
(HU) Carter (T. Murray)
(HU) D. Burke (Hynes, Sangster)
Goalies: (HU) Hynes, (BU) Weisman
Northeastern 5, Boston College 4 (OT)
1st Period
(BC) Army (Blossom, McCarran)
(NU) Cowie (unassisted)
(BC) Army (Antetomaso, Murphy)
(BC) Hammer (O'Neil)
2nd Period
(NU) Parks (Archambault, Turner)
(NU) McDougall (unassisted)
3rd Period
(BC) Hehir (M. Switaj, Cowles)
(NU) McDougall (Iskyan, Beadle)
Overtime
(NU) Turner (Ferdinandi, Parks)
Goalies: (BC) O'Connor, (NU) Demetroulakas

29th   February 2, 1981 (14,456)

Harvard 10, Northeastern 2
1st Period
(HU) Britz (Fusco, Code)
(HU) Olson (Murray, Watson)
(HU) Fusco (Burke, Connors)
(HU) Watson (Murray, Olson)
(NU) Filipe (Manchurek, Turnbull)
2nd Period
(HU) Turner (Martin, Code)
(HU) Falcone (Connors, Burke)
(HU) Watson (Murray, Olson)
(HU) Burke (Falcone, Fusco)
(HU) Olson (unassisted)
3rd Period
(NU) Beadle (Cowle, Hiltz)
(HU) Kukulowicz (Powers, Larson)
Goalies: (HU) Lau, (NU) Demetroulakas, Davidner
Boston College 5, Boston University 2
1st Period
(BC) Chisholm (Switaj, O'Dwyer)
(BC) Switaj (O'Neil, Griffin)
2nd Period
(BU) Johnson (O'Regan, Davies)
(BC) Hammer (Amidon, Griffin)
(BU) Johnson (Milton)

3rd Period
(BC) Ewanouski (Hehir, Sampson)
(BC) Sampson (Ewanouski, Hehir)
Goalies: (BU) Weisman, (BC) O'Connor

February 9, 1981 (14,456)

Boston University 9, Northeastern 2
1st Period
(BU) Milton (Davies, Whelton)
(BU) Johnson (Cotter, Davies)
2nd Period
(BU) Cotter (Johnson, Davies)
(BU) Milton (Fidler, MacLeod)
(NU) Filipe (Hiltz, Cowie)
(BU) Cotter (Johnson)
(BU) Fidler (Darling, Whelton)
(BU) MacLeod (Fidler, August)
(BU) Darling (Fidler, MacLeod)
3rd Period
(NU) MacDougall (Beadle, Frank)
(BU) Sinclair (Pierog, O'Regan)
Goalies: (BU) Barich, (NU) Demetroulakas, Davidner
Harvard 2, Boston College 0
1st Period
(HU) Larson (Turner)
2nd Period
No Scoring
3rd Period
(HU) Burke (Sheehy)
Goalies: (HU) Lau, (BC) O'Connor

30th   February 1, 1982 (14,673)

Boston University 5, Harvard 1
1st Period
(BU) Darling (Davies, Fenton)
(BU) Milton (Mutch, Davies)
2nd Period
(HU) Visone (Britz, M. Fusco)
(BU) O'Regan (Mutch, Milton)
3rd Period
(BU) Darling (Fenton, Davies)
(BU) Darling (Mutch, Milton)
Goalies: (HU) Lau, (BU) Barich
Boston College 3, Northeastern 2 (OT)
1st Period
(BC) Rauseo (O'Neil, Boudreau)
(BC) Cowles (Chisholm)
2nd Period
(NU) McKenney (Giovanucci, Manchurek)
3rd Period
(NU) McKenney (Cowie, Fahringer)
Overtime
(BC) Delaney (Cowles, Boudreau)
Goalies: (BC) O'Connor, (NU) Davidner

February 8, 1982 (14,673)

Northeastern 6, Harvard 5 (OT)
1st Period
(HU) Britz (Visone, M. Olson)
(HU) S. Fusco (Litchfield, G. Olson)
(NU) Fahringer (B. Cowie, G. Cowie)
2nd Period
(NU) Fahringer (B. Cowie, G. Cowie)
(HU) Kukulowicz (M. Fusco, Code)
(HU) G. Olson (Turner, Sheehy)
(HU) Britz (Litchfield, Watson)

3rd Period
    (NU) Manchurek (Giovanucci, McKenney)
    (NU) McKenney (Giovanucci)
    (NU) McKenney (Giavonucci)
Overtime
    (NU) J. Averill (Fahringer)
Goalies: (NU) Davidner, (HU) Better
Boston University 3, Boston College 1
1st Period
    (BC) Herlihy (O'Dwyer, Blossom)
    (BU) O'Regan (Pierog)
    (BU) Pierog (O'Regan)
2nd Period
    No Scoring
3rd Period
    (BU) O'Regan (Milton)
Goalies: (BC) O'Connor, (BU) Daskalakis

31st   February 7, 1983 (14,448)
Boston College 5, Harvard 4 (OT)
1st Period
    (BC) Chisholm (Campedelli)
    (HU) Chalmers (Britz, Visone)
    (BC) Mitchell (Monleon)
    (HU) Chalmers (Visone)
2nd Period
    (HU) Chalmers (Visone)
    (BC) Rauseo (Boudreau, Sweeney)
    (HU) Kukulowicz (Code)
3rd Period
    (BC) Blossom (Sweeney, Rauseo)
Overtime
    (BC) Rauseo (Sweeney)
Goalies: (BC) Switaj, (HU) Blair
Northeastern 4, Boston University 3
1st Period
    (BU) Pierog (LaGarde, Cappellano)
    (BU) Sinclair (O'Regan, Pierog)
2nd Period
    (BU) Sinclair (Pierog, O'Regan)
    (NU) Madigan (Fitzsimmons, B. Averill)
    (NU) J. Averill (Emerson, Fahringer)
3rd Period
    (NU) Bucyk (Kessler, B. Averill)
    (NU) Neary (Frank)
Goalies: (NU) Davidner, (BU) Daskalakis

February 14, 1983 (14,523)
Boston University 5, Harvard 4
1st Period
    (BU) LaGarde (August)
    (HU) Hartman (Griffin)
    (BU) Marshall (unassisted)
2nd Period
    (BU) Sullivan (Marshall, Cappellano)
    (HU) Griffin (Starbuck, Smith)
    (BU) Sullivan (August, LaGarde)
    (BU) Pierog (Sinclair, O'Regan)
3rd Period
    (HU) Burke (Wheeler, Follows)
    (HU) Burke (Follows, Cleary)
Goalies: (HU) McEvoy, (BU) Barich
Boston College 8, Northeastern 2
1st Period
    (BC) Sweeney (Blossom, Rauseo)
    (BC) Livingston (unassisted)
    (NU) O'Brien (Neary, Marshall)

2nd Period
    (BC) Brown (Monleon, McCarran)
    (BC) Sweeney (Livingston, Rauseo)
    (BC) Shea (Emery, McCarran)
    (BC) Livingston (Rauseo, Sweeney)
    (BC) O'Neil (Harlow, Griffin)
3rd Period
    (NU) Giovanucci (Frank, Manchurek)
Goalies: (BC) Switaj, Gordon, O'Hearn, (NU)
Davidner, Marshall

32nd   February 6, 1984 (14,451)
Northeastern 7, Harvard 3
1st Period
    (NU) Kinal (Mader, Fahringer)
    (NU) B. Averill (Heinbuck, Manchurek)
    (NU) Pratt (Heinbuck, Emerson)
    (NU) Isbister (J. Averill, Manchurek)
2nd Period
    (NU) Emerson (Heinbuck)
    (HU) Busconi (unassisted)
    (HU) Connors (Martin, Busconi)
    (HU) Barakeet (Kukulowicz, Visone)
    (NU) B. Averill (Neary)
3rd Period
    (NU) Pratt (Emerson, Heinbuck)
Goalies: (HU) Blair, (NU) Marshall
Boston University 6, Boston College 5
1st Period
    (BU) Gerlitz (Shaunessy, Mutch)
    (BU) Mutch (Marshall, Gerlitz)
    (BU) Lagarde (Cappellano, Matchett)
    (BU) Sullivan (Lagarde)
2nd Period
    (BC) Campedelli (Herlihy)
3rd Period
    (BC) Harlow (Campadelli, Bauseo)
    (BU) Delorey (Sullivan, Cappellano)
    (BC) Mitchell (Herlihy, Delaney)
    (BU) Pierog (Majkozak, Carlacci)
    (BC) Houle (Herlihy, McNamara)
    (BC) Campadelli (Rauseo)
Goalies: (BU) Daskalakis, (BC) Gordon

February 13, 1984 (14,451)
Boston College 5, Harvard 2
1st Period
    (BC) Brown (Whyte, Stevens)
2nd Period
    (BC) Stevens (Brown)
    (BC) Mitchell (Houle, Sweeney)
3rd Period
    (HU) Follows (Chiarelli)
    (BC) Harlow (Shea, Chisolm)
    (HU) Smith (Chiarelli, Cutone)
    (BC) Rauseo (Emery)
Goalies: (HU) McEvoy, (BC) Real
Northeastern 5, Boston University 2
1st Period
    No Scoring
2nd Period
    (BU) Cappellano (Lagarde, Majkozak)
    (NU) Bucyk (unassisted)
    (BU) Mutch (Shaunessy, Gerlitz)
    (NU) Heinbuck (Fahringer, Frank)
    (NU) B. Averill (Heinbuck, Kinal)

3rd Period
    (NU) Manchurek (unassisted)
    (NU) Bucyk (B. Averill)
Goalies: (NU) Marshall, (BU) Daskalakis

33rd   February 4, 1985 (14,451)
Boston University 5, Harvard 3
1st Period
    (BU) Ryan (Marshall)
    (BU) Sullivan (Marshall, Ryan)
2nd Period
    (BU) LaBrosse (unassisted)
    (BU) Majkozak (Sanders, Sveen)
    (HU) Fusco (MacDonald, Taylor)
    (BU) Cullen (Donatelli, Lowney)
3rd Period
    (HU) Benning (Taylor, Fusco)
    (HU) Smith (Fusco, Benning)
Goalies: (HU) Blair, (BU) Deraney
Northeastern 4, Boston College 2
1st Period
    (NU) Kinal (Heinbuck, MacInnis)
2nd Period
    (NU) Emerson (Marshall)
    (BC) Hodge (Boudreau, Stevens)
3rd Period
    (BC) Brown (unassisted)
    (NU) MacInnis (Kinal)
    (NU) Averill (Lori)
Goalies: (NU) Racine, (BC) Gordon

February 11, 1985 (14,451)
Harvard 6, Boston College 5
1st Period
    (HU) Smith (Fusco, MacDonald)
    (HU) Chiarelli (Busconi, Sweeney)
    (HU) Armstrong (Follows, Pawloski)
    (HU) Fusco (unassisted)
2nd Period
    (HU) Ohno (Janfaza, Carone)
    (BC) Hodge (McEachern, Stevens)
    (BC) Harlow (Mitchell, Sweeney)
    (BC) Herlihy (Livingston)
3rd Period
    (BC) Sweeney (Harlow)
    (BC) Brown (unassisted)
    (HU) MacDonald (Smith, Fusco)
Goalies: (HU) Devin, (BC) Real
Northeastern 4, Boston University 2
1st Period
    (NU) Neary (Whitfield, Lodin)
2nd Period
    (BU) Lowney (Cullen)
    (BU) Sullivan (Ryan, Marshall)
    (NU) Heffernan (Marshall, Emerson)
3rd Period
    (NU) Lori (Isbister)
    (NU) Lori (Isbister)
Goalies: (NU) Racine, (BU) Deraney

34th   February 3, 1986 (14,451)
Boston University 8, Northeastern 5
1st Period
    (NU) Isbister (O'Brien)
    (NU) Isbister (O'Brien, Pratt)
    (BU) Sveen (Sanders, Quinn)
    (NU) Buda (Marshall)

2nd Period
    (BU) Cullen (Lowney, Donatelli)
    (BU) Gerlitz (Marshall, Matchett)
    (BU) Sveen (Sanders, Labrosse)
    (BU) Cullen (Lowney, Octeau)
3rd Period
    (BU) Sanders (Ennis)
    (BU) Marshall (Matchett)
    (BU) Donatelli (Cullen, Lowney)
    (NU) Pratt (Whitfield, Neary)
Goalies: (NU) Racine, (BU) Taillefer
Boston College 4, Harvard 2
1st Period
    (BC) B. Sweeney (Houle)
    (BC) Houle (McLean, B. Sweeney)
    (BC) Harlow (McNamara, Hodge)
    (BC) Harlow (McLean)
2nd Period
    No Scoring
3rd Period
    (HU) Fusco (MacDonald)
    (HU) Fusco (Fawloski, MacDonald)
Goalies: (HU) Blair, (BC) Gordon

February 10, 1986 (14,451)
Harvard 7, Northeastern 1
1st Period
    (NU) Heinbuck (Rossi, Emerson)
    (HU) McDonald (Barakett, Fusco)
2nd Period
    (HU) Carone (unassisted)
3rd Period
    (HU) Fusco (Barakett, Benning)
    (HU) Ohno (Carone, Armstrong)
    (HU) D. Sweeney (McDonald, Fusco)
    (HU) Taylor (Janfaza, Cutone)
Goalies: (HU) McEvoy, (NU) Racine
Boston University 4, Boston College 1
1st Period
    (BU) Donatelli (Cullen, Octeau)
    (BC) Harlow (Hodge, Sweeney)
    (BU) Donatelli (Cullen, Shaunessy)
    (BU) Majkozak (Sveen, Sanders)
2nd Period
    No Scoring
3rd Period
    (BU) Marshall (Shaunessy, Octeau)
Goalies: (BU) Taillefer, (BC) Gordon

35th February 2, 1987 (14,451)
Boston University 6, Boston College 3
1st Period
    (BU) Sullivan (Cullen, Lowney)
2nd Period
    (BU) Sveen (Labrosse)
    (BU) Young (Octeau, Kelfer)
3rd Period
    (BU) Kelfer (Young, Donatelli)
    (BC) Hodge (Leetch, Stevens)
    (BU) Labrosse (Octeau, Sveen)
    (BC) Stevens (McLean)
    (BC) Stevens (Brown, McLean)
    (BU) Cullen (Sullivan, Lowney)
Goalies: (BU) Taillefer, (BC) Real

Northeastern 5, Harvard 4 (OT)
1st Period
    (NU) Rossi (unassisted)
    (HU) Barakett (Benning, Bourbeau)
2nd Period
    (NU) Birona (Rossi, Kiley)
    (HU) Bourbeau (unassisted)
3rd Period
    (NU) O'Brien (Lodin, Heffernan)
    (NU) MacInnis (O'Brien, Heffernan)
    (HU) MacDonald (Taylor)
    (HU) Barakett (Benning, Bourbeau)
Overtime
    (NU) Dowd (Pratt, Buda)
Goalies: (HU) McEvoy, (NU) Racine

February 9, 1987 (14,451)
Boston College 7, Harvard 6 (OT)
1st Period
    (HU) Barakett (Taylor, Bourbeau)
    (HU) Bourbeau (MacDonald)
    (BC) Leetch (Hodge)
    (HU) Armstrong (Barakett, Biotti)
2nd Period
    (BC) Schiefele (Hodge)
    (BC) Janney (Brown)
    (HU) MacDonald (Benning, Taylor)
3rd Period
    (HU) Young (MacDonald, Benning)
    (BC) Sweeney (Shea)
    (BC) Hodge (Janney, Stevens)
    (BC) Hodge (Stevens)
    (HU) Barakett (Young, Bourbeau)
Overtime
    (BC) Hodge (Leetch, Stevens)
Goalies: (HU) McEvoy, (BC) Littman
Boston University 4, Northeastern 3 (OT)
1st Period
    No Scoring
2nd Period
    (BU) Lowney (Sullivan)
    (BU) Thiesing (Donatelli)
3rd Period
    (NU) Dowd (Heffernan)
    (NU) Dowd (Lodin, Buda)
    (BU) Cullen (Lowney)
    (NU) O'Brien (Pratt)
Overtime
    (BU) Kelfer (Thiesing, Donatelli)
Goalies: (BU) Taillefer, (NU) Racine

36th February 1, 1988 (14,451)
Northeastern 4, Boston College 0
1st Period
    (NU) Mews (Rossi)
    (NU) Buda (Mews, Averill)
2nd Period
    (NU) O'Brien (Averill, Sullivan)
3rd Period
    (NU) Sullivan (O'Brien, Heffernan)
Goalies: (NU) Racine, (BC) Littman
Boston University 6, Harvard 4
1st Period
    (BU) Ronan (von Stefenelli, Kentala)
    (HU) Armstrong (Janfaza, Hartje)

2nd Period
    (HU) Vukonich (Melrose)
    (HU) Murphy (unassisted)
    (BU) Regan (Pesklewis, Sullivan)
    (BU) Sullivan (Dion, Kelfer)
    (BU) Headon (Kentala, Sullivan)
3rd Period
    (HU) Murphy (Vukonich)
    (BU) Tomlinson (Kelfer, Sacco)
    (BU) Kentala (Dion)
Goalies: (HU) Levin, (BU) Fish

February 8, 1988 (14,451)
Boston College 4, Harvard 2
1st Period
    (BC) Devereaux (Shea, Marshall)
    (HU) Donato (Murphy)
    (HU) Pawloski (Armstrong)
2nd Period
    (BC) Nolan (Devereaux, Shea)
3rd Period
    (BC) Shea (Stapleton, Devereaux)
    (BC) Shea (unassisted)
Goalies: (BC) Galuppo, (HU) Francis
Northeastern 6, Boston University 3
1st Period
    (NU) MacInnis (unassisted)
2nd Period
    (NU) Schure (Bivona, Russo)
    (NU) Mews (Buda)
3rd Period
    (BU) Sullivan (Kelfer, Kentala)
    (BU) Kelfer (Sacco, Kentala)
    (NU) Buda (Mews, Schure)
    (NU) O'Brien (Heffernan, Lodin)
    (NU) O'Brien (Lodin)
    (BU) McCann (Ryan, Labrosse)
Goalies: (BU) Fish, (NU) Racine

37th February 6, 1989 (14,448)
Harvard 5, Boston College 4
1st Period
    (HU) Donato (Murphy)
    (HU) Taucher (Donato, McCormack)
    (BC) Emma (Scheifele, Buckley)
    (HU) MacDonald (Donato, Ciavaglia)
2nd Period
    (HU) Young (Caplan, McCormack)
    (BC) Scheifele (Nolan, Emma)
    (HU) Bourbeau (MacDonald)
3rd Period
    (BC) Braccia (O'Neill)
    (BC) Braccia (Mullowney, Emma)
Goalies: (HU) Hughes, (BC) Littman
Boston University 5, Northeastern 4 (OT)
1st Period
    (BU) D. Sacco (McEachern, Sullivan)
    (NU) Grant (Jankowski)
    (NU) Buda (P. Sacco, Bivona)
2nd Period
    (NU) Roberts (unassisted)
    (BU) J. Sacco (M. Lappin, Tomlinson)
3rd Period
    (NU) Bivona (P. Sacco, Rossi)
    (BU) Kelfer (Dion, Sullivan)
    (BU) Sullivan (McEachern)

Overtime
(BU) C. Lappin (Dion, J. Sacco)
Goalies: (BU) Fish, (NU) Burchill

February 13, 1989 (14,448)
Boston College 4, Northeastern 1
1st Period
(BC) Franzose (Marshall)
(NU) Schiavo (Schure)
2nd Period
(BC) Pergola (Brown)
3rd Period
(BC) Sweeney (Molonis)
(BC) Sweeney (Heinze, Cleary)
Goalies: (BC) Galuppo, (NU) Burchill
Harvard 9, Boston University 6
1st Period
(HU) Young (Ciavaglia)
(HU) Howley (Hartje, Presz)
(HU) Vukonich (Donato, Murphy)
(BU) Lappin (Kris, Wood)
2nd Period
(BU) von Stefenelli (Kentala, Ronan)
(BU) Kelfer (McEachern)
(BU) Tomlinson (unassisted)
(HU) Weisbrod (Ciavaglia)
(HU) Vukonich (Donato, Sneddon)
(HU) McDonald (Young)
(BU) D. Sacco (McEachern, Sullivan)
(HU) Donato (Murphy)
3rd Period
(BU) J. Sacco (D. Sacco, M. Lappin)
(HU) Hartje (Presz, Roy)
(HU) Weisbrod (McCormack, Krayer)
Goalies: (HU) Roy, (BU) Fish

38th   February 5, 1990 (14,448)
Boston University 4, Boston College 3
1st Period
(BU) von Stefenelli (Sullivan, Tomlinson)
(BU) McEachern (Sacco, Amonte)
2nd Period
(BU) Legault (Sullivan)
(BC) Schafhauser (Glennon)
(BC) Guerin (Pascucci, Franzosa)
(BC) Emma (Pascucci, Heinze)
3rd Period
(BU) Ronan (Tomlinson, Legault)
Goalies: (BU) Cashman, (BC) Galuppo
Harvard 5, Northeastern 4
1st Period
(NU) Kellogg (Bivona, Schiavo)
(HU) Hartje (Murphy, Flomenhoft)
2nd Period
(HU) Young (Murphy)
(HU) Coady (Barringer, Popiel)
(NU) Saunders (Sullivan, Mews)
3rd Period
(NU) Schure (May, Sacco)
(NU) Roberts (Cyr, May)
(HU) Ciavaglia (Young, Vukonich)
(HU) Vukonich (Murphy, Young)
Goalies: (NU) Cole, (HU) Hughes

February 12, 1990 (14,448)
Boston College 8, Northeastern 4
1st Period
(NU) Saunders (Sullivan, Mews)
(NU) Schiavo (Cyr)
(BC) Heinze (Schafhauser, Emma)
(NU) Sullivan (Mews, Saunders)
2nd Period
(NU) Mews (Saunders)
(BC) Emma (Crowley, Heinze)
(BC) Glennon (Beran)
(BC) Farley (Pergola)
(BC) Emma (Heinze, Cleary)
(BC) Pergola (Farley)
3rd Period
(BC) Pergola (O'Neill)
(BC) McInnis (Cleary, Heinze)
Goalies: (BC) LaGrand, (NU) Hopkins
Boston University 8, Harvard 2
1st Period
(BU) Sacco (Legault, von Stefenelli)
(BU) von Stefenelli (Tomlinson, Ronan)
(BU) McEachern (Tomlinson, Ronan)
2nd Period
(BU) Sacco (McEachern, Amonte)
(BU) Tomlinson (unassisted)
(HU) Vukonich (Hartje)
(BU) Tomlinson (Ronan, Ahola)
(BU) McEachern (Sacco, Amonte)
3rd Period
(BU) Koskimaki (von Stefenelli, MacDonald)
(HU) Young (Vukonich)
Goalies: (HU) Roy, Francis, (BU) Cashman

39th   February 4, 1991 (14,448)
Boston College 5, Northeastern 3
1st Period
No Scoring
2nd Period
(NU) LaPlante (Schure)
(NU) Kenny (unassisted)
(BC) Glennon (O'Neill, Pergola)
(NU) Saunders (O'Connor)
(BC) Beran (Emma, Dennehy)
(BC) Farley (Beran)
3rd Period
(BC) Callahan (Beran, Pascucci)
(BC) Emma (unassisted)
Goalies: (NU) Cole, (BC) Galuppo
Boston University 8, Harvard 2
1st Period
(HU) Mallgrave (McCormack, Vukonich)
(BU) Tkachuk (McEachern)
(BU) Sacco (Dion)
(BU) Ronan (Tomlinson, Koskimaki)
(BU) Ronan (Tomlinson, MacDonald)
(BU) McEachern (Tkachuk)
2nd Period
(BU) Sacco (Tkachuk, McEachern)
(HU) Flomenhoft (Burke)
(BU) Amonte (McEachern)
3rd Period
(BU) LaChance (Tomlinson, Ronan)
Goalies: (HU) Roy, Hughes, (BU) Bradley

February 11, 1991 (14,448)
Northeastern 5, Harvard 0
1st Period
(NU) Schure (Kenny, Bishop)
(NU) Edgerly (Sullivan, Roberts)
(NU) Cowie (Edgerly, Sullivan)
2nd Period
(NU) Sacco (Taylor, Grossi)
3rd Period
(NU) Sullivan (Edgerly, Cowie)
Goalies: (NU) Cole, (HU) Francis
Boston University 8, Boston College 4
1st Period
(BC) Emma (Cleary, McInnis)
(BU) Krys (Sacco, Brownschilde)
(BC) Heinze (Spalla, Callahan)
(BU) Koskimaki (Ahola)
2nd Period
(BC) Cleary (Crowley, McInnis)
(BU) Amonte (von Stefenelli)
(BU) Amonte (McEachern, Tkachuk)
(BC) Franzosa (Heinze, Cleary)
(BU) Amonte (McEachern, Krys)
(BU) Friedman (Sacco, McCann)
(BU) Bavis (Tomlinson)
3rd Period
(BU) McCann (unassisted)
Goalies: (BU) Bradley, (BC) Galuppo

40th   February 3, 1992 (14,448)
Harvard 6, Boston College 4
1st Period
(HU) Coughlin (Konik, Martins)
2nd Period
(HU) Martins (unassisted)
(BC) Krayer (Spalla)
(HU) Coady (Cohagan, Baird)
(BC) Beran (Moran, Franzosa)
3rd Period
(HU) McCann (Burke)
(HU) Mallgrave (Flomenhoft, Burke)
(BC) Joyce (Rathbone)
(BC) Canavan (Spalla)
(HU) Burke (Flomenhoft, Mallgrave)
Goalies: (HU) Roy, (BC) LaGrand
Boston University 5, Northeastern 4
1st Period
(BU) Prendergast (Pomichter)
(BU) Lilley (Mark Bavis)
2nd Period
(BU) Pomichter (Prendergast)
(NU) Grossi (Saunders)
(NU) O'Connor (Saunders)
(BU) Lilley (unassisted)
(NU) Saunders (O'Connor, MacNair)
3rd Period
(NU) LaPlante (Schiavo, Aube)
(BU) D. Sacco (Prendergast, Brennan)
Goalies: (BU) Cashman, (NU) Cole

February 10, 1992 (14,448)
Boston College 5, Northeastern 3
1st Period
(NU) Kenny (Schiavo, Grossi)
(BC) Haggerty (Beran, Moran)

(NU) Bouchard (Foy)
(BC) Beran (Morgan)
2nd Period
(BC) Haggerty (Delay, Callahan)
(NU) Bishop (Lucas)
3rd Period
(BC) Spalla (Krayer)
(BC) Beran (Joyce)
Goalies: (BC) Singewald, (NU) Reynolds
Boston University 5, Harvard 2
1st Period
(BU) Prendergast (Sacco, Pomichter)
(HU) Burke (Flomenhoft)
(BU) Mike Bavis (Dion, Thorton)
(HU) Sneddon (Konik)
2nd Period
(BU) Brennan (Mark Bavis, O'Sullivan)
3rd Period
(BU) Prendergast (unassisted)
(BU) Mike Bavis (O'Sullivan, Koskimaki)
Goalies: (HU) Hughes, (BU) Cashman

41st February 1, 1993 (14,448)
Harvard 7, Northeastern 5
1st Period
(HU) Drury (unassisted)
(NU) Shields (Schiavo, MacNair)
(HU) Holmes (Mallgrave, Maguire)
(HU) Mallgrave (Flomenhoft)
2nd Period
(NU) Kellogg (Schiavo, MacNair)
(NU) Melong (Taylor, Shields)
(HU) Mallgrave (Body, Drury)
(HU) Mallgrave (Baird, Drury)
3rd Period
(HU) Farrell (Drury)
(NU) Grossi (Shields)
(HU) Gustafson (Karmanos)
(NU) Melong (Kellogg, Persson)
Goalies: (HU) Israel, (NU) Veisor
Boston University 8, Boston College 2
1st Period
(BU) Thornton (unassisted)
(BU) Pandolfo (Joubert, Lachance)
(BU) Thornton (Mike Bavis, Mark Bavis)
2nd Period
(BU) Brennan (Rausch)
3rd Period
(BC) Joyce (Spalla, Beran)
(BU) Wood (Mike Bavis)
(BC) Spalla (Chase)
(BU) Rausch (Pratt)
(BU) Joubert (Lachance)
(BU) Rausch (Koskimaki)
Goalies: (BU) Cashman, (BC) Sparrow, Singewald

February 8, 1993 (14,448)
Northeastern 4, Boston College 3
1st Period
(NU) MacNair (Schiavo)
(BC) Haggerty (Canavan, Spalla)
2nd Period
(BC) Callahan (Joyce)
(BC) Callahan (Hymovitz, Hall)

3rd Period
(NU) Schiavo (Grossi)
(NU) Grossi (Schiavo, Laplante)
(NU) Melong (Shields, Taylor)
Goalies: (NU) Veisor, (BC) Singewald
Harvard 4, Boston University 2
1st Period
(BU) Friedman (Sacco, Joubert)
(HU) Martins (Holmes, Flomenhoft)
2nd Period
(HU) Farrell (Drury)
(BU) Sacco (Foster)
3rd Period
(HU) Drury (Farrell)
(HU) Martins (unassisted)
Goalies: (HU) Tracy, (BU) Cashman

42nd February 7, 1994 (14,448)
Boston College 5, Northeastern 4 (2 OT)
1st Period
(BC) J. Callahan (Joyce, Harney)
(NU) Aube (Shields, Taylor)
2nd Period
(BC) Chase (Laferriere)
(BC) G. Callahan (Harney, B. Callahan)
(NU) MacNair (Webb)
3rd Period
(BC) Connolly (unassisted)
(NU) Shields (Schuhwerk)
(NU) Melong (Lupo)
1st Overtime
No Scoring
2nd Overtime
(BC) Joyce (J. Callahan, B. Callahan)
Goalies: (BC) Taylor, (NU) Veisor, Reynolds
Harvard 4, Boston University 2
1st Period
(BU) LaChance (Pandolfo, Thornton)
(HU) McCann (Maguire, Baird)
2nd Period
(HU) Coughlin (McCann)
3rd Period
(HU) Karmanos (Nielsen, Coughlin)
(HU) Martins (unassisted)
(BU) Thornton (Pomichter)
Goalies: (HU) Tracy, (BU) McKersie

February 14, 1994 (14,448)
Boston University 8, Northeastern 0
1st Period
(BU) Joubert (Coleman, Rausch)
(BU) Prendergast (Joubert, Pomichter)
2nd Period
(BU) Pandolfo (Bates)
(BU) Grier (Pandolfo, Donato)
(BU) Pomichter (Prendergast, Donato)
3rd Period
(BU) Joubert (Rausch, Prendergast)
(BU) Rausch (Donato, Friedman)
(BU) Bates (Pandolfo)
Goalies: (BU) Herlofsky, (NU) Reynolds, Veisor
Boston College 2, Harvard 1 (OT)
1st Period
No Scoring
2nd Period
(HU) McCann (Martins, Maguire)

3rd Period
(BC) Chase (Hymovitz, LaFerriere)
Overtime
(BC) Ashe (unassisted)
Goalies: (HU) Israel, (BC) Taylor

43rd February 6, 1995 (14,448)
Boston University 6, Northeastern 2
1st Period
(NU) Bouchard (Lupo, Melong)
(BU) Sylvia (Rausch, Wright)
(BU) Lachance (Joubert, Kelleher)
2nd Period
(BU) Prendergast (Brennan, Joubert)
(BU) Kelleher (Brennan, Joubert)
(NU) Bouchard (Collett, Shields)
(BU) Pandolfo (Brennan)
3rd Period
(BU) Rausch (unassisted)
Goalies: (BU) Herlofsky, (NU) Reynolds, Veisor
Boston College 7, Harvard 6
1st Period
(BC) McCarthy (LaFerriere, Callahan)
(BC) Haggerty (Masters)
(BC) Chase (Hymovitz)
(BC) B. Callahan (Canavan)
2nd Period
(HU) Nielsen (McLaughlin, Martins)
(BC) B. Callahan (Canavan)
(HU) Gustafson (Lonsinger, Holmes)
(HU) Coughlin (Sproule, Gustafson)
3rd Period
(BC) Chase (unassisted)
(HU) Martins (Higdon, Coughlin)
(BC) Hymovitz (Haggerty)
(HU) Karmanos (Halfnight, Lonsinger)
(HU) Martins (Coughlin)
Goalies: (HU) Tracy, (BC) Taylor

February 13, 1995 (14,448)
Northeastern 4, Harvard 2
1st Period
No Scoring
2nd Period
(NU) Collett (McGillis)
(HU) Gustafson (Karmanos)
(NU) Kelly (Lupo, McLong)
(NU) Parlon (unassisted)
(NU) Shields (Campbell, Bouchard)
(HU) Cohagen (Karmanos, Gustafson)
3rd Period
No Scoring
Goalies: (HU) Hermsdorf, (NU) Veisor
Boston University 5, Boston College 1
1st Period
(BU) Rausch (unassisted)
2nd Period
(BU) Prendergast (Lachance)
(BU) Rausch (Drury, Coleman)
(BU) Grier (O'Sullivan)
(BC) Lewis (Laferriere)
3rd Period
(BU) Wright (Lachance, Joubert)
Goalies: (BU) Herlofsky, (BC) Taylor

44th   February 5, 1996 (17,565)

Northeastern 4, Harvard 1
1st Period
    (NU) Campell (Schuhwerk)
2nd Period
    (NU) Peterson (McGillis)
3rd Period
    (NU) Campbell (Lupo, McGillis)
    (NU) Kayhko (Collett)
    (HU) MacDonald (unassisted)
Goalies: (HU) Tracy, (NU) Veisor

Boston University 4, Boston College 1
1st Period
    (BC) Harney (B. Callahan)
    (BU) Wright (O'Sullivan, Lachance)
2nd Period
    (BU) Grier (Kealty, Coleman)
3rd Period
    (BU) Ronan (Sylvia, O'Connell)
    (BU) Grier (unassisted)
Goalies: (BU) Noble, (BC) Taylor

February 12, 1996 (17,565)

Boston College 6, Harvard 2
1st Period
    (BC) Powers (O'Leary)
2nd Period
    (HU) Swenson (Famiglelli, Millar)
    (BC) Hymovitz (Reasoner)
3rd Period
    (BC) Hymovitz (Hemenway, Reasoner)
    (BC) Reasoner (Powers)
    (BC) Mittleman (Powers, O'Leary)
    (BC) Hymovitz (Reasoner, P. Masters)
    (HU) Higden (McCarthy, Miller)
Goalies: (HU) Tracy, (BC) Taylor

Boston University 11, Northeastern 4
1st Period
    (BU) Grier (Kelleher, Wood)
    (BU) Lachance (Coleman, O'Sullivan)
    (BU) Drury (Grier, Wood)
    (NU) Lupo (Shields, Campbell)
    (NU) McGillis (Kayhko, Campbell)
    (NU) McGillis (Lupo)
    (BU) Lachance (Pandolfo, O'Sullivan)
    (BU) Drury (O'Sullivan)
2nd Period
    (BU) Drury (unassisted)
    (BU) Pierce (Hynes, Walsh)
    (BU) Pandolfo (Lachance)
    (BU) O'Connell (Kelleher)
    (BU) Walsh (Pandolfo, Hynes)
    (BU) Grier (Pandolfo, Lachance)
3rd Period
    (NU) Campbell (Schunwerk, Persson)
Goalies: (NU) Veisor, Reynolds, (BU) Noble, McKersie

45th   February 3, 1997 (17,565)

Boston University 7, Harvard 1
1st Period
    (BU) Kelleher (Coleman, Degerman)
2nd Period
    No Scoring
3rd Period
    (BU) Sylvia (Bates, Johnson)
    (BU) Degerman (Drury)

    (BU) Drury (Poti, O'Connell)
    (HU) Chodorow (Storey, MacDonald)
    (BU) Donatelli (Heron)
    (BU) Pierce (Johnson, Kealty)
Goalies: (HU) Prestifilippo, (BU) Larocque

Boston College 4, Northeastern 1
1st Period
    (BC) Reasoner (Farkas, Bellefeuille)
    (NU) Barclay (Calla)
2nd Period
    No Scoring
3rd Period
    (BC) Masters (unassisted)
    (BC) Farkas (Bellefeuille)
    (BC) Caulfield (Mottau)
Goalies: (BC) Taylor, (NU) Robitaille

February 10, 1997 (17,565)

Northeastern 2, Harvard 0
1st Period
    No Scoring
2nd Period
    (NU) Campbell (Kearns, Mahoney)
3rd Period
    (NU) Kearns (Klyn, McGaughey)
Goalies: (HU) Prestifilippo, (NU) Robataille

Boston University 4, Boston College 2
1st Period
    (BC) P. Masters (C. Masters)
2nd Period
    No Scoring
3rd Period
    (BC) Reasoner (Bellefeuille)
    (BU) LaCouture (Bates)
    (BU) Walsh (Pierce, Coleman)
    (BU) Pierce (Heron, Coleman)
    (BU) Drury (Coleman)
Goalies: (BC) Taylor, (BU) Noble

46th   February 2, 1998 (17,565)

Boston University 4, Northeastern 1
1st Period
    (NU) Davis (Welch)
2nd Period
    (BU) O'Connell
    (BU) Corazzini (Perry, DiPenta)
    (BU) Sylvia (Heron)
3rd Period
    (BU) Drury (unassisted)
Goalies: (BU) Larocque, (NU) Robitaille

Harvard 5, Boston College 4 (OT)
1st Period
    (BC) Mottau (Caulfield)
    (BC) Pierandri (Masters, Mottau)
2nd Period
    (BC) Masters (Mulhern, Allen)
    (HU) Higden (Miller)
3rd Period
    (HU) Bala (unassisted)
    (BC) Allen (Reasoner, Mottau)
    (HU) Storey (unassisted)
Overtime
    (HU) Bala (S. Moore, Scorsune)
Goalies: (HU) Jonas, (BC) Clemmensen

February 9, 1998 (17,565)

Boston College 4, Northeastern 1
1st Period
    (BC) Lephart (Bellefeuille, Farkas)
2nd Period
    No Scoring
3rd Period
    (BC) Powers (Reasoner)
    (NU) Mischler (unassisted)
    (BC) Powers (Reasoner, Gionta)
    (BC) Pierando (Mulhern, Mottau)
Goalies: (BC) Clemmensen, (NU) Robitaille

Boston University 2, Harvard 1 (OT)
1st Period
    No Scoring
2nd Period
    (BU) Drury (Poti, Kelleher)
3rd Period
    (HU) Schwefel (Conklin)
Overtime
    (BU) Gillis (Poti)
Goalies: (BU) Larocque, (HU) Prestifilippo

47th   February 1, 1999 (17,565)

Northeastern 4, Harvard 3 (OT)
1st Period
    (NU) Hayward (Welch, Fahey)
    (HU) Adams (Miller)
2nd Period
    (HU) Schwefel (Nowack)
    (NU) Newson (Spiller)
    (NU) Levesque (Spiller)
3rd Period
    (HU) Scorsune (Storey, Schwefel)
Overtime
    (NU) Cummings (Zoller, Fahey)
Goalies: (HU) Prestifilippo, (NU) Braun

Boston University 3, Boston College 2 (OT)
1st Period
    (BU) Vuori (Baker)
    (BC) Farkas (Mottau)
2nd Period
    (BU) Corazzini (Baker, Cavanaugh)
    (BC) Farkas (Mottau, Masters)
3rd Period
    No Scoring
Overtime
    (BU) Bartlett (Heron)
Goalies: (BC) Clemmensen, (BU) Larocque

February 8, 1999 (17,565)

Boston College 6, Harvard 4
1st Period
    (HU) Stonehouse (Adams)
    (BC) Gionta (Bellefeuille, Orpik)
    (HU) Conklin (Allman)
2nd Period
    (HU) Turco (Storey)
    (BC) Farkas (Buckley)
    (BC) Hutchins (Pierandi, Mulhern)
3rd Period
    (BC) Gionta (Bellefeuille, Mottau)
    (BC) Hutchins (Pierandi, Orpik)
    (HU) Schwefel (Bala)
    (BC) Masters (Mottau)
Goalies: (HU) Jonas, Prestifilippo, (BC) Clemmensen

Boston University 4, Northeastern 2
1st Period
   (BU) Baker (O'Connell)
2nd Period
   (NU) Zoller (Welsh, Fahey)
   (BU) Bartlett (Hanson)
   (NU) Zoller (Holeczy)
   (BU) Corazzini (Perry)
3rd Period
   (BU) Degerman (Heron)
Goalies: (BU) Larocque, (NU) Braun

48th February 7, 2000 (17,728)

Boston College 6, Northeastern 0
1st Period
   (BC) Gionta (unassisted)
2nd Period
   (BC) Farkas (Lephart)
   (BC) Dolinar (Kolanos, Caulfield)
   (BC) Kolanos (Cass, Allen)
   (BC) Kolanos (Dolinar, Mottau)
3rd Period
   (BC) Kolanos (Farkas, Scuderi)
Goalies: (NU) Gilhooly, Braun, (BC) Clemmensen
Boston University 4, Harvard 0
1st Period
   (BU) Baker (Meyer, Aufiero)
2nd Period
   No Scoring
3rd Period
   (BU) Baker (Corazzini, Meyer)
   (BU) Chris Heron (Meyer, Aufiero)
   (BU) Baker (Sabo, DiPietro)
Goalies: (HU) Prestifilippo, (BU) DiPietro

February 14, 2000 (17,278)

Harvard 3, Northeastern 1
1st Period
   (HU) Alman (Chodorow, MacLeod)
   (HU) Moore (Turco, Schwefel)
2nd Period
   (NU) Fahey (Mischler)
3rd Period
   (HU) MacLeod (unassisted)
Boston University 4, Boston College 1
1st Period
   No Scoring
2nd Period
   (BC) Bellefeuille (Hughes, Gionta)
   (BU) Heron (Cavanaugh)
   (BU) Degerman (Dyment, Heron)
   (BU) Gillis (Meyer, Collins)
3rd Period
   (BU) Corazzini (Perry, Meyer)
Goalies: (BU) DiPietro, (BC) Kelleher

49th February 5, 2001 (17,565)

Boston University 6, Northeastern 4
1st Period
   (BU) Collins (Aufiero)
   (NU) Levesque (Mischler, Ryan)
   (BU) Corazzini (Mullen, Baker)
2nd Period
   (BU) Collins (Cavanaugh)
   (BU) Collins (Cavanaugh)
   (NU) Fahey (Levesque)

   (NU) Mischler (Levesque, Ryan)
   (BU) Gillis (Collins, Pandolfo)
3rd Period
   (NU) Jozefowicz (Fahey, Mischler)
   (BU) Corazzini (Pandolfo)
Goalies: (BU) Tapp, (NU) Gilhooly
Boston College 4, Harvard 1
1st Period
   (BC) Gionta (Cass, Scuderi)
   (BC) Kobasew (Scuderi, Orpik)
2nd Period
   (BC) Hughes (Eaves, Gionta)
3rd Period
   (BC) Voce (Gionta)
   (HU) Turano (unassisted)
Goalies: (BC) Clemmensen, (HU) Jonas

February 12, 2001 (17,278)

Northeastern 8, Harvard 7
1st Period
   (HU) Kinkopf (Cantanucci, D. Moore)
   (HU) Pettit (Moore, Capouch)
   (NU) Sullivan (Levesque, Fahey)
   (NU) Cummings (Ryan, Peterman)
   (HU) Barlow (D. Moore, S. Moore)
   (HU) Cantanucci (S. Moore, Kinkopf)
2nd Period
   (HU) Bala (Moore, Pettit)
   (NU) Levesque (Mischler, Jozefowicz)
   (HU) Capouch (Pettit, Bala)
   (NU) Fahey (Mischler, Cummings)
   (NU) Cummings (Lynch, Mastronardi)
3rd Period
   (HU) S. Moore (unassisted)
   (NU) Ryan (Mischler, Engbrecht)
   (NU) Hayward (Peterman, Ortlip)
   (NU) Mischler (Jozefowicz, Fahey)
Goalies: (HU) Jonas, (NU) Braun, Gilhooly
Boston College 5, Boston University 3
1st Period
   (BC) Forrest (unassisted)
   (BC) Kolanos (Scuderi)
2nd Period
   (BC) Kobasew (Kolanos, Cass)
   (BU) Skladany (Bussoli)
   (BU) Magowan (Collins, Tapp)
3rd Period
   (BC) Scuderi (unassisted)
   (BU) Pandolfo (Collins, Cavanaugh)
   (BC) Eaves (Voce, Gionta)
Goalies: (BC) Clemmensen, (BU) Tapp

50th February 4, 2002 (17,565)

Boston University 5, Boston College 3
1st Period
   (BC) Voce (Cass, Giuliano)
2nd Period
   (BU) Baker (unassisted)
   (BC) Alberts (Forrest, Murphy)
   (BU) Sabo (Pandolfo)
3rd Period
   (BU) Whitney (unassisted)
   (BU) Sabo (McConnell, Pandolfo)
   (BC) Forrest (D'Arpino, Giuliano)
   (BU) Pandolfo (Collins)
Goalies: (BC) Kaltiainen, (BU) Fields

Northeastern 5, Harvard 2
1st Period
   (NU) Ryan (Guerriero)
2nd Period
   (HU) Bernakevitch (Cavanaugh)
   (NU) Dudgeon (Mudryk)
   (NU) Ortlip (Herriman, Engbrecht)
3rd Period
   (NU) Ryan (Guerriero, Mastronardi)
   (NU) Ryan (Guerriero, Judy)
   (HU) Turano (Moore)
Goalies: (NU) Gibson, (HU) Grumet-Morris

February 11, 2002 (17,278)

Boston College 4, Harvard 0
1st Period
   (BC) Voce (Hennes, Adams)
   (BC) Eaves (Voce, Adams)
2nd Period
   (BC) D'Arpino (Giuliano, Dolinar)
3rd Period
   (BC) Cass (Peterson, Dolinar)
Goalies: (HU) Crothers, (BC) Kaltiainen
Boston University 5, Northeastern 3
1st Period
   (BU) Maiser (Klema)
2nd Period
   (BU) Whitney (unassisted)
   (NU) Lynch (Fahey)
   (NU) Lynch (unassisted)
   (NU) Fahey (Ortlip)
3rd Period
   (BU) Pandolfo (Miller, Meyer)
   (BU) Maiser (Klema, Magowan)
   (BU) Baker (Whitney)
Goalies: (BU) Fields, (NU) Gibson

Olympians and NHL Players

Beanpot Players in the Olympic Games

Boston College Eagles		Boston University Terriers		Harvard University Crimson	
Year	Player	Year	Player	Year	Player
1932	Joe Fitzgerald	1936[2]	John Lax	1932[2]	John Chase
1952[2]	Len Ceglarski		Paul Rowe		John Garrison
	Jack Mulhern	1948	Jack Garrity		Alfred Winsor (Coach)
1956	Wellington Burtnett	1952[2]	Red Czarnota	1936[2]	John Garrison
	Frank O'Grady	1956[2]	Dick Rodenheiser		Frank Stubbs
1964	Tom "Red" Martin	1960[1]	Dick Rodenheiser	1948	John Garrison (Coach)
1968	John Cunniff	1972[2]	Tim Regan		Goodwin Harding
	Paul Hurley		Herb Wakabayashi (Japan)	1952[2]	Bob Ridder (Manager)
	Jim Logue	1976	Dick Lamby	1956[2]	Bill Cleary
1972[2]	Kevin Ahearn	1980[1]	Jim Craig		Bob Ridder (Manager)
	Tom Mellor		Mike Eruzione (Captain)	1960[1]	Bill Cleary
	Tim Sheehy		Jack O'Callahan		Bob Cleary
1984	Gary Sampson		Dave Silk		Bob McVey
1988	Greg Brown	1988	Clark Donatelli		Bob Owen
	Craig Janney		Scott Young	1976	Dan Bolduc
	Brian Leetch (Captain)	1992	Clark Donatelli (Captain)		Ted Thorndike
	Kevin Stevens		Scott Lachance	1984	Mark Fusco
1992	Greg Brown		Shawn McEachern		Scott Fusco
	David Emma		Joe Sacco		Tim Taylor (Asst. Coach & GM)
	Scott Gordon		Keith Tkachuk	1988	Alan Bourbeau
	Steve Heinze		Scott Young		Scott Fusco
	Marty McInnis	1994	John Lilley		Lane MacDonald
	Tim Sweeney		David Sacco		Ben Smith (Asst. Coach)
1994	Ted Crowley		Adrian Aucoin (Canada)[2]	1992	Ted Donato
	Ian Moran	1998	Tony Amonte		Ted Drury
	Brian Leetch		Keith Tkachuk		C. J. Young
1998	Bill Guerin	2002	Tony Amonte	1994	Joe Bertagna (Asst. GM)
	Brian Leetch		Keith Tkachuk		Peter Ciavaglia
2002	Bill Guerin		Chris Drury		Ted Drury
			Scott Young		Tim Taylor (Coach & GM)
			Tom Poti		Alain Roy (Canada)[4]

[1] Gold-medal winner

[2] Silver-medal winner

[3] Bronze-medal winer

NHL Players

Boston College

Player	BC Years	NHL Team(s)	Years
Harvey Bennett	1972–73	5 Teams	1974–79
Doug Brown	1987–91	3 Teams	1987–
Greg Brown	1986–90	3 Teams	1990–95
Dom Campedelli	1982–85	Montreal	1985–86
Ted Crowley	1989–91	Hartford	1993–94
David Emma	1987–91	NJ, Boston	1992–97
Jeff Farkas			
Matt Glennon	1987–91	Boston	1991–92
Scott Gordon	1982–86	Quebec	1989–91
Bill Guerin	1989–91	NJ, Edmonton, Boston	1991–
Scott Harlow	1982–86	St. Louis	1987–88
Steve Heinze	1988–91	Boston	1991–
Ken Hodge	1984–87	3 Teams	1988–93
Paul Hurley	1964–68	Boston	1968–69
Craig Janney	1985–87	5 Teams	1987–
Brian Leetch	1986–88	NYR	1987–
David Littman	1985–89	Buffalo, Tampa Bay	1990–93
Marty McInnis	1988–91	NYI, Calgary	1991–
Tom Mellor	1968–72	Detroit	1973–75
Ian Moran	1991–93	Pittsburgh	1995–
Mike Mottau			
Joe Mullen	1975–79	4 Teams	1981–97
Bill O'Dwyer	1978–82	LA, Boston	1983–90
Marty Reasoner	1996–98	St. Louis	1998–
Gary Sampson	1978–82	Washington	1983–87
Tim Sheehy	1985–89	Detroit, Hartford	1977–80
Paul Skidmore			
Tommy Songin	1973–77	Boston	1978–81
Kevin Stevens	1983–87	4 Teams	1987–
Bob Sweeney	1982–86	4 Teams	1986–96
Tim Sweeney	1985–89	4 Teams	1990–96

Boston University

Player	BU Years	NHL Team(s)	Years
Peter Ahola	1989–91	4 Teams	1991–94
Tony Amonte	1989–91	Chicago	1991–
Adrien Aucoin	1991–92	Vancouver, NYI	1994
Ron Anderson	1969–72	Washington	1974–75
Shawn Bates	1993–97	Boston, NYI	1997–
John Bethel	1976–79	Winnipeg	1979–80
Rich Brennan	1991–95	Los Angeles	1996–2000
Bob Brown	1970–72	NE Whalers	
Jim Craig	1976–79	3 Teams	1979–84
John Cullen	1983–87	4 Teams	1988–98
John Danby	1969–72	NE Whalers	
Cleon Daskalakis	1980–84	Boston	1984–87
Rick DiPietro	1999–00	NYI	2000–
Clark Donatelli	1984–87	Minnesota, Boston	1989–92
Chris Drury	1994–98	Colorado	1998–
Dale Dunbar	1981–85	Vancouver, Boston	1985–89
Jim Ennis	1985–87	Edmonton	1987–88
Paul Fenton	1979–82	7 Teams	1984–92
Mike Fidler	1974–76	4 Teams	1976–83
Doug Friedman	1990–94	Nashville	1995–99
Mike Grier	1993–96	Edmonton	1996–
Bob Gryp	1968–72	Boston, Washington	1973–76
Ric Jordan	1970–72	NE Whalers	
Ken Kuzyk	1972–76	Cleveland Barons	1976–78
Scott Lachance	1990–91	Vancouver	1991–
Dan Lacouture	1996–97	Edmonton, Pittsburgh	1997–
Dick Lamby	1976–78	St. Louis	1979–81

Player	BU Years	NHL Team(s)	Years
John Lilley	1991–93	Anaheim	1993–96
Kaj Linna	1991–95	Nashville	1995–98
Shawn MacEachern	1988–91	Boston, Ottawa	1991–
Rick Meagher	1973–77	4 Teams	1979–82
Paul Miller	1977–80	Colorado	1981–82
Jack O'Callahan	1976–79	Chicago, New Jersey	1982–89
Paul O'Neil	1971–73	Vancouver, Boston	1973–76
Tom O'Regan	1979–83	Pittsburgh	1983–86
Chris O'Sullivan	1993–96	Calgary, Anaheim	1996–2000
Jay Pandolfo	1992–96	New Jersey	1996–
Tom Poti	1996–98	Edmonton	1998–
Ed Ronan	1987–91	4 Teams	1991–98
David Sacco	1988–93	NYI	1994–96
Joe Sacco	1987–90	Washington	1990–
Scott Shaunessy	1983–87	Quebec	1986–87
Dave Silk	1976–79	3 Teams	1979–86
Mike Sullivan	1986–90	Phoenix	1990–
Keith Tkachuk	1990–91	Phoenix, St. Louis	1991–
Dave Tomlinson	1987–91	3 Teams	1991–95
Nick Vachon	1990–91	NYI	1996–97
Phil von Stefenelli	1987–91	Boston, Ottawa	1995–97
Bill Whelton	1978–81	Winnipeg	1980–81
Scott Young	1985–87	St. Louis	1987–

Harvard University

Player	HU Years	NHL Team(s)	Years
Craig Adams	1996–99	Carolina	2000–
Danny Balduc	1972–75	Detroit, Calgary	1978–84
Greg Britz	1979–83	Toronto, Hartford	1983–87
Peter Ciavaglia	1987–89	Buffalo	1991–93
Ted Donato	1987–91	Boston, NYI	1991–
Ted Drury	1989–91	4 Teams	1993–
Mark Fusco	1979–83	Hartford	1983–85
Jack Hughes	1976–80	Colorado	1980–82
Dave Hynes	1969–73	Boston	1973–75
Craig MacDonald			
Steve Martins	1991–95	Hartford, Ottawa	1995–
Bob McManama	1970–73	Pittsburgh	1973–76
Kirk Nielsen	1992–96	Boston	1997–98
Neil Sheehy	1979–83	3 Teams	1983–92
Don Sweeney	1984–88	Boston	1988–
Tripp Tracy	1992–96	Carolina	1997–98
C.J. Young	1986–90	Calgary, Boston	1992–93

Northeastern University

Player	NU Years	NHL Team(s)	Years
Sandy Beadle	1979–81	Winnipeg	1979
Randy Bucyk	1980–84	Montreal, Calgary	1985, 90
Art Chisolm	1958–61	Boston	1960–61
Rob Cowie	1987–91	Los Angeles	1994–96
Scott Gruhl	1977–78	LA, Pittsburgh	1981–88
Dan McGillis	1992–96	Edmonton, Philadelphia	1996–
Chris Nilan	1976–79	3 Teams	1978–91
Bruce Racine	1984–88	Pittsburgh, St. Louis	1991–96
Brian Sullivan	1987–91	New Jersey	1991–92
Jim Walsh	1976–79	Buffalo	1981–82

Participants List

Boston College

Adams, John	2001–02
Aiken, Paul	1960–63
Ahearn, Kevin	1967–70
Ahern, Charlie	1970–72
Alberts, Andrew	2001–02
Albrecht, Mark	1973–76
Allen, Bobby	1997–01
Allen, Whitney	1965–68
Amidon, George	1977–81
Annecchiarico, Dave	1976–80
Apprille, Thomas	1962–64
Army, Bill	1976–80
Arnold, Peter	1978–79, 1980–82
Ashe, Tom	1992–96
Augustine, Joe	1975–78
Babine, Bob	1951–54
Baier, John	1972–74
Barger, Steve	1977–78
Barrett, Paul	1974–78
Barron, Michael	1984–86
Bartholomew, Kevin	1975–76
Barton, Jim	1969–71
Bastarache, Raymond	1966–69
Bellefeuille, Blake	1996–00
Bennett, Harvey	1970–73
Beran, Marc	1989–93
Bilafer, Paul	1954–55
Blossom, Lee	1979–83
Boudreau, George	1981–85
Boyle, Robert	1957–59
Braccia, Rich	1985–89
Breen, Edward	1962–63, 1964–65
Brown, Doug	1982–86
Brown, Greg	1986–87, 1988–90
Buckley, Brendan	1995–99
Buckley, David	1985–89
Buckley, Jerry	1991–95
Bunyon, Ned	1956–58
Burnett, John	1969–70
Burns, Brian	1976–80
Burtnett, Wellington	1950–53
Byrne, Arthur	1964–65
Cadagan, John	1955–58
Callahan, Brian	1993–97
Callahan, Greg	1992–96
Callahan, Jack	1990–94
Callahan, John	1960–63
Callow, Don	1969–71
Campedelli, Dominic	1982–85
Cananvan, Rob	1991–95
Canniff, John	1951–52, 1953–54
Carey, Paul	1954–55
Carlson, Brad	1993–97
Carroll, Edward	1953–56
Carroll, Joseph	1950–53
Casey, Joe	1977–79
Cass, Bill	1999–2002
Cassidy, Myles	1955–58

Caulfield, Kevin	1996–2000
Cedorchuk, Steven	1966–69
Ceglarski, Tim	1986–87
Celeta, Joseph	1954–55, 1956–57
Chase, Don	1992–96
Cheevers, Rob	1986–89
Chisholm, Jim	1980–84
Cisternelli, James	1952–54
Clarke, Gordie	1965–68
Cleary, Joe	1988–92
Clemmensen, Scott	1997–01
Coakley, Edward	1956–57
Cohen, Jeff	1965–68
Colleran, Joseph	1952–53
Conceison, Bob	1971–72
Connolly, Jeff	1993–94
Connolly, Mike	1987–88
Cooper, Bob	1971–72
Cornish, Robert	1964–66
Correia, Mike	1994–95, 1996–99
Costa, George	1950–52
Cowles, Jeff	1978–82
Cronin, Jack	1969–72
Cronin, Mike	1977–78
Crowley, Ted	1989–91
Cunniff, John	1963–66
Cusack, Jack	1957–60
Daley, Billy	1958–61
D'Arcy, Ray	1971–74
D'Arpino, Anthony	1999–00, 2002
Delaney, Chris	1981–82, 1983–84
Delaney, Sean	1987–89
Delay, Mike	1988–92
Delay, Tim	1987–89
Dempsey, Dick	1952–55
Dennehy, Mark	1987–91
D'Entremont, Charles	1953–56
Devereaux, John	1984–88
Dolinar, Ales	1998–02
Donlan, William	1954–55
Dowling, Steve	1965–68
Downes, Eddie	1962–65
Doyle, Jim	1972–74
Driscoll, Brian	1975–76, 1977–79
Driscoll, Charles	1959–62
Duffy, David	1961–64
Duffy, Jim	1951–52
Duncan, Clark	1958–60
Dyer, Phil	1963–66
Dziama, Justin	2002
Eaves, Ben	2000–02
Ellis, Doug	1978–82
Emery, Darren	1988–89
Emery, Bob	1982–86
Emery, Edward	1950–52, 1954–55
Emma, David	1987–91
Emmons, William	1950–53
Ewanouski, Mike	1977–81
Famigletti, Bob	1958–61

Farkas, Jeff	1996–00
Farley, Sean	1987–91
Fernald, Joe	1973–77
Ferriter, Bob	1973–77
Fidler, Joe	1971–73
Flaherty, Peter	1962–65
Flavin, Frederick	1964–65
Flynn, Mike	1966–69
Flynn, Tim	1974–75
Forgues, Gerad	1953–54, 1955–56
Forrest, J.D.	2000–02
Fox, Donald	1954–57
Franzosa, David	1988–92
Fuller, Dick	1964–67
Gagliardi, Richard	1953–56
Galuppo, Sandy	1987–91
Gervasi, Michael	1984–88
Giles, Kenneth	1960–63
Gionta, Brian	1997–01
Giuliano, Jeff	1998–02
Glennon, Matt	1987–91
Glynn, Brendan	1975–76
Godfrey, Scott	1969–72
Gordon, Scott	1982–86
Grant, George	1960–62
Griffin, Dan	1980–84
Guerin, Bill	1989–91
Haggerty, Ryan	1991–95
Haley, Bob	1970–71
Hall, Todd	1991–93
Hammer, Paul	1977–81
Hanlon, John	1981–82
Harlow, Scott	1982–86
Harney, Joe	1993–97
Harrington, Jack	1978–79
Harris, Toby	1993–97
Hart, Rich	1972–75
Havern, Ned	2001–02
Hayes, Ed	1971–72
Hehir, Bobby	1977–81
Heinze, Steve	1988–91
Hemenway, Ken	1994–98
Hennes, Ty	2000–02
Herlihy, Jim	1981–85
Higgins, Neil	1970–73
Hodge, Kenneth	1984–87
Hogan, Billy	1960–63
Horton, Kevin	1970–71
Hosford, Joseph	1950–52
Houle, Kevin	1982–86
House, Skip	1975–78
Hughes, Marty	1997–01
Hughes, Owen	1958–61
Hurley, Paul	1965–67, 1968–69
Hutchins, Tony	1996–00
Hymovitz, David	1992–96
Jangro, Joseph	1956–59
Janney, Craig	1985–87
Johnson, Woody	1964–67
Joyce, John	1990–94
Kaltiainen, Matti	2001–02
Kane, Richard	1955–58
Kearns, Francis	1962–65

Keaveney, Joe	1970–71
Kelleher, Tim	2000–02
Kelly, Paul	1999–00
Kennedy, Bill	1976–78
Kennedy, Shawn	1986–89
Kenty, Ed	1970–73
Kierstad, Allan	1963–66
Kiley, Robert	1951–54
Kimball, Kevin	1970–73
King, Jim	1971–74
Kinsman, Fred	1964–67
Kobasew, Chuck	2000–01
Kolanos, Krys	1999–01
Kopecky, William	1984–85
Krayer, Jim	1991–95
Kupka, Bob	1964–67
Kyle, Walt	1976–78
Laferriere, Rob	1992–95
LaGrand, Scott	1989–92
Lambert, Chuck	1971–74
Larkin, Francis	1960–61
Latshaw, Thomas	1961–62, 1963–64
Lawrence, Ray	1970–71
Leahy, Taylor	2001–02
Leary, Bill	1954–57
Leetch, Brian	1986–87
Leetch, Jack	1960–63
Leetch, Richard	1964–65
Leonard, Robert	1957–60
Lephart, Mike	1997–01
Lewis, Timmy	1994–96
Littman, David	1985–89
Livingston, David	1981–85
Logue, James	1958–61
Looney, Brian	1988–89
Lowry, Jack	1975–76
Lufkin, Paul	1961–64
Lufkin, Tom	1963–64, 1965–66
MacCarthy, Barry	1966–69
Madden, John	1957–59
Maguire, William	1951–54
Mahoney, Thomas	1956–58
Manganaro, Sal	1991–93
Marenholz, Otto	1978–79, 1980–81
Marin, Carl	1954–57
Marsh, John	1962–64
Marshall, Chris	1989–90
Marshall, Paul	1985–89
Martin, Mike	1973–77
Martin, Thomas	1958–61
Masters, Chris	1995–99
Masters, Peter	1993–97
McCarran, Joe	1979–81, 1982–83
McCarthy, Charlie	1959–62
McCarthy, Mike	1991–95
McClellan, Bob	1977–78, 1980–81
McCool, Steve	1987–88
McDonough, Billy	1980–84
McDonough, Dan	1974–77
McEachern, Joe	1984–85

McElaney, Edward	1963–64	Putnam, Willy	1966–69
McGuire, John	1975–78	Quinn, Francis	1953–56
McHale, Clifton	1992–96	Rathbone, Jason	1988–92
McInnis, Marty	1988–91	Rauseo, Ed	1980–84
McIver, Donald	1950–51,	Real, Shaun	1984–87
	1952–53	Reardon, Bob	1970–73
McLaughlin, Andy	1995–99	Reardon, Ed	1974–77
McLean, John	1983–84,	Reasoner, Marty	1995–98
	1985–87	Redmond, Dale	1974–75
McLennan, Mark	1997–01	Reilly, John	1987–88,
McManama, Ben	2001–02		1989–91
McNamara, John	1982–86	Riley, Mark	1972–75
McPhee, George	1966–69	Riley, Richard	1958–60
Mellor, Tom	1969–71,	Riley, Rob	1974–78
	1972–73	Robertson, Mike	1966–67
Michaud, Richard	1954–57	Rudman, Robert	1958–60
Miller, Robbie	2001–02	St. Pierre, Duke	1987–88
Milton, Bruce	1983–85	Saltmarsh, Sherman	1950–53
Mishler, Todd	1980–82	Sampson, Gary	1978–82
Mitchell, Tim	1981–85	Scarry, Leo	1973–74
Mittleman, Ryan	1995–96	Schafhauser, Pat	1989–91
Monahan, John	1971–74	Scheifele, Steve	1986–89
Monleon, Robin	1980–84	Schilling, Paul	1967–70
Moore, Gordie	1979–82	Scuderi, Rob	1997–01
Moran, Ian	1991–93	Shanley, Vin	1969–72
Morse, Pete	1969–70	Shannon, Ryan	2001–02
Mottau, Mike	1996–00	Shea, Daniel	1984–88
Moylan, John	1963–66	Shea, Neil	1982–86
Moylan, Joe	1954–57	Sheehan, David	1956–57
Mulhern, Matt	1995–99	Sheehy, Paul	1954–57
Mullen, Jim	1963–66	Sheehy, Tim	1967–70
Mullen, Joe	1975–79	Shenk, Tim	1986–89
Mullowney, Mike	1959–60	Shocket, Ari	1995–96
Mullowney, Mike	1985–89	Siblo, Robert	1952–54
Murphy, Mark	1978–82	Sico, Mike	1970–71
Murphy, Patrick	1964–66	Singewald, Josh	1991–95
Murphy, Ryan	2001–02	Skidmore, Paul	1975–79
Murray, Tom	1971–72,	Smith, Ed	1957–60
	1973–74	Smith, Jeff	1978–82
Nelson, Norman	1962–63	Smith, Paul	1953–54,
Nolan, Len	1970–72		1955–56
Nolan, Bill	1986–90	Smith, Richie	1972–76
O'Connor, Bob	1979–82	Smith, Terry	1974–75
O'Connor, Roderick	1961–62	Smythe, Tim	1968–70
O'Dwyer, Billy	1978–82	Snyder, John	1967–68,
O'Grady, Frank	1950–53		1969–70
O'Leary, Jamie	1994–98	Songin, Tom	1974–77
O'Neil, Mike	1979–83	Spalla, Michael	1990–94
O'Neil, Paul	1974–75	Sparrow, Mike	1991–93
O'Neill, Donald	1957–59	Spina, Dave	2001–02
O'Neil, Jack	1967–68	Stapleton, Christopher	1984–88
O'Neill, Jeff	1987–91	Stevens, Kevin	1983–87
Orpik, Brooks	1998–01	Stickney, Brett	1991–93
Orr, John	1982–86	Sullivan, Eddie	1960–63
Parlato, Tom	1971–72	Sullivan, John	1967–70
Pascucci, Ron	1989–93	Sullivan, Tom	1974–76
Pergola, Dave	1987–91	Sweeney, Bob	1982–86
Pergola, David	1957–60	Sweeney, Tim	1985–89
Peterson, Brett	2000–02	Switaj, Billy	1980–83
Picard, Randi	1970–71	Switaj, Mark	1977–81
Pierandri, Nick	1995–99	Taylor, Greg	1993–97
Pitts, Alvan	1955–58	Taylor, Harvey	1971–72
Pors, Robert	1959–60	Taylor, Ryan	1993–95,
Powers, Andy	1995–99		1996–97
Powers, John	1969–71	Tiernan, James	1954–56
Powers, Mike	1972–73	Timmins, Norbert	1952–53
Prevett, Jim	1966–68	Toczylowski, Charlie	1967–70

Toran, Ralph	1962–65	Carlacci, Cesare	1981–84
Vassil, Basil	1953–54	Carnevale, Dan	1980–83
Voce, Tony	2000–02	Carriere, Arthur	1955–58
Wainwright, David	1993–97	Carruthers, Jack	1955–58
Walker, A.J.	2002	Carter, Lyman	1963–65
Walker, Jeffrey	1986–89	Carver, Davide	1960–62
Walsh, Ron	1957–60	Cashman, Scott	1989–93
Warren, John	1961–62	Cavanaugh, Dan	1998–2001
Welch, Jerry	1979–80	Chausse, Scott	1979–80
Whyte, David	1986–87	Cicoria, Anthony	1952–53,
Willis, Fred	1968–69		1955–58
Wilkens, Bill	1973–77	Cleary, Paul	1952–53
Wilson, Jeremy	1999–00	Coleman, Jon	1993–97
Wray, Chris	1979–81	Comeau, Alien	1962–64
Wright, Tom	1973–82	Collins, Brian	1999–2002
Yandle, Buddy	1973–74	Collins, Ralph	1953–54
Yetten, Ned	1971–74	Connolly, T. J.	1980–84
York, Jerry	1964–67	Connors, Eddie	1960–63
Young, Kerry	1974–77	Conte, Vic	1963–66
Zygulski, Scott	1989–93	Cooke, John	1965–68
		Corazzini, Carl	1997–2001
Boston University		Corriveau, John	1977–79
Abbott, Darrell	1966–69	Cotter, Bill	1977–81
Abbott, Larry	1970–72	Cournoyea, Raymond	1970–73
Ahola, Peter	1989–91	Craig, Jim	1976–79
Aiken, John	1954–55	Creighton, Larry	1956–59
Alger, Rich	1995–97	Crisafulli, David	1966–67
Amonte, Tony	1989–91	Crocker, Robert	1954–55
Anderson, Ron	1970–72	Cronin, John	1999–2002
Aucoin, Adrian	1991–92	Cross, James	1958–59
Aufiero, Pat	1998–2002	Crozier, Steve	1983–84
August, Jerry	1979–83	Cullen, John	1983–87
Baker, Jack	1998–2002	Dahlberg, Dave	1989–93
Bannerman, Chris	1973–75	Dakin, James	1967–69
Barich, Bob	1979–83	Danby, John	1969–72
Barker, Fred	1981–82	Darling, Bob	1980–84
Bartlett, Russ	1997–99	Daskalakis, Cleon	1980–84
Bassi, Fred	1964–67	Davenport, Larry	1967–70
Bates, Shawn	1993–97	Davies, Rob	1978–82
Bavis, Mark	1989–93	Decker, Wayne	1967–70
Bavis, Mike	1989–93	Decloe, Dick	1972–73
Beauchain, Chuck	1988–89	Degerman, Tommi	1996–2000
Bethel, John	1976–79	Delorey, Joe	1981–85
Bise, Chris	1990–94	Denihan, Mike	1960–63
Bishop, William	1972–75	Denning, Jerry	1950–54
Blainey, William	1959–60	Deraney, Bob	1984–87
Boileau, Bob	1976–79	Devlin, Patrick	1973–76
Boily, Serge	1966–69	Dion, Tom	1987–92
Bradley, John	1987–91	DiMella, Mike	1998–2001
Bradley, Robert	1952–54	DiPenta, Joe	1997–99
Brady, Dan	1969–72	DiPietro, Rick	1999–2000
Brennan, Rich	1991–95	DiVincenzo, Ron	1957–59
Brown, Peter	1972–76	Dolloff, Steve	1970–73
Brown, Robert	1970–72	Dooley, John	1958–59
Brownschidle, Mark	1988–92	Donate, Dan	1991–94
Bryand, Ted	1969–70	Donaldson, Coleman	1969–70
Buckton, Bill	1973–76	Donatelli, Clark	1984–87
Buell, Robert	1954–55	Donatelli, Peter	1994–98
Burdett, Danny	1980–81	D'Orio, Frank	1964–65
Burlington, William	1972–75	Driscoll, Leonard	1953–55
Burns, John	1952–55	Drury, Chris	1994–98
Burrowes, Guy	1969–72	Dudley, Robert	1974–77
Bussoli, Mike	1999–2002	Dunbar, Dale	1980–85
Cahoon, Don	1969–72	Dupuis, Robert	1955–58
Callaghan, Kevin	1979–80	Durocher, Brian	1974–78
Campbell, Ryan	1997–98	Dwyer, Thomas	1952–55
Cappellano, Joe	1982–84	Dyment, Chris	1998–2002

Name	Years	Name	Years	Name	Years	Name	Years
Eberly, Glen	1961–63	Kelfer, Mike	1985–89	McCann, Peter	1972–73	Robinson, William	1959–60
Emery, Keith	1997–2001	Kelleher, Chris	1994–98	McClellan, John	1973–77	Rodenheiser, Richard	1951–53
Ennis, Jim	1985–87	Kelley, Paul	1950–52	McConnell, Brian	2001–02	Ronan, Ed	1987–91
Enright, Pat	1957–60	Kelley, Raymond	1951–54	McComb, John	1954–55	Ronan, Dan	1995–99
Eruzione, Mike	1973–77	Kentala, Ville	1986–89	McCormack, William	1957–60	Ross, Ken	1961–62, 1963–65
Fay, Gary	1973–77	Kimball, Tim	1977–81	McCurdy, Russ	1958–61	Ross, Tom	1963–66
Fennie, Bruce	1963–66	King, Scott	1995–96	McEachern, Shawn	1988–91	Rosseau, Robert	1951–54
Fennie, Mark	1967–68	Kinlin, Sarge	1955–58	McFaun, Francis	1961–63	Rowan, Robert	1960–63
Fenton, Paul	1978–82	Klapes, George	1979–83	McKersie, J.P.	1991–96	Roy, Travis	1995–96
Fenwick, William	1969–70	Klema, David	2001–02	McInnis, Bennett	1961–63	Russell, Bernie	1951–52
Ferreira, Jack	1963–66	Koskimaki, Petteri	1989–93	McLachian, Peter	1964–67	Ryan, Tom	1984–88
Ferullo, Shawn	1993–97	Krys, Mark	1987–91	Meagher, Rick	1973–77	Ryan, Wayne	1965–67
Fidler, Mark	1977–81	Kuzyk, Kenneth	1972–76	Meagher, Terry	1973–76	Sabo, John	1999–2002
Fidler, Mike	1974–76	Labrosse, Eric	1984–88	Meagher, Tony	1976–80	Sacco, David	1988–89, 1990–93
Fields, Sean	2000–02	Lachance, Bob	1992–96	Meehan, Ronald	1953–54		
Fila, Andy	1964–65	Lachance, Scott	1990–91	Melanson, John	1976–78, 1979–80	Sacco, Joe	1987–90
Fish, Peter	1984–89	LaCouture, Dan	1996–97			Sampson, Alden	1961–62, 1963–64
Fitzgerald, Peter	1960–62	LaFort, Bryan	1988–89	Meyer, Freddy	1999–2002		
Flynn, William	1960–62	LaGarde, Denis	1981–84	Miller, Bryan	2001–02	Sanders, Scott	1984–88
Foreman, Brian	1984–86	LaGarde, Mike	1970–73	Miller, Paul	1977–80	Shannon, Art	1952–53
Foster, Stephen	1989–90, 1991–93	Lamby, Dick	1976–78	Mills, Robert	1952–53	Shaunessy, Scott	1983–87
		Lappin, Chris	1987–88	Milton, Bruce	1980–82	Shaunessy, Steve	1986–88
Fox, John	1975–79	Lappin, Mike	1987–88	Morton, Vincent	1977–79	Sheen, Colin	1997–2001
Friedman, Doug	1990–94	Larocque, Michel	1995–99	Mullen, Mark	2000–02	Silk, Dave	1976–79
Gama, Glen	1968–69	Leahy, John	1959–61	Mullen, Mickey	1976–80	Simpson, Steve	1979–81
Gerlitz, Paul	1982–86	Leatherbee, Harold	1977–80	Mullins, Vince	1976–77	Sinclair, Marc	1979–83
Giandomenico, Paul	1969–72	LeBlond, Bill	1976–80	Murphy, John	1953–56	Skladany, Frantisek	2000–02
Gillis, Nick	1997–99, 2000–01	Lee, Richard	1951–53	Murray, Robert	1969–72	Smith, Les	1980–81
		Legault, Alexandre	1989–91	Mutch, Kevin	1982–84	Smith, Robert	1960–63
Gilmour, Brian	1964–67	Levin, Henry	1955–57	Nieland, Scott	1977–80	Sobeski, Mike	1964–67
Giuliotti, Andy	1958–60	Lilley, John	1991–92	Noble, Tom	1994–98	Spinney, Don	1959–62
Glover, James	1972–75	Linna, Kaj	1991–95	O'Callahan, Jack	1975–79	Stanfield, Vic	1972–75
Goegan, Grant	1978–80	Little, Tim	1981–83	O'Connell, Albie	1995–99	Stirling, Steve	1968–71
Goguen, Don	1959–62	LoPresti, Dave	1998–99	O'Connell, Dennis	1963–66	Sullivan, Chuck	1982–85
Gowing, Wayne	1968–71	Lowell, James	1972–73, 1974–75	Octeau, Jay	1983–87	Sullivan, Mike	1986–90
Gray, Mickey	1966–69			O'Neil, Paul	1972–73	Sullivan, William	1955–58
Greeley, Steve	2000–02	Lowney, Edward	1983–87	O'Neil, Bill	1976–79	Sunderland, Robert	1973–76
Green, Richard	1962–64	Luimes, John	1980–81	O'Regan, Tom	1979–83	Suterland, Allan	1956–57
Grier, Mike	1993–96	Lumley, Donald	1965–67	O'Sullivan, Chris	1993–96	Sweeney, William	1955–58
Gryp, Jerry	1972–73, 1974–76	MacDonald, Darin	1987–91	O'Sullivan, Kevin	1989–93	Sveen, Jeff	1984–87
		MacDougall, Jack	1988–89	Pandolfo, Jay	1992–96	Sylvia, Mike	1994–98
Gryp, Robert	1969–72	MacGregor, Brad	1982–84, 1985–86	Pandolfo, Mike	1998–2002	Sylvia, Robert	1962–65
Gurberg, Marvin	1953–54			Parker, Jack	1965–68	Taillefer, Terry	1983–87
Hanson, Bobby Jr.	1996–2000	MacLeod, Daryl	1977–81	Perry, Scott	1997–2001	Tanner, Ronald	1958–59
Hatton, Bruce	1968–69	MacLeod, David	1957–58, 1959–61	Pesklewis, Matt	1986–89	Tansey, William	1957–58
Headon, Peter	1985–89			Pidgeon, John	1976–77	Tapp, Jason	1998–2002
Heffernan, Daniel	1956–57	MacLeod, Donald	1955–58	Pierce, Bill	1993–97	Thiesing, David	1983–87
Herlofsky, Derek	1991–95	Magowan, Kenny	2000–02	Pierog, Mark	1980–84	Thornton, Steve	1991–95
Heron, Chris	1996–2000	Mahoney, David	1959–62	Pomichter, Mike	1991–94	Thornton, Peter	1969–72
Hetnik, Marc	1975–79	Maiser, Justin	2001–02	Poti, Tom	1996–98	Tiano, John	1982–84
Higgins, James	1960–62	Majkozak, Tony	1982–86	Powers, Buddy	1972–75	Tkachuk, Keith	1990–91
Hinch, William	1966–69	Manning, Mike	1954–56	Pratt, Jon	1990–94	Todaro, James	1963–66
Hughes, Paul	1959–61	Manty, Scott	1981–82	Prendergast, Mike	1991–95	Tomlinson, David	1987–91
Hyndman, Mike	1967–70	Marden, Matt	1975–78	Preston, John	1986–87	Toomey, Richard	1967–70
Hynes, John	1994–96	Marquis, Robert	1957–60	Priem, Ryan	1999–2002	Toperzer, Frank	1951–53
Jackson, William	1963–64	Marshall, Don	1979–80	Quebec, Greg	1996–2000	Trentini, Ron	1988–90
Jacques, Jon	1991–93	Marshall, Peter	1982–86	Quinn, Billy	1958–61	Totuny, Charles	1952–53
Jantzi, Michael	1980–81	Martell, Robert	1962–65	Quinn, David	1984–88	Urbanski, Barry	1959–61
Jarasitis, Al	1958–60	Marzo, Peter	1973–76	Quinn, Jim	1964–67	Valle, Richard	1967–68
Jenkins, Jon	1991–94	Matchett, Chris	1982–86	Quinn, Joe	1954–57	Vachon, Nick	1990–91
Johnson, Gregg	2000–02	Matterazzo, John	1986–87	Radoslovich, Matt	2001–02	Von Stefenelli, Phil	1987–91
Johnson, Shane	1993–97	Maus, Blaine	1968–69	Rausch, Ken	1991–95	Vuori, Juha	1997–2000
Johnson, Todd	1977–81	Mays, Chris	1980–84	Regan, Rob	1986–90	Wakabayashi, Herb	1966–69
Jordan, Ric	1970–72	McBride, John	1960–63	Regan, Tim	1969–72	Walsh, Brendan	1995–96
Joubert, Jacques	1992–95	McCann, Chris	1987–91	Riley, William Jr.	1965–68	Warner, David	1971–73
Kealty, Jeff	1994–98	McCann, James	1966–69	Robbins, William	1972–76	Warren, Andy	2000–02
Keith, Forbes	1957–59	McCann, Pete	1958–61	Robillard, Joe	1972–74		

The Beanpot: Fifty Years of Thrills, Spills, and Chills

Weisman, Jeff	1978–82	Burke, Dustin M.	1952	Daly, John S.F.	1963	Green, Gerald W.	1986
Weis, Bob	1977–78	Burke, Kevin F.	1974–76	Dea, Murray P.	1977–79	Griffin, James M.	1983
Werner, Kris	1985–88	Burke, Kevin M.	1965–66	DeFord, William, Jr.	1959	Grimble, Donald L.	1967–68
Weston, Bob	1997–99	Burke, Timothy P.	1990–92	DeFreitas, Richard J., Jr.	1989–92	Grumet-Morris, Dov	2002
Whalen, Paul	1951–53	Burnes, Andrew P.	1971–72	DeMichele, Daniel F.	1969–71	Gund, Gordon	1961
Whelton, Bill	1978–81	Burnes, Kennett F.	1964–65	Demment, Montague W.	1966	Gurry, Christopher J.	1968–70
Whiting, Warren	1953–54	Burns, Robert A.	1980–81	Desmond, Lawrence L.	1971–73	Gustafason, Cory G.	1992–95
Whitney, Ryan	2001–02	Busconi, Brian D.	1982–85	Devin, John P.	1985–88	Guttu, Lyle R.	1956–58
Wisener, David	1971–73	Butterworth, George W. III	1959–60	DeVoe, Michael W.	1986–87	Haley, Paul R.	1974–76
Wood, Doug	1992–96	Byrd, Leverett S.	1972–74	Diercks, William E.	1967–69	Halfnight, James A.	1996–99
Wood, Ian	1985–89	Callanan, William S.	1961	Donato, Edward P.	1988–91	Hampe, Kevin F.	1971–73
Wood, James	1964–67	Cantanucci, Jared	1999–2002	Dorman, Bradley P.	1984	Hands, David	1972–74
Wright, Eddie	1967–69	Caplan, Joshua C.	1986–89	Downes, Gregory	1959–60	Haney, Richard W.	1985–87
Wright, Matt	1993–97	Capouch, Peter	1999–2002	Downes, James E. II	1963	Harrington, Alden C.	1966
Yetten, Peter	1968–71	Cardone, Nicholas E.	1985–87	Driscoll, Terrence T.	1969–70	Harris, Nathaniel L., Jr.	1952
Young, Scott	1985–87	Carney, Mark J.	1986	Drury, Theodore E.	1990–91,	Hart, Timothy J.	1984
Zanetti, Mario	1951–53	Carr, Kevin M.	1974–76		1993	Hartje, Tod D.	1987–90
		Carr, Robert H., Jr.	1966–68	Duffy, Gifford R.	1979–80	Hartmann, Ralph P.	1984
Harvard University		Carter, Graham M.	1979–80	Dunbar, Robert P.	1958	Hatch, Morgan P.	1952
Abbot, David M.	1948–50	Cavanagh, David J.	1970–72	Duncan, Leslie R.	1958–59	Havern, Robert A.	1970–72
Adams, Craig D.	1996–99	Cavanagh, Joseph V.	1969–71	Dunderdale, John J.	1978–79	Heintzman, Thomas G.	1960–62
Aiken, John J.	1974–76	Cavanagh, Tom	2002	Durno, Stanley B.	1969–71	Henderson, John W.	1960
Allen, J. Aaron	1990	Celi, Mario J.	1955–56	Dwinell, James F. III	1960–62	Hermsdorf, Stephen G.	1994–95
Allen, Richard A	1956	Chalmers, Gregory R.	1982–83,	Early, Brian F.	1996	Hess, Gregory M.	1991–92
Allman, Trevor G.	1997–2000		1985	Elliott, John D.	1971–73	Higdon, Henry G. III	1995–98
Almy, Edward P.	1953–55	Chase, George W.	1953	Ericson, Leif M.	1999–2002	Higginbottom, George H.	1957–59
Alpine, A. Dean	1960–62	Chiarelli, Peter E.	1984–87	Evans, Peter J.	1980–81	Hodder, Melville T.	1960
Anderson, Robert G.	1959–61	Chodorow, Brett H.	1997–2000	Evans, Philip R.	1978	Hogan, Leigh P.	1973–75
Andrews, Stephen W.	1978–79	Ciavaglia, Peter A.	1988–91	Falcone, Philip A.	1981–84	Holmes, David U.	1957
Armstrong, Scott J.	1985–88	Clark, Dennis P.	1966	Famigletti, Brian T.	1995–98	Holmes, Thomas B.	1993–96
Armstrong, Steven J.	1985–88	Clark, Forrester A., Jr.	1958	Fanning, Charles F., Jr.	1963	Hornig, James A.	1969
Bailey, James A. I'	1955–57	Clark, Kyle	1999–2000	Farden, R. Scott	1985–86,	Horton, Douglas L.	1980
Baird, Christopher M.	1991–94	Clark, Robert L.	1964–66		1988	Horton, Wiliam R., Jr.	1976–77
Baker, Benjamin B.	1961–62	Clasby, Richard J.	1952–54	Farrell, Brian P.	1991–94	Howe, Reginald H. II	1962
Bala, Christopher B.	1998–2001	Cleary, Richard S.	1959	Ferrari, Marco J.	1994–97	Howell, A. Harold, Jr.	1961–63
Balboni, Maurice	1957–59	Cleary, Robert B.	1956–58	Filoon, John W., Jr.	1959	Howley, Paul T.	1987–89
Barakett, Timothy R.	1984–87	Cleary, William J., Jr.	1954–55	Fischer, Richard S.	1957–59	Hozach, William J.	1975–77
Barlow, Blair A.	2001–02	Cleary, William John III	1984–85	Fitzsimmons, William R	1965–66	Hubbard, E. Amory	1952–53
Bartlett, Joseph W. II	1955	Coady, James D.	1992	Flaman, Terrance E.	1968–70	Hughes, Charles W. II	1989–92
Bauer, Robert T., Jr.	1967–69	Cochrane, John G.	1977–79	Fletcher, George C.	1989	Hughes, George S.	1977–79
Beadie, David M.	1958	Code, Kenneth S.	1981–84	Flomenhoft, Steven T.	1990–93	Hughes, John F.	1977–78
Beckett, William H. M.	1960–62	Cohagan, Perry A.	1992–95	Flynn, Charles B.	1954–56	Hyland, Robert G.	1995–98
Bell, David S.	1975–77	Coleman, Robert M.	1965	Flynn, Rob	2002	Hynes, David E.	1971–73
Benning, Mark K.	1985–88	Colins, William E. III	1959	Follows, Peter C.	1984–86	Hynes, John B.	1978–80
Benson, Richard D.	1978–81	Colt, James D.	1954	Forbes, C. Stewart	1959–61	Ikauniks, Romuald	1962–64
Bent, Michael E.	1996	Conklin, Brice H.	1997–99	Fowkes, Robert J.	1977	Ingalls, Theodore S.	1960–61
Bernakevitch, Brendan	2002	Conners, David M.	1980–81,	Francis, Michael B.	1988–91	Israel, Aaron M.	1993–94
Bertagna, Joseph D.	1971–73		1983–84	Fredo, Robert F., Jr.	1966–68	Jahncke, Redington T.	1972
Better, Steven J.	1982	Connolly, Brian D.	1991–92	Freeman, Gordon L., Jr.	1969–70	Janfaza, Andrew E.	1985–88
Biotti, Christopher J.	1986–87	Connor, David G.	1962	Fried, Robert J.	2001–02	Janicek, Steven A.	1974–75
Blair, Grant A.	1983–86	Connors, David M.	1980–81,	Fryer, William J.	1963–64	Johnson, Barry F.	1969
Blakey, Richard B.	1963		1983	Fusco, Mark E.	1980–83	Johnston, David L.	1961–63
Bland, Robert P.	1960–62	Cook, Bryan W.	1976–78	Fusco, Scott M.	1982–83,	Jonas, Oliver H.	1998–2001
Bliss, Edward P.	1953–55	Cooledge, W. Scott III	1953–55		1985	Jones, David R.	1969–71
Bliss, William L.	1950–52	Coolidge, Thomas J., Jr.	1952–54	Gardner, Augustus P.	1991–92	Jorgenson, Gerald W.	1961–63
Body, Louis Frederick V.	1991–94	Cooney, Edward A., Jr.	1955	Garfield, Michael R.	1963	Karmanos, Jason R.	1993–96
Bolduc, Daniel G.	1975	Copeland, John T.	1956–57	Garrity, John P., Jr.	1966–68	Kelley, Paul M.	1957, 1959
Bourbeau, Allen H.	1986–87	Corkery, William J.	1971–73	Garrity, Jonathan P.	1977–80	Kelley, Robert C.	1978–79
Bowman, Robert T.	1987	Corning, Nathan E.	1952	Gauthier, David R.	1975	Kennish, Ian T.	1993–94
Bray, John R.	1952–54	Coughlin, Benjamin M.	1992–95	Gillie, Bruce L.	1958	Kerner, Jamin F.	1997–98,
Breistroff, C. Michael	1991–93	Craigen, Joseph C.	1994–97	Ginal, Michael E.	1997–99		2000
Brignall, James T.	1963	Crehore, Joseph F.	1954–56	Glaser, Howard H.	1957	Kilpatrick, David J.	1991–92
Britz, Gregory J.	1980–83	Crocker, Prescott B.	1963	Gonzalez, Jorge R.	1964–66	Kim, Aaron Y.	2000–02
Bullard, Lyman G., Jr.	1977	Crosby, David B.	1959–61	Goodenow, Robert W.	1972–74	Kinasewich, Eugene	1962–64
Burke, Charles J.	1977	Cutone, Mario V.	1984,	Graney, Michael	1958–60	Kinkopf, Abraham R.	2001–02
Burke, David M., Jr.	1979–81,		1986–87	Grannis, David L. III	1960–62	Kolarik, Tyler S.	2001–02
	1983	Dagdigian, Steven T.	1975	Greeley, Walter F.	1952–53		

Northeastern University

Caputo, Perry	1980	Ferguson, Sheldon	1975	Igo, Richard	1954	Mancuso, Joe	1999–2002
Casey, Thomas	1960–61	Ferdinandi, Dale	1977–80	Isbister, Rod	1983–86	Mansfield, John	1967
Cavanaugh, Richard	1955–57	Fidler, Joseph	1975	Iskyan, Paul	1979–82	Marshall, Charles	1981–82
Celata, Jack	2002	Filipe, Paul	1979–82	Jacobs, Timothy	1981	Marshall, Scott	1983,
Chaisson, John L.	1971–73	Finch, Duncan	1973–76	Jankowski, Mike	1989		1985–86
Chisholm, Arthur	1959–61	Fitzgerald, Thomas	1974–75	Jeanneault, Ronald	1965–67	Marshall, Tim	1982–85
Christie, Monte	1965–67	Fitzgerald, Walter	1962–64	Johanson, Don	1955–57	Martel, James	1973–76
Clegg, William	1972	Fitzsimmons, Paul	1983–86	Johnson, Richard	1955–57	Mason, James	1974–75
Coates, Mark	1975–78	Flanagan, Paul	1989–92	Johnston, J. Philip	1960–62	Massey, Peter	1986–87
Coates, Matt	2002	Fletcher, Richard	1962–63	Jones, Stephen	1975	Mastronardi, Joe	2000–02
Cole, Tom	1989–92	Flowers, John	1978	Jordan, Donald	1970–71	Mattie, Michael E.	1958
Coleman, David	1963	Ford, Kenneth	1980	Joyce, John	1968	May, Andy	1987–90
Collet, Mike	1994–96	Forselius, Charles	1988	Jozefowicz, Mike	1998–01	McCabe, Don	1981–82
Condon, Daniel	1972–74	Foy, Chris	1990–93	Judy, Tim	2002	McCann, Timothy	1967
Connelly, Joseph	1961	France, Robert	1975–78	Kaminski, Erik	1996–97	McCarty, Edward	1966–68
Connelly, John	1950–52	Frank, Craig	1981–84	Kayhko, Arttu	1996–97	McDougall, Mike	1986–88
Coombes, John	1967	Frier, David	1962–63	Kearns, Justin	1995–98	McDougall, Paul	1979–82
Costa, Richard	1969–71	Furnald, Stephen	1970–71	Keating, Matt	1998–2001	McElholm, James	1959–61
Cotter, William	1971–72	Gannon, Mark	1977	Kelley, Roy	1952–54	McElroy, James	1975–78
Cowie, Brad	1982–83	Gaudet, Ronald	1960–62	Kellogg, Bob	1990–93	McGaughey, Tony	1997
Cowie, Gerard	1979–82	Gennings, Kert	1979	Kelly, Jason	1992–95	McGee, Kevin	1980
Cowie, Rob	1988–91	Giatrelis, John	1954	Kennedy, Walter	1981–82	McGillis, Dan	1993–96
Cronin, Donald P.	1958–59	Gibson, Keni	2002	Kenny, Rob	1990–92	McGranahan, Dean	1964,
Cronin, Gerard M.	1959–61	Gilbody, John	1953–54	Kerr, Edward	1957–58		1966–67
Cull, Dean	1991	Gilardi, Chris	1991	Kessler, Bill	1982–84	McGrath, Mark	1960
Cummings, Brian	1998–01	Gilhooly, Mike	2000–02	Kiley, Gerry	1984–87	McKenna, William	1973–75
Cunniff, Chris	1987	Giovanucci, Glenn	1981–83	Kimura, Robert	1983–86	McKenney, D. Scot	1981–82
Curtin, Sean	1989–92	Goclowski, Eric	1997	Kinal, Roman	1984–87	McMillen, Michael	1977
Cyr, Keith	1989–92	Gold, Elijah	1993	Klyn, Brad	1994–97	McNamara, Leonard	1951–53
Daniels, Thomas	1968–70	Gordon, Steven	1971	Koslowski, Thomas	1968	McPhedran, Evan	1973–75
Davidner, Mark	1980–83	Grande, Marc	1996	Lally, Robert	1952–55	McPhee, Neil	1963–64
Davis, Bobby	1998–00	Grant, Robbie	1988–90	Lawn, William	1954, 1956	Meisner, William	1971
De Blois, Robert	1964–66	Green, Marcus	1973–76	Lambert, George	1957–59	Melong, Jason	1992–95
Deck, Darrell	1975–77	Grossi, Dino	1990–93	Lambert, G. Howard	1953	Metz, James	1976–77
Delaney, Kevin	1970–72	Grover, Donny	2002	Laplante, Sebastien	1990–93	Mews, Harry	1987–90
Delaney, William	1960–62	Gruhl, Scott	1977–78	LeBoeuf, R. Carl	1960	Milewski, Jim	1984
Demetroulakos, George	1980–83	Guerette, Robert	1956	Ledoux, Michael	1976–78	Mischler, Graig	1998–2001
Dempsey, William	1971	Guerriero, Jason	2002	LeFort, Peter	1950–52	Mitchell, Francis	1956–58
Derby, Mark	1977–80	Gulon, John	1977–80	Leger, John	1965–67	Moon, Thomas	1963–65
Desjardins, Jacques	1968–69	Haglund, Bob	1998–99	Lehman, Robert	1959	Moore, Charles	1963
DesJardins, Robert	1973–74	Haldane, Robert	1975–76	LeNormand, Edward	1963–65	Moffatt, Dennis	1972–74
Desroiers, Paul	1963	Hallenborg, Charles	1966	Levesque, Willie	1999–2002	Montgomery, Jonathan	1980–81
Devlin, Michael	1975–77	Haidy, Marty	1987	Levis, Bruce	1978	Morrison, Ralph	1970–71
DeWolf, Clyde	1951,	Hampe, James	1968–70	Leu, James	1965–67	Moynihan, Robert	1960–62
	1954–55	Handler, Mitch	1982	Leu, Kenneth	1968–69	Mudryk, Jared	2002
Doherty, Philip	1950–53	Harper, Greg	1979	Lodin, Claude	1985–88	Murphy, Jay	1996
Doherty, William	1952–54	Harrington, Cornelius	1958	Long, Chris	1986	Murphy, Joseph	1974–76
Dowd, Brian	1985–88	Harrison, John	1979	Lori, Mark	1984–85	Mutch, Tom	1987–88
Dudgeon, Ryan	2001–02	Hartney, Walter E.	1958	Lovell, John	1972–74	Nathe, Bryan	2002
Duffy, Harold	1951–54	Hartney, William	1965	Lucas, Geoff	1992–95	Neary, Greg	1983–86
Dunkle, Allan	1972–74	Harvey, Doug	1978–79	Lupo, Dan	1993–96	Newson, Billy	1997–2000
Dupont, David	1998	Harvey, Frank	1976	Lynch, Chris	1999–2002	Nilan, Christopher	1977–79
Dupere, Leo	1962–64	Hayes, Adam	1992–93	Lynch, David	1960–61	Nolfi, Philip	1973
Dutczak, Edward	1960–62	Hayes, Michael	1980	MacCausland, Robert	1967–69	O'Brien, David	1985–88
Dwyer, Jeremy	1980	Hayward, Leon	1999–2002	MacDonald, R. Bruce	1962	O'Brien, Mike	1982
Eagan, Joe	1992	Heagle, Richard	1968–69	MacDonald, Sean	1998–2001	O'Brien, Michael	1983, 1985
Eberly, Daniel	1970–72	Heerter, Richard	1955	MacGillivray, Charles	1964–66	O'Brien, Paul	1963
Edgerly, Derek	1991–92	Heffernan, Kevin	1985–88	MacInnis, Joe	1985–88	O'Connell, Philip	1965–67
Ellis, Randy	1980	Heinbuck, Jay	1983–86	MacKinnon, Gerald	1980	O'Connor, John	1956–58
Engbrecht, Arik	1998,	Herriman, Jaron	2002	MacLean, Brian	1962–63	O'Connor, Tom	1991–94
	2000–02	Heisler, Robert	1975–76	MacNair, Darryl	1992–95	Ortlip, Eric	2001–02
Emerson, Stewart	1983–86	Hiltz, Jeff	1979–82	Madden, Thomas	1950–52	O'Shaughnessy, Jim	1987
Eramo, Glenn	1969	Holeczy, Roger	1997–2000	Mader, Milan	1984	O'Sullivan, Shawn	1984
Eremian, Daniel	1971	Holmes, Michael	1975–78	Madigan, Jim	1982–85	Pagliarulo, Paul	1973–74
Fahey, Jim	1999–2002	Hopkins, Scott	1990–91	Mahoney, Brad	1997	Palmer, John H.	1959–61
Fahringer, Brian	1981–84	Huck, Charles	1973–76	Manchurek, Kenneth	1981–84	Palone, Patrick	1963

Paresky, Arthur	1957–59	Santonelli, Mike	1996	Thornton, Gary	1965–67
Parks, Larry	1978–80	Sarkisian, Martin	1965	Tierney, David	1962
Parlon, Tom	1992–95	Sarno, Joseph	1967–69	Tingley, Lawrence	1969–71
Pasinato, Maurizio	1981–84	Saunders, Matt	1989–92	Toal, Terry	1972–74
Payette, Chris	1984	Scherer, Paul	1971–73	Toews, Aaron	1997–98
Pecararo, Dave	1987–88	Schiavo, Jay	1989–90,	Tudrick, Brian	2001–02
Penney, David	1994–95		1992–93	Turcotte, Donald	1965–67
Perreault, Peter	1976	Schofield, Steve	1987–89	Turnbull, Rick	1981–82
Persson, Tomas	1994–96	Schultz, John	1990	Turner, Wayne	1977–80
Peterman, John	1998–2001	Schure, Peter	1988–91	Twombly, David	1981, 1984
Peters, Robert B.	1958	Schuhwerk, Rick	1994–97	Utano, Chris	1992
Petersen, Eric	1994–97	Seabury, William	1964–66	Valade, Jay	1987
Picard, Ray	1951–53	Selig, Scott	2001–02	Vasiliev, Dmitri	1996–97
Pitts, Robert J.	1958	Sheehan, Bob	1995–98	Vaughan, Jeff	1994–97
Poile, David	1968–70	Shephard, Mark	1971	Veisor, Mike	1993–96
Polak, Gregory	1986	Sherlock, David	1973–76	Vient, Walter	1959–61
Porter, Eric	1966–68	Shields, Jordon	1993–96	Vorderer, Frederick	1954–56
Power, Kevin	1963	Sibulkin, Jay	1974–76	Walker, John	1952
Powers, Stephen	1962–64	Simmons, Mark	1977–79	Walker, Orlando	1978
Pratt, Greg	1984–87	Smith, Richard	1951–52	Wallace, Stephen	1971
Purcell, John	1951–53	Smith, Richard F.	1953–56	Walsh, James	1957–59
Puttick, Andrew	1998	Smith, Robert	1955–56	Walsh, James	1977–79
Quinn, Thomas	1972	Southorn, William	1973	Walter, Robert	1969
Racine, Bruce	1985–88	Spence, Wayne	1961, 1963	Waterman, Frank	1960, 1962
Raus, Martin	1986–89	Spiller, Rich	1999–2000	Watson, John	1953
Reardon, Sean	1976	Spofford, David	1957–59	Watson, Sidney	1954–55
Reise, Norman	1973–76	Sterling, Gordon	1950, 1952	Webb, Dean	1962
Reschny, Trevor	2001–02	Stewart, James	1979–80	Webb, Hart	1994–95
Reynolds, Todd	1992,	Sullivan, Brian	1988–91	Weiss, Ben	1996–99
	1994–96	Sullivan, Brian	2000–02	Weissbach, Lawrence	1959–61
Ricciardi, Robert	1979	Sullivan, John	1966–68	Welch, Kevin	1998–2001
Rich, P.J.	1982	Summers, Patrick	1977	Wenham, Mark	1956–58
Richardson, John	1976	Sunderland, Robert	1970	White, Alan	1957–59
Ridpath, John	1985–88	Suprenant, Paul	1958, 1960	Whitfield, Bill	1985–87
Rizzo, Joseph	1964	Sutton, Scott	1999	Whynot, Donald	1954
Roberts, Mike	1989–91	Sweeney, Matt	1988–89	Wieczorek, Bob	1982
Robitaille, Marc	1997–98	Swiriduk, John	1955–56	Wilkens, David	1978–79
Rossi, George	1962–64	Tanner, Lorne	1968	Wilkins, Paul	1977
Rossi, Rico	1986–89	Taylor, Donald	1967–68	Wilkinson, Geoff	1996–97
Russo, Paul	1988–89	Taylor, Hobart	1975	Williams, Donald	1968
Ryan, Mike	2000–02	Taylor, Mike	1992–94	Williamson, Edward	1953–55
Sabroski, Walter	1952	Taylor, Robert	1991	Wilson, John	1960
Sacco, Paul	1989–92	Thayer, Thomas	1971–73	Yaworski, Rod	1979–80
Salvucci, Donald	1957–59	Thomas, Brent	1996–99	Yeadon, Foster	1956
Sandford, Michael	1975–78	Thomson, Brian	1988	Zoller, Ryan	1999–2000

ACKNOWLEDGMENTS

I'd like first and foremost to thank Beanpot tournament director Steve Nazro for his invaluable assistance and for making this book project a reality.

I'd also like to offer special thanks to Jack Grinold, Beanpot Committee Secretary and de facto tournament historian. His extensive knowledge and unwavering support lightened the undertaking of an endeavor of this magnitude.

Thanks are also due to the Beanpot schools' athletic directors for giving this book the necessary approval to make it possible: Gene DeFilipo, Boston College; Gary Strickler, Boston University; Bob Scalese, Harvard University; and Ian McCaw, Northeastern University.

The cooperation of the sports information departments of each Beanpot school was vital to creating an accurate record of fifty years of tournament play: Dick Kelley and Lizz Summers, Boston College; Pete Charboneau, Ed Carpenter, and Rick Young, Boston University; John Veneziano and Jamie Weir, Harvard University; Ben Miller, Northeastern University; and John Norton, Beanpot statistician.

Special thanks also goes to Don Skwar, Joe Sullivan, and Lisa Tuity at the *Boston Globe*, and Mark Torpey, Joe Thomas, and John Cronin at the *Boston Herald*.

My associate, Paul Simpson, was involved in this project since its inception. His long hours spent on the manuscript from beginning to end are greatly appreciated.

Finally, I'd like to thank my editor, John Weingartner, for his guidance and expertise, and for allowing the game to go into overtime with a successful result.